Nineteenth Century German Plays

The German Library: Volume 31
Volkmar Sander, General Editor

Franz Grillparzer
Johann Nepomuk Nestroy
Friedrich Hebbel

NINETEENTH CENTURY GERMAN PLAYS

King Ottocar's Rise and Fall
The Talisman
Agnes Bernauer

Edited by Egon Schwarz in collaboration with
Hannelore M. Spence

CONTINUUM · NEW YORK

1990
The Continuum Publishing Company
370 Lexington Avenue, New York, NY 10017

The German Library
is published in cooperation with Deutsches Haus,
New York University.

Printed in the United States of America

Library of Congress Cataloging-in-Publication Data

Nineteenth century German plays / edited by Egon Schwarz in
collaboration with Hannelore M. Spence.
        p.   cm.
    Contents: King Ottocar's rise and fall / Franz Grillparzer — The
Talisman / Johann Nepomuk Nestroy — Agnes Bernauer / Friedrich
Hebbel.
    ISBN 0-8264-0331-X. — ISBN 0-8264-0332-8 (pbk.)
    1. German drama—19th century—Translations into English.
2. English drama—Translations from German. I. Schwarz, Egon,
1922–   . II. Spence, Hannelore M. III. Grillparzer, Franz,
1813–1863. King Ottocar's rise and fall. IV. Nestroy, Johann,
1801–1862. Talisman. V. Hebbel, Friedrich, 1813–1863. Agnes
Bernauer.
PT1258.N5   1990
832'.70809436—dc20   89-49311
                                                                  CIP

Acknowledgments will be found on page 263,
which constitutes an extension of the copyright page.

Contents

Introduction

At the beginning of the nineteenth century there were Heinrich von Kleist and Georg Büchner, at its end Gerhart Hauptmann, all internationally admired, performed, emulated. Such towering successes are rare. But this does not mean in the least that the intervening decades were the dramatic wasteland that some critics have invented. The advent of Austrian playwrights in the early nineteenth century, for example, permanently enriched the German stage, and in addition to a number of lesser but perfectly respectable talents such as Grabbe, Gutzkow, and Wildenbruch, the enormous dramatic achievements of Friedrich Hebbel (1813–63),[1] from the early *Maria Magdalene* (1844) to his last work *Demetrius* (1864), must be regarded as summits of stagecraft worthy of representing and continuing the great dramatic tradition of Germany.

Franz Grillparzer's (1791–1872)[2] birth actually antedates Büchner's by a generation, but it is with him that Austrian writing spectacularly enters the realm of literature where it has occupied a special and disproportionately large place ever since. Grillparzer was the author of novellas and poems, historical, and theoretical writings about literature, but first and foremost he was a master of the stage, and many of his dramatic masterpieces from *Der Traum ein Leben* (1840) to the posthumously published *Die Jüdin von Toledo* (1873) are of such magnitude that it would detract from their importance to say that they "fill a gap" in German drama, real or imagined.

After years of great material and intellectual deprivation, Friedrich Hebbel managed to get an education and to travel. He too wound up in Vienna where he spent the last two, very productive, decades of his life. But his speculative and theoretical propensities, influenced by the dominant thinker of the age, Georg Wilhelm Friedrich

Hegel (1770–1831), reveal his Northern origin and orientation. Like Grillparzer he was a gifted poet, a writer of narrative and reflective prose, but above all a dramatist. Most of his plays are tragedies in which exceptional individuals are pitted against the state and indeed the spirit of the times. Anticipating a major shift in the mentality of mankind and thus located at the threshold of a new historical epoch, they are crushed by the existing order. There is no religious or other metaphysical consolation to compensate for their inexorable defeat, except the realization by the audience that the struggle of the heroes and, more often, heroines, be they of humble or royal extraction, has helped bring about a more enlightened era in human history. In *Agnes Bernauer* (1855) too, the conflict arises from a clash between private and public values, between love and *raison d'état*. The dynastic system, prevailing almost everywhere in Europe, triumphs, but the intensity of the personal bonding, despite huge class differences, the plug for women's rights on the one hand and the disregard for human happiness and the dispassionate brutality of the powers representing the status quo on the other, opens up a utopian vision and prepares the minds of the spectators for a drastic change of values.

As a writer having grown up in a multiethnic, multinational empire, Grillparzer necessarily developed a different attitude toward the state in which he saw the main force of cohesion in a centrifugal society. He was aware of the disruptive threat represented by every political movement, every severe criticism of the dynasty, every bureaucratic initiative, indeed every individual act. He was therefore extremely skeptical of self-assertion, experiment, and adventure and developed a quietistic view of history that places him squarely in the Biedermeier style of life following the exile of Napoleon and the repressive order established by Metternich in the wake of the Congress of Vienna. He became a disgruntled minor official in the Austrian bureaucracy who struggled to keep up his literary activities on the side. Even though he suffered as a writer from the existing censorship, as a citizen he rejected the revolutionary movement of 1848 after an initial period of consent. Like Hebbel he chose his subjects mostly from history but with the intent of extolling the benefits of tradition and restraint. Without of course entirely proscribing action, more often than not his dramatic works tend to restore a *status quo ante bellum* disturbed by the innovative hubris of a dynamic personality oblivious to domestic values and the precarious equilibrium of societal forces.

While Hebbel needs an innocent victim to construct his tragedy, Grillparzer eschews tragedy altogether, whenever possible preferring to show the prevalence of traditionalist legitimacy over a megalomaniac character who confuses his restless ambition with strength and his accidental triumphs with the approval of history. Such is the case, at any rate, in *King Ottocar's Rise and Fall* (1828). What might have been the tragedy of a royal reformer who is frustrated by the inertia and the vested interests of his contemporaries, turns into a festival play celebrating the reigning dynasty of the Hapsburgs. In act 3 the long speech by Ottocar of Horneck whose rhymed chronicle was Grillparzer's main historical source, a paean of praise for the beauties of the Austrian scenery as well as the Austrian national character, purposefully violates dramatic convention but manages to identify the ancient poet with the modern one and to assign to literature the task of stabilizing legitimate authority. Similarly, by giving the thirteenth-century girl who presents a bouquet of flowers to Rudolph I, the founder of the Hapsburg dynasty, the name of Grillparzer's own fiancée, Katharina Fröhlich, a venerable continuity is alluded to: the historic emperor is subtly confused with the currently reigning one and the fact that there always will be a Hapsburg is firmly established in the viewer's mind.

This emphasis on visibility is a profoundly characteristic trait of Austrian drama. In his plays Hebbel portrays the clash of values, a battle of abstract ideas. In his plays Grillparzer resorts to symbolic representation by introducing portents that embody the meaning of history in a painterly rather than in a dramatic fashion. In act 1 the usurper Ottocar stands proudly upright, successfully defying the old order. In the middle act he is seen kneeling before his opponent, humiliated in the eyes of the populace by the very forces of tradition upon which he has trampled. In the final act he lies prostrate on the ground, defeated in body and spirit. Few spectators of the time would have failed to compare his fate to Napoleon's.

The many "objective correlatives" in the play, the seductive paper messages and verses, the swords and velvet cushions, the pomp and circumstance of power, the sight of the legitimate emperor who humbly straightens out the dents in his own helmet, the huddled and hooded figure of Ottocar, a beggar in his own palace, forced to hear the invectives of his subjects—all of these strangely poetic but basically undramatic elements introduce a fairy-tale atmosphere into Grillparzer's play. For the source of this one does not have to look far. They are echoes of the Viennese popular stage, functions of the magic farces that attracted nightly a cross section of Austrian society, from the working classes to the aristocracy, to the suburban theaters that Grillparzer knew so well. In contrast to the Protestant austerity of the German drama of Lessing and Schiller, Kleist and Hebbel, the Catholic South had maintained an uninterrupted tradition of sumptuous theatrical spectacles and succulent playacting. In Vienna a genre had developed where the ordinary world was mixed with fantastic ingredients, where everyday life was presided over by an Olympus of Greek and other gods, powerful divinities who held the threads of human fortune in their whimsical hands, but generously interspersed their lofty speeches with Viennese dialect and casually referred to local events or local celebrities. That is the stuff comedies are made of, the art of *ridendo dicere verum,* not tragedies. Extravagant costumes, allegorical figures of every description, stage machinery that defied gravity, Hanswurst, a clown in many guises who had been banned long ago from the sober stages of Germany, dance and song characterized the Viennese popular theater, and playwrights who were also actors were feverishly active keeping the voracious stages in the populous suburbs supplied with this kind of fare, unashamedly plagiarizing the international theater scene as well as each other.

The best of these magic or fairy-tale playwrights was Ferdinand Raimund, a celebrated actor on the very stage for which he wrote successful farces. While he was frustrated during his lifetime in his hope to be performed in the famous *Burgtheater,* the stage of the social and intellectual elites, he succeeded in creating the best of the Viennese "magic" plays, *The King of the Alps or the Misanthrope.* The way the central character is forced to confront himself, to acknowledge his own abhorrent manner with growing distaste, and to distance himself more and more from his own behavior is owed to the fantastic transformations and impersonations possible only in the Viennese "machine comedy."

Johann Nepomuk Nestroy (1801–62),[3] a rival of Raimund for the favor of the audiences, was also an author-actor tied to the suburban fairy-tale farce of Vienna. But he soon left its conventions behind and became one of the most prolific and incisive stage satirists of all time. With irrepressible humor, aphoristic wit, and an unfailing instinct for the potentials of the stage, he lambasted the social and political contradictions of his day. Thus, if Raimund's *Misanthrope* can be seen as a psychological comedy, Nestroy's *Talisman* (1840) has predominantly sociosatirical traits. The recognition is growing that it is the wittiest play of an author who must be regarded as the greatest comedy writer in the German tongue for whom comedy was not a sideline but a compelling mission as it was for Goldoni or Molière. Nestroy surpasses the authors of individual brilliant comedies such as Lessing, Kleist, and Brecht with his ever-flowing humor and carefree transition from folksy fun to philosophical insight. There is no lack of popular and even slapstick comedy in the *Talisman*. It contains an abundance of local insinuations and erotic innuendoes, wordplays and quoteworthy aphorisms, a net of cleverly woven speeches and counterspeeches. But all this light banter serves a higher purpose, the uncovering of hidden desires and vanities, the exposure of a superficial society, mercilessly constructed along class lines.

The talisman, which gives the work its title, is a hairpiece the purpose of which is to cover the central figure's red hair, which has become a liability arousing prejudice and condemning the protagonist to an existence as a starving vagabond. The red hair may be replaced by any other characteristic deviating from the norm, a different skin color, an exotic slant of the eye, nose or lips, the wrong religion, or having been born on the wrong side of the tracks. In other words, the arbitrariness of the offending characteristic and its exchangeability indicated that in the *Talisman* we have before us the prototype of the comedy as allegory. With its blatant and improbable automatism of success, failure and final happy ending, the impudent manipulation of men through society, the *Talisman,* admired already by Kierkegaard, is one of the best of Nestroy's nearly one hundred comedies.

In Hebbel's tragedy with all its harshness one could still see the adumbration of a more humane society. Grillparzer's festival play seems to warn against modern experiments that aim to replace an imperfect present with a worse future, in keeping with the author's famous dictum that the world was moving from humanism through nationalism to barbarism. In this light, *King Ottocar,* despite its apparent Hapsburg conservatism, is still deeply attached to a humane vision of society. In Nestroy's play society is more closely scrutinized, its collective vanities and prejudices are made accountable, its unsound structure, shot through with corruption, injustice and deprivation, is criticized. Still, the confidence in the individual has not yet vanished. It is shown that an enlightened mind can bring light to the hidden corners of the social edifice and drive away the shadows. Although self-centeredness cannot be erased since it is the driving impulse behind the individual, its ill effects can be exposed and lessened. Enlightenment has not yet lost all its power.

German and Austrian drama does not stop there. Be it in tragedies or comedies, it records the gradual erosion of reason and ultimately the global destruction of humane values. As this was largely the work of the twentieth century, it became the burdensome task of twentieth-century playwrights to show these disastrous losses on the stage.

E. S.

Notes to the Introduction

1. Friedrich Hebbel

Born March 18, 1813, Wesselburen in Dithmarschen, West Germany; died Dec. 13, 1863, in Vienna, Austria.

Impoverished family; worked between the ages of 15 and 22 as scribe for a church warden; autodidact. Amalie Schoppe payed for his studies in Hamburg (1835). Elise Lensing became his lover and supported him. Their children died in childhood.

1836	Studied law in Heidelberg, later Munich.
1839	Returned to Hamburg on foot.
1840	Finished drama *Judith*.
1841	*Genoveva*.
1842	First collection of poems; trip to Copenhagen (received two-year travel grant from Danish king).
1843	Trip to Paris. *Maria Magdalene*.
1844	Doctor's degree from the University of Erlangen. Trip to Italy.
1845	Vienna.
1846	Married Christine Enghaus, actress.
1847	*Ein Trauerspiel in Sizilien* and *Julia*.
1848	*Herodes und Mariamne*.
1849	*Der Rubin*.
1852	*Agnes Bernauer* (published 1855).
1854	*Gyges und sein Ring*.
1860	*Die Nibelungen*, Trilogy (premiere 1861, in Weimar), *Demetrius*, fragment (published posthumously in 1864).

2. Franz Grillparzer

Born Jan. 15, 1791, Vienna, Austria; died Jan. 21, 1872, Vienna, Austria.

Middle class family; mother highly musical, committed suicide 1819; studied law, entered Civil Service 1813, director of the Financial Archives 1832, retired in 1856.

Sappho, performed in the Burgtheater 1818, brought him fame.

Conflict with hypersensitive court society and capricious police censorship. After failed reception of *Weh dem, der lügt,* Grillparzer withdrew from public life and kept all plays written thereafter locked up.

Met Katharina Fröhlich in 1821. She became his fiancée; he stayed in connection with her all his life but did not marry her. Travels to France, England, Italy, Greece. During his last years honors were heaped upon him. He became a member of the Imperial Academy of the Sciences; was awarded an honorary doctorate in Leipzig; named member of the "Herrenhaus" (His answer: "Much too late").

1816 (Performed 1817): *Die Ahnfrau.*
1818–20 (Performed 1821): *Das Goldene Fließ,* Trilogy.
1823 (Performed 1825): *König Ottokars Glück und Ende.*
1826–27 (Performed 1828): *Ein treuer Diener seines Herrn.*
1817–31 (Performed 1834): *Der Traum ein Leben.*
1820–29 (Performed 1831): *Des Meeres und der Liebe Wellen.*
1834–37 (Performed 1838): *Weh dem, der lügt.*
1872 Premiere in Prague: *Die Jüdin von Toledo.*
Premiere: *Ein Bruderzwist in Habsburg.*
Premiere: *Libussa.*
Best known novella: *Der arme Spielmann,* 1847.

3. Johann Nepomuk Nestroy

Born Dec. 7, 1801, Vienna, Austria; died May 25, 1862, Graz.

1822	Opera singer and actor in Amsterdam, Brünn, Graz, and Preßburg.
1831ff.	Vienna as comic and dramatic writer at the Theater an der Wien and Theater in der Leopoldstadt (Carl-Theater).
1833	*Der böse Geist Lumpazivagabundus.*
1835	*Zu ebener Erde und erster Stock.*
1836	*Die beiden Nachtwandler.*
1840	*Der Talisman.*
1841	*Das Mädl aus der Vorstadt.*
1842	*Einen Jux will er sich machen.* (Source of Thornton Wilder's *The Matchmaker* and the musical *Hello, Dolly*).
1844	*Der Zerrissene.*
1846	*Der Unbedeutende.*
1847	*Der Schützling.*
1848	*Freiheit in Krähwinkel.*
1849	*Lady und Schneider.*
1849	*Höllenangst.*
1849	*Der alte Mann mit der jungen Frau.*
1849	*Judith und Holofernes.*
1854–60	Director of the Carl-Theater.

Apart from the three selections in this volume, additional plays of the German nineteenth– and twentieth-century canon may be found in other volumes of The German Library. They include: Friedrich Schiller: *Intrigue and Love* and *Don Carlos* (volume 15); *Wallenstein* and *Mary Stuart* (volume 16); Johann Wolfgang von Goethe: *Faust* (volume 17, in preparation); *Egmont, Iphigenia, Tasso* (volume 18, in preparation); Heinrich von Kleist: *The Broken Pitcher, Amphytrion, Penthesilea, Prince Frederick of Homburg* (volume 25); Georg Büchner: *Danton's Death, Leonce and Lena, Woyzeck* (volume 28); Arthur Schnitzler: *Flirtations, La Ronde* (volume 55); Gerhart Hauptmann: *Before Sunrise, The Weavers* (volume 57, in preparation); Frank Wedekind: *Spring's Awakening*, et al. (volume 58, in preparation); Friedrich Dürrenmatt: *Romulus the Great* and *The Visit* (volume 89); Max Frisch: *Don Juan, or the Love of*

Geometry; as well as excerpts from others (volume 90). Theoretical writings on drama from Lessing through the present may be found in: *Essays on German Theater* (volume 83), including selections from Franz Grillparzer ("On the Nature of the Drama" and "A Letter Concerning Fate"), Georg Wilhelm Friedrich Hegel (from "The Philosophy of Fine Art"), and Friedrich Hebbel ("A Word about the Theater"). Volumes on additional authors are in preparation, such as: *Baroque Plays* (volume 71); Gottfried Ephraim Lessing (volume 12); *Storm and Stress* (volume 14); *Expressionist Plays* (volume 66); Bertolt Brecht (volume 75); and *Contemporary Plays* (volumes 96 and 97).

KING OTTOCAR'S
RISE AND FALL

Franz Grillparzer

CHARACTERS

PRIMISLAUS OTTOCAR, *King of Bohemia*
MARGARET OF AUSTRIA, *widow of Henry of Hohenstaufen, his wife*
BENESH OF DIEDITZ ⎫
MILOTA, *his brother* ⎬ *the Rosenbergs*
ZAVISH, *their nephew* ⎭
BERTA, *daughter of Benesh*
BRAUN OF OLMUETZ, *the King's Chancellor*
BELA, *King of Hungary*
CUNIGUNDA OF MASSOVIA, *his granddaughter*
RUDOLPH OF HAPSBURG
ALBRECHT *and* RUDOLPH, *his sons*
FREDERICK OF ZOLLERN, *Burgrave of Nuremberg*
HENRY OF LICHTENSTEIN ⎫
BERTOLD OF EMERBERG ⎬ *Austrian knights*
The elder MERENBERG ⎫
SEYFRIED MERENBERG ⎬ *Styrian knights*
FREDERICK PETTAUER ⎭
HERBOTT OF FUELLENSTEIN
ORTOLF OF WINDISCHGRAEZ
LADY MERENBERG
PALTRAM VATZO, *Burgomaster of Vienna*
The BURGOMASTER of Prague
IMPERIAL HERALD
The SEXTON of Goetzendorf

The CHANCELLOR of the Archbishop of Mainz
ELIZABETH, *lady-in-waiting to Margaret*
LADY-IN-WAITING to Cunigunda
ENVOYS of the German Electoral Assembly
NOBLES *and* CLERGY of Bohemia, Austria, Styria, Carinthia
SOLDIERS

Act 1

The castle at Prague: Queen Margaret's *antechamber. Doors right and left; the one at the right leads to the inner rooms. Before this door* Seyfried Merenberg *stands guard, leaning on his halberd; enter* Lady Elizabeth *and another lady-in-waiting from the* Queen's *chamber*

ELIZABETH: Run, Barbara! Quick! Fetch Master Nicholas!
    The Queen looks well enough, but looks deceive.
                (to a servant who enters)
    Have you the balm? Give it to me, good friend.
    O sad, unhappy day! My poor, poor lady!
MERENBERG *(enters):* How fares the Queen?
ELIZABETH: Better than you would think;
    Although it's clear the strain has taxed her powers.
MERENBERG: Who's there with her?
ELIZABETH: The Count of Hapsburg, sir.
    Oh, that I lived to see this day!
                (exit into the Queen's *chamber)*
MERENBERG: My son!
SEYFRIED *(has been standing leaning on his halberd, lost in thought):* Yes, father?
MERENBERG: You heard the news?
SEYFRIED: I heard.
MERENBERG: And say to it?
SEYFRIED: That it's not true!
MERENBERG: Not true?

SEYFRIED: No, father. And I'm so stirred to anger by it
   That I should like to take this halberd here
   And crush those liars' heads in, one and all.
MERENBERG *(steps back):* Ah me, my son! Why would you strike
   your father?
   I too believe it.
SEYFRIED: You too?
MERENBERG: My son, I *know!*
SEYFRIED: How could a noble and a knight like him, a king
   Like him, so sin against his plighted word,
   Forsake the wife that's bound to him by wedlock?
   Have I not served him since my days as page,
   And was he not a mold and pattern to me
   Of noble conduct?
MERENBERG: There's none that turns to evil
   But he was good before he made the turn.
SEYFRIED: No virtuous act, no valiant deed of mine
   But shamed me when I sought to liken it
   To his high nobleness of soul and body.
   The other day he cut me to the quick:
   He sent me from him while he fought the Huns!
   He thinks, perhaps, there's still the old affection
   For Berta Rosenberg. You know the story.
   Oh, could I but wash out the single stain
   Upon his life that else is fair and clean!
   Feel sure, though, it was they that led him on.
   These Rosenbergs! The father—Faugh, the pander!
MERENBERG: Think as you will, but doubt not this one thing:
   The Queen must go, both she and those who serve her.
   They have the worst, the uttermost, to fear.
   I shall start home to Merenberg today,
   Our family seat. You, too, must go from here.
SEYFRIED: But father!
MERENBERG: You must! This foolish trust of yours
   Shan't bring you to the block, if I can help it.
   You'll follow me, or seem to; but in Bruck
   A trusty servant will be waiting with fresh horses;
   And while they think you're safe at home with me,
   You'll be in Germany before they know.

The Queen refuses to address the Empire
Now she's in trouble; but *I will*, God helping.
I'll not stand by and see my liege-lord's daughter
Exiled from home and country, shelterless.
You'll go to Frankfort, and this letter here
   (opens his jacket and shows where the letter is hidden)
Give to the Archbishop of Mainz.— No more!
Someone is coming!
     (moves away from him)
      Secrecy and haste!
One day too late is thirty years too early!
    (Enter Benesh of Dieditz *and* Milota)

BENESH: Wasn't Lord Zavish here?
SEYFRIED *(turns away):* I have not seen him.
BENESH: He just rode through the gate!
MILOTA: Brother, be calm!
BENESH: "Be calm!" I'm calm enough. The King will never dare!
 Am I not Rosenberg? Is not our house
 Stronger than any other in the realm?
 You think he'd dare? Disgrace like this? Why, nonsense!
 But I'll find out who started such a tale;
 And then I'll smite him; thus, and thus, and thus!
 Him, and his sons and heirs!
    (Enter Berta Rosenberg)
BENESH: You, little fool?
 Why are you here? Away! Go to your room.
BERTA: I cannot stay; I feel too restless there.
 They hurry through the halls; with frightened eyes,
 They whisper news too terrible to tell.
 Say, father; is it true?
BENESH: How should I know?
 Away! Begone!
BERTA: O God! A word of kindness!
 (walks toward Seyfried *but starts back as she sees who it is)*
 Why, Merenberg! You, whom I ought to flee,
 You, of all men! Yet, you're a human being.
 I did you wrong past measure, Merenberg;
 But don't take vengeance *now*. See! I will kneel.
    (she kneels)

Say, is it true?

SEYFRIED: What, Berta?

BERTA: Is it true?
The King puts her away?

SEYFRIED: My father says so.

BERTA: And others say so, too.— And now he weds—
My shame comes late—is this a time for shame?—
And now he weds anew—and whom?

SEYFRIED *(pityingly):* Not Berta
Of Rosenberg.

> *(With a cry* Berta *presses her face to the ground)*

BENESH *(to* Seyfried*):* Who told you?— Girl, come here!

MILOTA *(goes toward* Berta*):* Come, niece! Come on; this is no
place for you.

BERTA: O Seyfried, save me!

SEYFRIED: Your leave, Lord Milota!
If you dare even put your hand on her,
I'll thrust you through the body with my pike.

BENESH: Even if I—?

SEYFRIED: All one!

BENESH: You'd keep a daughter
From her father?

SEYFRIED: Oh, if you had only kept her,
She would not now lie sobbing at our feet,
Until my heart turns over in my bosom.

BENESH: We'd better wedded her to you, no doubt?

SEYFRIED: Far better that, sir, than such shame as this.

BENESH: My daughter!

SEYFRIED: Hands off! She trusted herself to me;
And I am one to keep faith with a trust!

BENESH: My sword shall answer!

SEYFRIED: Put by!— Don't be afraid, dear girl.

> *(Enter* Zavish; *he pauses at the door and laughs loudly)*

ZAVISH: Ha, ha, ha, ha!

BENESH *(turns around quickly as he sees* Zavish*):* It's you? God
sends you to us.

ZAVISH: Why this dispute, my noble-minded hunters;
This heat and rage about the quarry's pelt?
Sir Bruin trots through hill and dale unworried

And one fine day he'll let you feel his claws.
Fair cousin, good morning!
                              (to Seyfried*)* And you, good huntsman,
    Put up your dart and smooth your ruffled brow;
    I am no game for you!
BENESH: Tell us what happened.
MILOTA: Yes, nephew, speak.
ZAVISH: Speak? Tell? What would you hear?
BENESH: The King—
ZAVISH: has met and roundly thrashed the Huns
    At Croissenbrunn.[1]
                              (to Milota*)* You, uncle! Weren't you there?
BENESH: Who asks for news of that?
ZAVISH: The treaty's signed.
    To Austria—
BENESH: No, no!
ZAVISH: To Styria—
BENESH: You'd mock me?
ZAVISH: Well, what do you want to know?
BENESH: The King and Margaret—
ZAVISH: Oh, their marriage is dissolved.
BENESH: That's down in black and white?
ZAVISH: And signed and sealed.
    Before this day is done, the Queen leaves for Vienna.
    From there—
BENESH: Is there no talk—? Confound you!—
    With whom—? *(to* Berta*)* Be quiet, you! With whom the King—?
ZAVISH: I see!
    With whom the King will make a second marriage?
    With whom else, surely, than that lady yonder,
    Your daughter! Oh, you played your cards so shrewdly!
    You brought the girl where he would chance on her;
    Decked her in finery till she outshone the fairest;
    And what the poor thing lacked in wit, you gave her
    From your own store. Who ever heard such discourse?
    The Queen of Sheba talks but half as well.
    And then—oh, how do I know what you did?
    In short, he's lost his head; and mind my words,
    He'll come at once and sue for Berta's hand!

BERTA *(leaps to her feet):* The Queen, the Queen! To fall at her feet
and die!

(exit into the Queen's *chamber)*

ZAVISH: Ha, ha, ha, ha!

MERENBERG: Lord Zavish!

ZAVISH: Why, let's be merry!

The King's to wed, and we'll dance at the feast.

(to Seyfried*)*

You too, once on a time, paid court to her?

That's not so strange. Why, even I, one night,

At wine, came close to loving those pink cheeks.

Your hand, my friend, for we have much in common.

(Seyfried turns away*)*

MILOTA: Why play the madman? Just be plain and brief:

Who is it the King is marrying?

ZAVISH: As brief

As was your question shall my answer be:

It's Cunigunda of Massovia,

King Bela's grandchild.[2]

BENESH: May Hell's fire consume him!

ZAVISH: It was yourselves sought to dissolve his marriage;

For years bent every effort to that end.

Well, it's dissolved—and he weds Bela's grandchild.

BENESH *(beats his forehead):* Betrayed, deceived, and cheated!
Shameful! Shameful!

ZAVISH: Don't knock so loudly at the gate of thought!

If it closed then, don't open it today.

BENESH: You mock us now, though you approved the scheme.

ZAVISH: I gave approval? To such crazy nonsense?

BENESH: Yes, you. And you!

MILOTA: You said the plan was sure.

BENESH: Bring her to me! Bring me the girl, I say!

She must not live! Not she, nor I. Oh!— Oh!—

SEYFRIED *(calls across to them):* You blame the girl. Why don't you
blame yourselves?

What grounds had you to think that for your daughter

The hand of Majesty, of her own King—

ZAVISH: Why, sir, there's ground enough for such a thought.

A Merenberg were mad to look so high;

But we, whose line descends from Rome's imperial city,
From those patricians who subdued the world,
And, as Ursini, still stand next that throne
From which St. Peter's might rules over rulers,
We have a right to reach for royal crowns;
Our daughters have a right, assured and free,
To wed the noblest title on this earth,
And— Ha, ha, ha, ha, ha!

MILOTA *(has sat down):* Confound his laughter!

ZAVISH: The daughter's mad; the father tears his hair;
And we bring proof how ancient is our line!
Though it were older than the angels' fall,
The King can nod, and crash, it lies in ruin.

BENESH: Before I fall, revenge!

(seizes Milota*):*

Brother, revenge!

MILOTA: I've just been thinking; and I plan to act.

ZAVISH: Are you astir, old square-hewn Milota?
Aye, now the King must tremble for his life!

BENESH: If you—if you refuse to help our cause,
You are no Rosenberg; a knave. That's so?

MILOTA: That's so.

ZAVISH: No doubt! How shall we do the deed?
Next time at mass, crowd close beside the King
And stamp hard on his foot; the pain is dreadful.
There's your revenge.

BENESH: He's mocking us again?
My head, my head!— He is no Rosenberg!

MILOTA: Come, brother; let's be gone. A man who laughs
When shame is on his house, deserves—

ZAVISH: Halt, friend!
What right have you, you two, to rail at me?
You who on public streets cry out for vengeance
To walls that hear not—and to ears that do!
Conspire in marketplaces and rebel at home!
Lord Merenberg, smart people, they, you'll grant me.
But for a man that's drunk with wine or rage
Cool air is the best cure, in either case.
And so let's seek the open, worthy sirs.
Our house burns with too hot a flame to quench;

Let us at least warm both our hands before it.
The King's my liege-lord; and enough is said.
MILOTA *(approaches him):* I wonder, friend, if you say all you think.
What do you take us for?
ZAVISH *(loudly):* For worthy folk.
What no man tells, you're not the ones to guess;
Though if you guessed, you'd go and tell it out.
But look! The door of the Queen's chamber opens.
She's coming! With her the Lord High Confessor,
The Count of Hapsburg. Let us leave, at once!
We might disturb them in their hour of prayer.
(They move away as the Queen *comes out of her chamber; with
her is* Rudolph of Hapsburg; *she is followed by two servants who
are carrying the unconscious form of* Berta Rosenberg *in a chair;*
Lady Elizabeth *supports her)*
MARGARET *(enters; turns toward the* Rosenbergs *as they with-
draw):* They draw away like great black thunder-clouds
Which drop their bolts and seek the rising sun.
(turns toward Berta*)*
Take her; look to it that her needs are tended;
And shortly I shall come myself to see.
RUDOLPH: Your Majesty is over kind, perhaps.
*(*Berta, *surrounded by her relatives, is borne away. The two*
Merenbergs *also leave the stage)*
MARGARET: The girl herself is hardly wicked; just weak
Of wit, and vain and silly; and so misled.
Her cousins though, her relatives and friends:
Great stubborn Milota, and Benesh, loose of tongue,
And Zavish, that's the worst I think of all,
They talked to her of riches, power, the throne—
Their proud ambition so far out-reached itself—
And turned a head that was not hard to turn.
I long had watched the three, my Lord the King's
Bad angels, working stealthily at the bonds
That were already few and weak enough,
And Ottocar scarce longer felt as bonds.
I heard them feigning sympathy, and feeding
For their own purposes his wish for heirs
Born of his body to come after him—

A wish we cannot justly chide a king for.
But if a birthright springs from wrong, what then?
They were the ones who fostered busily,
Without recess, this marriage's annulment,
Almost before the King had given the order,
Hoping to set one of their own house,
This poor young girl that struggles now with madness,
Upon the throne Bohemia's rulers hold.
How often have I watched her at the feasts,
Bedecked with finery, with crowds about her,
While I sat quite alone and nursed old grief.
The King had eyes for naught but her young charms,
And ears for her desires; his lips' stern threat
Was tempered to a gentle flattery.
But she was gay, and proud, and all too happy,
And looked at me with something of contempt.
Then I felt pity for the luckless victim,
And told myself that when her fall had come
I must be kind, and helpful to her sorrow.
O Ottocar, how great the load you bear!

RUDOLPH: Because of wrong he's done another, do not
Forget the greater wrong to you, my lady.

MARGARET: Oh, do not think that I excuse the King;
Let me be ever far from praising evil!
His treatment of me is unjust and wrong;
And when I come before him, I shall say so.
I am not young, but never hid the fact.
If grief has dimmed the beauty of my face,
Why, he had seen me when he sought my hand.
He feels, no doubt, my lack of gaiety.
If he'd be gay, why did he come a-wooing
To an unhappy queen, a queen of tears,
Crushed to the grave by all her loved ones' death?
With my own eyes, in that Apulian prison
Whose cruel walls had filled my heart with dread,
I saw my husband, Henry, King of Rome,
The all too gentle son of iron Frederick,
Where he lay slain by hands that were close kin;
And slain the little sons in whom we hoped,

That I had borne him ere my womb was closed.
Since then no joy has dwelt in this void bosom,
Each smile has fled in fear before my lips
That grief and pain have put their seal upon.—

What reasons do they give why we must part?
I know the first: I've not borne him a child,
Nor am I like to bear a child again—
Because I will not, not because I can't.
And Ottocar knew that before he wed me,
For I had told him, and he found it good.
My rich inheritance in Austria
It was he had his mind on; and with him
His father, Wenceslaus, greedy for land.
What is it the King asks for? Children, heirs?
It were better a beggar child sat on the throne
Than princes whom wrong and injustice sired.
What more do they allege, what further reasons?
RUDOLPH: You two are kin, too close for proper marriage.[3]
MARGARET: When I was but a maid, I heard them tell
About a Bela— Was that his name?— And Geysa,
And they were brothers and had daughters. One
Wedded an Austrian prince, and one a Czech,
A hundred years ago. The King is jesting!
Why, every royal house is kin to every other,
And dispensations are not hard to get!
Nor was a word said of it when we wed.
RUDOLPH: The recollection came when it best served him.
MARGARET: Oh, do not think that I am grieved to go;
That I shall miss the honors paid me here.
No, no. Could I but now, this very moment,
Put far behind me every regal pomp,
And go to Haimburg where my fathers dwelt;
Where, when my husband died, I sought retreat
And wept to think how our two sons had fallen!
Oh, let the King dismiss me at this hour,
And I will thank him as I never thanked him.
But my fair name I bid him leave untouched;
The bond that joins us he must leave unsullied

Or else these years that we have passed together
Become a loathsome sin and an offense!
I never sought to wear this crown. I dwelt
At Haimburg in seclusion with my sorrow
And scarcely heard how all my people suffered
While fire and pillage laid my country waste.
Hungarians here, Bavarians there, the Czechs,
They ravaged Austria with fire and sword,
Bringing the fair land of my sires to ruin.
Then they convened, the Lords, at Triebensee
To find, it might be, one to end this mischief;
And they sent envoys north to Meissenland
To get a Prince from there, Constantia's son,
Who was a Babenberger and my sister.
The envoys, though, were caught by Wenceslaus
The Wily, who then was ruling in Bohemia.
He used them for his ends, and never ceased
From asking, threatening; promises and presents,
Until his son, until this Ottocar
Was chosen by the Lords to rule the land.
One man was pleased, the other not; new war
Now flamed the hotter through my country's fields.
And then to me, to Castle Haimburg, came
My country's Lords and told me all their woe;
And that there was one cure, but only one:
If I would strengthen his strong right with mine,
If I would marry Ottocar, and so
Unite Bohemia's lands and Austria.
I answered, "No!"—remembering my husband
To whom my heart was true inside his tomb.
So then they led me to the battlements
And showed me all the fire-scarred land. The fields
Were bare, the houses empty, their owners dead.
I saw a piteous wailing throng about me,
Women and children, bleeding, wounded bodies,
Entreating me to save them, for I could.
My heart was stirred, and yielded; and I promised.
Not long thereafter they brought Ottocar
And showed him to me as my future husband.

With black eyes peering out beneath black brows
He stood apart, abashed, uncertain; studied
One who was growing old while he was young.[4]
But mindful only of my country's need,
I went and spoke to him with friendly words;
And we were wed. I never grew to love him,
I never asked myself if I could love him;
But quietly I served his needs; and as I served him,
A feeling came and dwelt within my heart
That knows love's pain and hurt, though it knows nothing
Of the happiness of love.—That is our story.
You cannot think that I am loath to leave.
Yes, I will go. The marriage, though, must stand.
There is no ground or reason to dissolve it.

RUDOLPH: They speak of one, I hear: that you, at Treves,
After King Henry died who was your husband,
Vowed solemnly that you would wed no more.
It's doubtless false.

MARGARET: No, it is true.
It was no *solemn* vow, though; at least no vow
To force the Church to call our marriage void.
But yet, I gave my word—and should have kept it.
At Treves I lay in prayer before our God
And promised my dead husband, promised Henry,
To keep fast faith with him and never wed.
No man should ever put his hands upon
The least of these my fingers, my robe's hem;
Nor any woman, even, kiss my lips
Which had touched his with pure and deep affection.
I gave my word and bade disaster come
Upon my guilty head if e'er I broke it.
Disaster, as I see, has found me out.
Once more I say it was no *solemn* vow.
I made it but to me and Henry's shade.
It was a promise, though; I should have kept it.

RUDOLPH: What word, my lady, shall I take the King?

MARGARET: How quick we are to blame as wrong in others
What we ourselves, though less indeed, have done!

Say to King Ottocar, Lord Duke of Hapsburg,
I leave the matter wholly to his conscience.
What he decides will meet with my assent.
RUDOLPH: You acquiesce?
MARGARET: Say, rather, I don't refuse.
RUDOLPH: But they are asking, too, that you concede
The lands of Austria and Styria,
Your family's demain.
MARGARET: That's done already.
RUDOLPH: But that bestowal followed from your marriage.
The marriage is dissolved: the deed is void.
MARGARET: I'll reaffirm it.
RUDOLPH: You must not forget,
Those lands are both imperial fiefs
Reverting to the Empire, not your own.
MARGARET: What rights I have in them I'll gladly yield.
Say that to Ottocar; and bid him stay
His hand from every unjust act. No wrong,
However small, will go unpunished. And now, farewell.
(Trumpets and noise in the street. Enter the elder Merenberg*)*
MERENBERG: The King!
MARGARET: O God in Heaven, it is too much!
I'll go to seek new strength from Thee in prayer.
(dismisses the two men with a gesture and goes to her chamber.
Exeunt Rudolph *and* Merenberg, *left)*

* * *

Throne room with Gothic arches and columns; throne halfway
back, right. In the foreground on each side, a table with a rich
covering, and an armchair. Martial music, blaring of trumpets, and
cheers of the populace outside. Enter Bohemian magnates and
knights, rear. They arrange themselves in rows, some beside the
throne and some opposite it. Left, forward, a deputation of the City
of Prague, the Burgomaster *at its head. Rear center, a group of*
Tartar[5] envoys. Enter the Chancellor
CHANCELLOR: The King!
ALL: Long live King Ottocar!
OTTOCAR *(enters hastily at the rear. He is in full armor, but without*

his helmet): I thank you, gentlemen.

(pauses before the Tartar envoys *who have knelt)* Who are these
men?

CHANCELLOR: The envoys, Sire, of the Khan of Tartary;
He greets you, and offers friendship and alliance.

OTTOCAR: Have them get up!—You hear? Up off the floor!
Strange people, they; and not less strangely armed.
Show me your sabre.

(takes it and tests its balance)

Much too sharply curved.

(swings it once in the air)

You lose the blow's full force. You'd better change it.
A curved blade has its uses; but the weight
Must lie close to the point. One of my horsemen
With his broad sword could deal with ten of you.

(returns the sabre)

What wear you else? That tuft of hair you have,
What good is that? To aid the foe, of course;
To twine his hands in, drag you off your horse,
And slit your throat at ease. Were I their king,
I'd have them all shorn, in a single night.
Tell them to go and come again tomorrow.

(Exeunt Tartars)

OTTOCAR *(comes forward)*: Well, gentlemen, we hope our work has
pleased you.

From this day on the Huns won't break your rest.
We've chased them out.— What else is there to do?

(to the deputation of the City of Prague who have come forward)
Who are you?

BURGOMASTER: We are the Mayor and Council, Sire,
Of your loyal and devoted city, Prague.

OTTOCAR: What do you want?— Ah!—

(throws himself in an armchair, left front)

Tell me your business.

(to the servants)

I'm weary; help me to get this armor off.

(Two servants set to work to remove his armor)

BURGOMASTER: Most mighty King! Monarch invincible!
Swift Fame brought word of your great victory
And—

OTTOCAR: Fuellenstein!

FUELLENSTEIN *(comes forward)*: I'm here, most gracious Sire!

OTTOCAR: How was the place called where we chased the Huns?

FUELLENSTEIN: It's Croissenbrunn.

OTTOCAR: Tom Fool, that was our camp!
  You think I don't remember where my base was?
  I mean the place where our horses made the charge
  That won the day.

FUELLENSTEIN: They call the spot Marchegg,
  Because the River March bends sharply there.

OTTOCAR: Marchegg!⁶ That's what I'll have them call the town
  I'm going to build there in memory of our triumph.
  Marchegg shall be the markstone of my fortune;
  And I'll go on from there, for who can stay me?
  And every passerby till earth's last day
  Shall tell of Ottocar and how he won the fray.
          (has arisen; to the servants)
  Well, what's the matter?— I see! You want my leg.
          (sits down again)
  You, Burgomaster, lend a hand and loose the greave.
  That's not the way! Hands off! Why waste good time?
   (rips the greave off and throws it into the center of the hall)
  Just where the March bends, across it, on a hill,
  Sat old King Bela high up on his seat,
  And Heinrich Preussel stood nearby—I saw it—
  Who, like the boy in the peepshow, pointed out
  The field to him and how the battle went;
  Which troops were which, and so forth and so on.
  At first his men fought well; but when Count Hapsburg
  Burst forth of a sudden with his heavy horse
  And every soul that cursed in Hunnish fled
  Back to the March, and all their tangled beards
  Stuck up like reedgrass where the water's dammed—
  Where is Count Hapsburg? Heigh, by God in Heaven,
  He fought that day! A quiet fellow, mostly;
  But when he charges, like the Fiend himself.
  Where is Count Hapsburg?

SERVANT: Shall we call him, Sire?

OTTOCAR: No, no!— When Bela saw the rout, he had
  No further need of an expositor.

He thrust his two hands in his tousled locks
And tore them cruelly. "Eh, man," thought I,
"Don't trouble to do that; we're better at it."
But now that he's our friend and an ally,
We must say only good and kindly things.
Well, are you done at last?

(arises)

My hat and cloak!
What progress in the city, Burgomaster?
Or have you slept the while?— That hat's too tight!
    (to the servant who is at a loss what to do)
Hell's fire, another hat!— Now then, what say you?
The wall about the Visherad[7] is built?

BURGOMASTER: Yes, Sire.

OTTOCAR: The bridge across the Moldau, too?

BURGOMASTER: We laid the last stone on it yesterday.

OTTOCAR: Yes, because you knew that I'd be here today.
  I bade you clear the lower city for
  The Germans that I sent you. Is it done?

BURGOMASTER: Your pardon—

OTTOCAR: Is it done?

BURGOMASTER: Your Highness—

OTTOCAR: Yes?

BURGOMASTER: Not yet.

OTTOCAR: And why not, wrath of God; why not?

BURGOMASTER: We wished to ask your Highness just once more
  Before we drove these loyal Czechs to exile—

OTTOCAR: To exile? Who said exile? No such thing!
  I said to send them to Chrudim[8] and give them
  Land for their farms and homes thrice what they'd had,
  And pay back threefold what the journey cost.
  But they must leave the quarter where they are.
  I say they must. *Must*, God's Blood! Do you grasp it?
  Oh, I know what you like, you old Bohemians:
  Sit on your heels where dross and rubbish gather,
  And dirty windows shut out half the light;
  Consume today what yesterday brought in,
  And harvest just enough to feed tomorrow;
  Sundays a feast, on holidays rude dancing;

You've eyes and ears for nothing else.
That's what you like, but I won't have it so.
You drag a drowning man out by the hair
And I'll catch you and choose a tender spot;
I'll put the Germans where your fur is thick
To nip and pinch till smart and anger rouse you
From your dull torpor and you kick out
Like a roweled horse. You're thinking of the times
Your Princes sat beside the hearth and wore
A shameful soot-black pot in their escutcheon.
That's not my way, God's Death!
(shows the cloak the servants have put on him)
Look here, you men!
This cloak was bought in Augsburg. See the gold,
The velvet, the embroidery, the make!
Can you do that here in Bohemia?
I say you shall, by God! I'll teach you how!
This Prague of yours shall stand on equal footing
With London and Paris, Vienna or Cologne.
The countries that looked down on you and scorned you,
I've brought them to their knees with my strong sword.
Hungary flees us, Bavaria keeps the peace;
And Austria and honest Styria,
Lands by the Adriatic, German soil,
I've made them mine and added to my kingdom.
I've made Bohemia's name known far and near;
From far and near her glory hears its echo.
I might have slept as calmly as my fathers
And let you sleep the way your fathers did.
Whom have I done this for? For you!
But you'll do your part, too, I pledge my word.
I've dragged you half-way up the mountain side;
Now climb the other half or break your necks.
(turns away from them)
See to it that the Germans have their quarters.
(the Chancellor *enters and approaches the* King*)*
OTTOCAR: What now?
CHANCELLOR: The Queen, as you commanded, Sire.

OTTOCAR *(turns back to the burghers)*:
That too, that too, I've done on your account.
No man but holds his peace at home above
All price. I've made the sacrifice that you
And yours may live henceforth in peace and quiet.
Lest, when I die, my realm remain without
An heir, my work a toy of civil discord,
I've put my wife, Queen Margaret, aside
Since there's no hope of issue to us two;
And have, not without risk, assumed new bonds.
                    (turns to the whole assemblage)
Indeed, my Lords, you all shall know the facts.
In confirmation of the new-made peace
King Bela offered me the hand in marriage
Of Cunigund, his grandchild, only daughter
Of Michael, Lord Duke of Massovia.
Now, since the Bishops of the Realm have long
Condemned my marriage with Queen Margaret,
And many other reasons speak against it—
For in the first place she is old and barren
And there's no hope she'll ever have a son;
And then she is akin to me, somehow,
I never know in what degree, and lastly—
But what's the use of all this one-two-three?
For first and next and lastly it must be!—
The Queen will come and sign a document
And reaffirm bestowal of her lands;
And you are gathered here as witnesses.
                    (ascends the throne)
CHANCELLOR *(has spread his papers on the table at which the* King
*has been seated and now advances to the center of the hall
holding an official document in his hand)*: Silence! Respect for
their Majesties! In the King's name!
*(Queen Margaret, clad in a cloak with a long train and wearing a
crown, enters, extreme front, left. She is escorted by* Hapsburg
and Merenberg, *and is followed by her ladies-in-waiting)*
CHANCELLOR: Illustrious Queen and Lady, Margaret,
Duchess of Austria and of Styria,
Widow of Henry, lately King of Rome,
Now consort of Bohemia's Majesty:

Who is the spokesman of your royal cause?
MARGARET: Myself.
    (with a gesture of refusal to Merenberg *as he steps forward)*
        No need, Lord Merenberg. Myself!
    Alone I'll bear the stigma of his wrath,
    And speak, and suffer also, I alone.
CHANCELLOR: The circumstance—
MARGARET: I know.
CHANCELLOR: I shall proceed.
    A holy synod, assembled at Vienna,
    Guido presiding, Legate and Cardinal,
    His title from San Lorenzo in Lucina,
    Has given judgment on the marriage bond
    That joins you to our gracious lord and liege.
    Whereas through Bela, King of Hungary,
    And Geysa, his brother, your respective grandsires,
    You are akin to our afore-said monarch
    By cousinship within the fourth degree;
    And whereas further it appears that you,
    Upon the death of your first lord and consort,
    Of Henry, King of Rome, of glorious memory,
    Did in the Convent of St. Catherine at Treves
    Make vow that you would never wed again—
MARGARET: It was no *solemn* vow.
OTTOCAR: It's written here! Continue.
CHANCELLOR: Therefore—
                    (Blare of trumpets outside)
OTTOCAR: What's that?
SERVANT: The Nobles, Sire,
    And Clergy of Austria are in the castle.
    They bring with them their country's ducal crown.
OTTOCAR: Bring them in. They're just the witnesses we need.
(Nobles and Clergy of Austria enter bearing before them the ducal
                    crown on a cushion)
LICHTENSTEIN *(as spokesman):* Your valiant sword, exalted Prince
    has put
    An end to strife with Hungary and shown
    Who shall be King in this fair land of ours.
    The quarrel, with woe and bloodshed, now is ended.

With lightened hearts we come once more to pay
Our homage, until now not in full force.
                              (*turns to Margaret*)
But you, before all else, illustrious Queen,
And noble offspring of the race of heroes
That long held sway in Austria with honor—
OTTOCAR: Enough of that! Just find your place and wait.
New homage means less than old fealty;
Best keep it once, rather than promise twice.
                              (*to the* Chancellor)
Continue!
CHANCELLOR: And therefore they have given judgment
That your afore-said union is no more
A fact; and they declare it null and void.
The bestowal of your family heritage
Of earlier date, in freehold to your husband
Remains in force; and they herewith do charge you
To reaffirm it lest sometime doubts arise.
To you, as life-estate, will be assigned
The City of Krems, and Polan around Horn,
And Grevenberg, by Ottocar, our Liege.
MARGARET: You've reached the end?
CHANCELLOR: I have, illustrious Lady.
MARGARET: There's much still I might offer in rejoinder!
OTTOCAR: Why do it? The judgment will remain in force.
MARGARET: Yet I submit!
OTTOCAR (*descends from the throne*): That's done. And now what
   else?
MARGARET: And go from here as they request.
OTTOCAR (*coming up to her*): I'm glad I find you wise and reason-
   able:
That is the Margaret I've always known,
And have respected always, then and now.
It's not the itch of youth that's wild and mad,
It's not the hot and heady urge for change
That bids me leave you. No, it is my country,
Which in me weds, unweds, and weds again.
As high as any man can rear his greatness,
So high has Ottocar upraised his own.

Here I am King; Moravia feels my strength;
Austria, Styria, I've won in battle;
My uncle must soon die and leave me Carnten;
    (lowers his voice so Margaret *alone can hear)*
In Hungary close by I have my hand:
The nobles look to me, the discontented;
Silesia's well-disposed; and Poland, like
A storm-racked ship, must soon make port with me.
    (raises his voice again)
From the Baltic to the Adriatic Gulf,
From Inn to Vistula with its cold shores
There's none whom Ottocar does not command.
The world since Charlemagne has never seen
A realm as wide and great as that I rule.
Why, even the crown of Charlemagne himself
Seems not so high but it might suit my brow.
Just one thing's lacking, which lacking, I lack all:
An heir to take my empire when I'm done.
If I would cap and crown what I have built,
Why, Margaret, I'm sure, will not refuse me.
MARGARET: I give, and gladly; to you more than myself.
  And not for my own good, but yours, I'm moved
  To say a further word and warn you.
  If it please you, come where we may speak alone.
OTTOCAR: You can speak here. Only where Kings are gathered,
  Is Ottocar the King in company.
  These men are subjects.
MARGARET *(quickly):* They are, sir; but how long?
  The very matter of my warning words.
    (comes closer to him)
  For all these lands, my family's heritage,
  They came to you when you and I were wed.
  Now that I go, and I go very gladly,
  Rebellion once more swings his hissing torch;
  And you have foes—
OTTOCAR: Are you some baker's wife
  Who wed her foreman with her shop as dowry,
  And fear the magistrates will come from town
  And drive me off the moment you're away?

(turns halfway round toward the Austrian Estates)
I hold them, see, in this right hand of mine;
Let them just make one move if they've the courage.
MARGARET: On every side of you are knaves and traitors.
OTTOCAR: Would you teach Ottocar to know his men?
I go my way. What blocks my path, must fall.
MARGARET: Don't cast my words aside with such contempt!
Before your feet yawns ruin, Ottocar!
(Repeated blasts of trumpets)
SERVANT *(enters):* The Styrian Estates wait at the door
And ask for audience at your gracious pleasure.
OTTOCAR: Let them come in.— You see now, Margaret?
The event does not confirm your dark foreboding.
(The Styrian Estates *enter, preceded by the ducal crown on a cushion)*
SPOKESMAN *(kneels before* Margaret*):* Illustrious Lady—
MARGARET *(motions him away):* Not to me!
OTTOCAR: Here, if you please!
It is the King who makes his wife a Queen.
You need not speak; I know what you are after.
I've fought to win your country from the Huns,
And what I've won, no man shall take away;
Not even you, if you should ever try.
Just find your places and await what comes.
I tell you also, look at me very closely;
And then, when next you enter, you'll know at once
Whom you should kneel to.
(The Styrians take their places in the same row with the Austrians, opposite the throne, those who carry the crown in front)
OTTOCAR: Now, one final matter.
You have the covenant here, Lord Chancellor?
The deed of gift to me of Margaret's lands?
CHANCELLOR: Not I. Her Majesty—
OTTOCAR: You have it, Margaret?
MARGARET: It lies locked in a casket on the altar
In my own chapel.
OTTOCAR: Why then, I'll send for it.
MARGARET: No human eye has ever seen the treasure
That casket keeps for me beneath its lock.

It lies beside my husband's precious likeness,
Beside sad relics of my two dead sons,
Beside the blood-stained arrowhead that pierced
My brother's heart on River Leitha's bank.
I pray your leave to go.
OTTOCAR: Just as you please.
(Trumpets and cheers outside)
SERVANT *(enters):* Oh, sir!
OTTOCAR: What now?
*(Enter the Estates of Carinthia, knights and peasants all together,
    with the ducal crown before them on a cushion)*
OTTOCAR: Who are they?
MARGARET: Shall I go?
OTTOCAR: I pray you, do. You see me much engaged.
    What! Still more crowns?
(Exit Margaret)
SERVANT: Most gracious Sire, the King
    Of Hungary is here—
OTTOCAR *(goes to the men who are carrying the crown):* What men
    are you?
SPOKESMAN: The Duke of Carnten, Sire, your Grace's uncle—
OTTOCAR: Is he dead?
SPOKESMAN: He is, your Majesty; and so,
    By virtue of the testimony contract
    Made with your Grace, his land and crown are yours.
OTTOCAR: Those who don't get his land, may mourn for him.
    You're welcome here, my worthy men of Carnten.
    Just add your crown to those two others there
    And let me feast my eyes upon the royal sight.
*(The Carinthians take their places in a row with the Austrians and
                    Styrians)*
OTTOCAR: They're shouting still. What is it?
SERVANT: I told you once!
    The King of Hungary, sir, rides through the gates.
    With him are envoys of the Imperial Diet
    Who bear the double eagle as their standard.
    They're shouting—
VOICES *(outside):* Ottocar, the German Emperor!
VOICES *(inside the hall):* Hail Ottocar, the German Emperor, hail!

OTTOCAR *(on foreground):* Now, earth, stand fast!
  You never yet have borne a greater man!
  (hastens back to welcome the King of Hungary.

While Ottocar *is so occupied,* Merenberg *walks over to* Bertold
Emerberg *who is in the extreme foreground, left, the first of the
Austrian nobles)*
MERENBERG *(whispers):* There is a letter hidden in this kerchief;
  See that my son receives it. He understands.
  I'm off for Merenberg. And bid him hasten.
  (drops the handkerchief and moves away; Emerberg *picks it up.*

Enter the King of Hungary *with his retinue and accompanied by*
Ladislaus *and by* Cunigunda *in a cloak and an Hungarian cap)*
OTTOCAR *(goes to welcome him):* Illustrious Sire and Father, if God
  wills—
BELA *(steps back):* Before I answer, permit these men to speak.
  (The Embassy of the Imperial Diet moves forward)
FIRST AMBASSADOR: The Princes of the Holy Roman Empire,
  Gathered to choose an Emperor at Frankfort,
  Send us to you, Prince of Bohemia.
  In searching for a man to guide the realm
  As Emperor, they've turned their eyes toward you;
  But it does not befit us to elect
  A man as liege who might refuse election;
  And so we've come to ask you, puissant King,
  If, when the council offers you the crown,
  You will take up the burden of the Empire.
  Do not refuse! You know the ancient saying:
  The Imperial Eagle will make his home at last
  In the Lion's nest. So now, magnanimous Lion,
  *(seizes a shield with the figure of a lion upon it that stood beside
    the steps of the throne, and raises it high in the air)*
  Receive the Eagle as he flies forlorn;
  Give him strong shelter from his many foes!
OTTOCAR: Ha! What is this? Who has done this to me?
  Why, that is not Bohemia's white lion!
  That lion's red!
RUDOLPH *(comes toward the center of the stage from where he has*

been standing beside the throne, right front): It's Hapsburg's lion,
  Sire!
The shield is mine. I left it as I came.
SECOND AMBASSADOR: Are you the Count of Hapsburg?
RUDOLPH: Yes, I am.
SECOND AMBASSADOR: You, in Bohemia?
RUDOLPH: Back from the Prussian wars.[9]
OTTOCAR: Enough.— You'll wait, my Lord Ambassador,
  Until you're called again.
                    (turns to King Bela)
                                    Most Noble Prince,
  My duty calls me doubly to you now.
BELA: But first let me present my grandchildren.
  This one is Ladislaus; my heir, when I am gone.
  The other one—
OTTOCAR: I did not know, King Bela,
  You had two grandsons.
BELA: You don't suspect?
                    (to Cunigunda)
  See! You're not welcome here.
CUNIGUNDA: Yet it was I
  Who most especially wished to win your favor.
  Can I not find a place among your soldiers?
  *(throws off her horseman's cloak and Hungarian cap; she is
                    wearing a woman's dress)*
ZAVISH *(stands not far from her, left; loudly):* How fair a soldier!
CUNIGUNDA *(turns in his direction):* Who said that?
OTTOCAR *(angrily):* Who spoke?
ZAVISH *(also turns to look):* It seemed to come from there, from the
  far corner.
CUNIGUNDA *(quickly):* Why, it was—wasn't *you!* You wouldn't dare
  Tell me it wasn't when I stood so close.
  Your Highness will forgive this sudden visit.
  They wished to let me cool my heels outside;
  But I preferred the inside, so I came.
RUDOLPH *(who has taken his old position, right front):* Oh, what a
  rude and ruthless haste is this!
                    (Queen Margaret *returns with the documents)*
OTTOCAR *(starts toward her):* Not now!

MARGARET *(supports herself by a chair):* O God! Will none help me
  away?

MERENBERG *(steps forward):* Who aids the Queen?

OTTOCAR: Who was it summoned you?
  Who was it gave you leave to quit your place?
  It's not the first time, either, you have meddled.
          *(*Merenberg *returns to his place)*

MARGARET *(in a faint voice):* Oh, let me go! Will no one help me?

RUDOLPH: Here is my arm, illustrious Queen and Lady;
  Hapsburg was still the refuge of the wronged.

OTTOCAR: Who bade you interfere?

RUDOLPH: Who needs a bidding
  When none can say him nay?

OTTOCAR: Do not forget
  I rule this land.

RUDOLPH: Which I can leave at will.
  I fought beneath your flag because I chose,
  And not for pay; and you may keep your thanks.
  I'm not your subject.

OTTOCAR: Not one step further!
  Wait till he speaks who has the right to speak.

SECOND AMBASSADOR *(steps forward):* Then I will give this Princess
  my protection,
  I, Chancellor of the Archbishop of Mainz,
  Sent by him with the Electoral Embassy
  That I might listen while the others speak.
  You know me, Count of Hapsburg?

RUDOLPH: No, in truth.

SECOND AMBASSADOR: Once in the forest close by Basel you found
  A priest who bore the sacrament to comfort
  A sick man, but stood helpless on the bank,
  His way barred by the raging stream. Did you
  Not give him your own horse to speed his errand?

RUDOLPH: That priest—?

SECOND AMBASSADOR: And did you not another time
  Give escort to the Archbishop of Mainz
  Through hostile lands, through war and flame and death,
  When he was journeying to the Pope in Rome?
  He often told his clerk to seek you out,

To talk with you, and learn something of you.
Do you not recognize the clerk again?
RUDOLPH: You're he?
SECOND AMBASSADOR *(turns to the assembly)*: I ask, for Lady
 Margaret,
 As Princess of the Empire, a safe and open way.
 Lord Count of Hapsburg, give your arm to her.
 We shall escort her where none can disturb her.
 In the name, then, of the Holy Roman Empire,
 Make way for Margaret, Duchess of Austria!
   (They escort Queen Margaret *out of the hall)*
OTTOCAR: When I'm your Emperor, you'll sing a different tune.
FIRST AMBASSADOR: Will it please your Majesty to make us answer?
ZAVISH *(pushes his way forward)*: You come to steal our King from
 us, our liege?
 Is he not mighty? What need has he of you?
 He reigns on earth as the Lord God in Heaven.
 The Empire brings in troubles and no profits.
 Leave him in peace and take your gifts to Germans.
 You give because you need. Leave our King alone!
OTTOCAR: He speaks not badly, Lord Ambassador.
 There's much that must be remedied in the Empire.
 There's many a stubborn neck to bend, and break.
 I see till now your master's been your servant.
 As sovereign of Bohemia I am rich;
 God fend that I become a needy Emperor.
 However, you're to wait. We might be pleased
 To look upon your plea with greater favor.
    (turns to Cunigunda*)*
 And now I'm yours, with all my soul and body.
ZAVISH: Long live King Ottocar!
   (Cheers and blare of trumpets)
VOICES *(on all sides)*: King of Bohemia!
 Austria! Styria! Carnten! Carniola!
 The German Emperor! Long live Ottocar!
   (The curtain falls.)

Act 2

Verandah with a marble balustrade some three feet high at the back; it is assumed that beyond this balustrade the garden descends in a series of terraces. Front, both sides, doors; beside them, statues. The main entrance is between the columns at the left side of the balustrade.

ZAVISH *(enters laughing):* I've fallen in love! Alas! My heart is lost!
    Good people, lend me aid! Ha, ha, ha, ha!
    The way she looked at me with those black eyes,
    The proud Hungarian! It won't help her much.
    And, by the God of miracles, she's fair!
    An untamed full-blood filly who fears a rider
    And fights the bridle that's to hold her in.
    And other things progress to please God well.
    The Austrians have taken to their heels
    Since Margaret left as though they fled the plague;
    One right, one left, but each and every one
    To Frankfort where the Electors sit. Now, now!
    They mean no harm. They only wish to urge
    Our Ottocar be picked to head the Empire.
MILOTA *(off-stage):* Bring him in here for now.
ZAVISH: Whom have they got?
(Enter a troop of armed men with a prisoner, Seyfried Merenberg.
   Milota, *in full armor, follows; he has a sealed letter in his hand)*
MILOTA: The King's still at the tourney?
ZAVISH: Yes, he is.
    Why look! Young Merenberg! With such an escort!
MILOTA: His father, the black traitor, sent him off
    To take this letter to the Archbishop
    Of Mainz. He must have bidden him make haste—
SEYFRIED: He did, he did!
MILOTA: But the young man, whose way
    Led him straight past the door where Brother Benesh
    Now dwells with Berta, his daughter and our cousin,—
    He wished to see his old love once again;
    And so they caught him and sent him here to us.

ZAVISH: What? With our little cousin? Not with Fair Berta?
SEYFRIED: They told me she lay sick with fever, sick
  And crazed. I hoped to see with my own eyes
  If she still lived. And all I did was put
  My father's head and mine in hostile hands,
  Fool that I was—the blind, accursed fool!
MILOTA: Here is his letter, marked with name and place.
SEYFRIED: Lord Zavish, listen! I never cared for you;
  I always thought you false and double tongued.
  My father tells me, though, I don't know men.
  Oh, show me, sir, that I did not know you!
  Give me the letter, let us destroy it here.
  With me do as you please; I ask no mercy.
  I'll only plead, I once did you a favor:
  I think you know the time you and your friends
  And relatives let rather curious words
  Escape your lips, in the Queen's ante-chamber.
  I didn't run hot-foot to tell the King,
  As I might have done and should have done, perhaps;
  For I still loved and honored Ottocar
  As consort of my country's sovereign Lady
  And as my true and honorable liege.
ZAVISH: You hear, friend Milota?
MILOTA: Who cares for him?
ZAVISH: The letter is in order.
          (reads)
                    To his Lordship,
  The archbishop of Mainz. You're lost, my friend,
  If such a letter ever reached the King.
SEYFRIED: Sir, you can save me.
ZAVISH: Yes, I know.— These men
  Are to be trusted?
         (points to the soldiers)
MILOTA: Yes. Why do you ask?
ZAVISH *(weighs the letter in his hand)*: The letter may hold much—
  or may hold little:
  A merest drop of venom—
      (quickly puts the letter behind his back)
                    a sea of doubt.

(turns toward the guards)
You may go home. Give our respects to Benesh.
MILOTA: What are you doing?
ZAVISH: Begone!

(Exeunt the guards)
ZAVISH: And you, my friend,
What will you give if I save you this once?
SEYFRIED: My life—
ZAVISH: No need! Just keep that for yourself.
You're good at jumping, too?
MILOTA: Zavish!
ZAVISH: Come on!
Here is your letter. Take it!

(leads him to the balustrade)
Now jump!
(Seyfried *jumps the balustrade*)
MILOTA: Why, you are mad!
ZAVISH: Heigh! How the lad can run!
MILOTA: He'll get away!
ZAVISH: Come back! Did you entrust
Yourself to me? Then if so, why not trust me?
And I know best what's right and what is not.
Some day it may disclose itself to you.
Besides, he's just a boy; my heart is soft!
Ha, Ha!— Don't stop to talk. Things are afoot
To which I feel no wish for witnesses.
You promised me free rein in this affair.
Then go!
MILOTA *(turns around just as he leaves):* You won't return and
share the jousting?
ZAVISH: No, I've already laid my arms aside;
The prize is mine. Now go! The moment's here,
And, knocking like a creditor, demands its own.

(Exit Milota)
ZAVISH: And there she is! Coming toward me down the path
With just one maid-in-waiting at her side.
I must be quick!
*(turns toward a statue of the Goddess of Love which stands left
front)*
Goddess of Love, chaste Venus,

The faithful spouse of thy most charming consort,
I do beseech thee, give me thy protection.
*(produces a sheet of paper, climbs up to the statue on a ledge of
the pedestal and puts the paper under the half raised foot of the
goddess)*
Let none but her find what I trust to thee.
They're coming.— I must wait a little.— Now!
(jumps down and hastens away as if ashamed

At the same moment enter Queen Cunigunda *and her* lady-in-
waiting, *left rear)*
CUNIGUNDA: Wasn't that Rosenberg? The brazen fellow!
Have him come back.
LADY-IN-WAITING *(calls into the wings):* Lord Zavish, please come
here!
The Queen commands. Come here! You must!
(Zavish returns, twisting his cap in embarrassment)
CUNIGUNDA: I do not know, sir, if I'm fully sane,
Or whether I've fallen a prey to feverish dreams
Of late. Or are you really quite as shameless,
As mad, as— No, the language lacks a word;
Derangement might serve partly to express it—
As shamelessly deranged as you pretend?
The day I came, your voice was shrilly raised—
It's true! I stood three steps away and *know* it!
Since then you follow me about with eyes—
With eyes that I'll not try to find a word for;
The thought of them's enough to make me fume.
(comes nearer to him)
Just now, in dancing, when I gave my hand,
Yes, brazen fellow, yes! You dared to *press* it!
Who am I, sir; and who are you?
ZAVISH: Forgive!
CUNIGUNDA: Is that the way you treat queens in your land?
If I were not too proud to stir the King
To wrath in my own cause; if things were here
The way they are at home in Hungary,
Where women also have a right, a voice,
And power to do what they think good to do,
A queen is not just consort of the king,

But really rules; you'd rue what you have done.
ZAVISH: Forgive!
CUNIGUNDA: And now: Forgive! First bold and brazen, daring,
And now so servile that it sickens me.
What was it you were hiding by that statue?
ZAVISH: That statue?— Is there something there?
CUNIGUNDA: A paper.
ZAVISH: A paper? Why, of course!
CUNIGUNDA (*to* lady-in-waiting, *who obeys*): Go take it down.
What's written on this sheet?
ZAVISH: I do not know.
CUNIGUNDA: You put it there yourself.
ZAVISH: I did? Oh, no!
CUNIGUNDA: Just now, as I came up.
ZAVISH: I wasn't here;
I came from over there.
CUNIGUNDA: By holy Heaven,
I must be mad! My head spins like a top.
Are these things trees? And are those earth and air?
I say I saw it. I stood three steps away
And saw you hide the paper by the statue.
ZAVISH: Then, if you saw it, most exalted Lady,
It must be so, though it had never been.
CUNIGUNDA: What's written on the paper?
ZAVISH: Merely fancies
That flamed up from a poet's fervent heart.
CUNIGUNDA (*to* lady-in-waiting): Bring it here!
(*unfolds the paper and reads the superscription*)
"To the Fairest One." You're insolent!
Take back this witness of your brazen folly.
(*throws the paper at his feet*)
Don't ever dare approach my side again
Or else the *King* shall punish such an outrage.
ZAVISH (*picks up the paper and kneels with it before the* lady-in-waiting): Now, lady, know; I am your loyal knight.
The secret long has burned and seared my breast.
In these few lines I dared to make confession;
My lady, I am lost, if I offend.
(*rises: exit*)

CUNIGUNDA: Why, I can't keep from laughing, he's so daft!

LADY-IN-WAITING: Look, Majesty, before you'd wink an eye
I've won myself a knight and troubadour.

CUNIGUNDA: What makes you think his words were meant for
you?
He has his eyes on me—so proud and brazen!

LADY-IN-WAITING: But, Majesty, what of it? Just to imagine
That such a knight would pay me court is sweet.

CUNIGUNDA: That such a knight—! You'll have me laughing soon!

LADY-IN-WAITING: Yes, gracious Queen, in all Bohemia
None can compare with Zavish Rosenberg.
His stately walk, his noble port and carriage,
And all his many noble gifts of body,
You saw them, Majesty, no less than I.
But he leads all who bear the name of knight
In valor, too; heroic mold of heart;
And he was long at school in Padua
And can make rhymes and sing them to the lute.

CUNIGUNDA: So much the worse!

LADY-IN-WAITING: Your Majesty is jesting!

CUNIGUNDA: At home in Hungary they pay zither players
With coins, and with contempt.

LADY-IN-WAITING: Not so with us.
There's many a noble vies with troubadours;
This very Zavish has won many a heart
With songs he sang to the music of his lute.
(opens the paper)
You shall soon see.

CUNIGUNDA *(has sat down)*: He'll surely pay for this.

LADY-IN-WAITING *(reads)*: "To the Fairest One." I take the words
with thanks.
O hand of snow—

CUNIGUNDA: "O hand of snow?" What does that mean.

LADY-IN-WAITING: Snow-white.

CUNIGUNDA *(takes off her glove and looks at her hand)*: How does
he know? He never saw my hand;
My glove at most.

LADY-IN-WAITING *(reads)*:
O hand of snow

That's yet so hot—
(Cunigunda *stamps her foot*)
LADY-IN-WAITING: What is it, Majesty?
CUNIGUNDA: You may read on.
I mean, do just whatever pleases you.
LADY-IN-WAITING:
O hand of snow
That's yet so hot;
O fiery eyes
That warm us not:
CUNIGUNDA: I wish they glowed so hot that I could scorch you;
And then I'd torture him till I'm avenged.
LADY-IN-WAITING:
Those sweetest lips
Speak cruelly;
The surging bosom
With steel doth vie.
CUNIGUNDA: Be still!
LADY-IN-WAITING:
O eyes, bring warmth;
O breast, grow soft;
O hand—
CUNIGUNDA: I tell you, you're to hold your tongue!
LADY-IN-WAITING: Am I to have no pleasure in my conquest?
CUNIGUNDA: The little fool! She must think he means her!
(*rises*)
Oh, if only I could leave this land, could go
To Hungary and be with my own people!
I counted there! Was free to roam about,
This way or that, wherever pleasure called.
Old as he was, my father did my will;
The princes too, his friends; and everyone
Who bore the name of man in that broad realm,
Who had some life and fire, and dash and daring.
And then they summoned me to far-off Prague;
They said a king was ruler there who, young
And strong, was married to an older woman,
And yearned for someone ardent like himself,
Whose breast was swelling with his own bold temper.

I come and find that he is—old; yes, old!
Or, are his hair and beard not streaked with grey?
They say it's wars that made them so. What of it?
Is he not gruff and cross like all old men?
And overbearing, uncontrolled? God save me!
I did not come here to be meek and silent!
But all the rest, they flatter, beg, and fawn.
Their blood is slow, their hearts are cold and white—
Except this Rosenberg. In Hungary,
With us, he'd hold his head up, proud and bold,
Like that high-mettled captain of the Kumans,[10]
The first and best of Hungary's strong vassals.
And he is like him, too, in face and form.
But *he* was brave, a gay and gallant knight,
Was straight and open in his aims and acts;
While this Bohemian's a fawning coward,
Degrades himself, and smirches all his worth.

        (Sound of trumpets outside)

CUNIGUNDA: What's that?

LADY-IN-WAITING: It means the tourney's done, I think.
The prizes will be given to those who won.
That duty will be yours since you're the Queen.

CUNIGUNDA: They'll send us word.—Give me that scrawl you have.
I heard it once, but hardly caught the sense.

        (takes the paper)

LADY-IN-WAITING: Lady, his Majesty is close at hand,
And all the rest. They're coming from the jousts.

(Enter Ottocar with Milota and Fuellenstein; behind them are knights and ladies coming from the tourney, among them the First Imperial Ambassador)

OTTOCAR *(to those behind him):* If he insists upon it, bring him here.

        (to Cunigunda as he comes up)

The winner of the tournament just ended
Refused to take the prize except from you.
Well, Connie, how are you?

        (starts to take her by the chin, but she steps back)

CUNIGUNDA: Quite well.

OTTOCAR: Good Lord!

She's out of sorts, must be.— Oh, Milota!
(walks with Milota *to the other side of the stage, front)*
Young Merenberg escaped?
MILOTA: Yes, Sire, he did.
OTTOCAR: The devil! How did the letter come to light?
MILOTA: In the way that young folk have, he boasted of it.
There is no doubt. They saw the thing itself.
OTTOCAR: And the address? The Archbishop of Mainz?
MILOTA: The very same.
OTTOCAR: And Wolkersdorf is gone?
MILOTA: And Hartneid Wildon. All the Austrians.
Now that Queen Margaret's no longer here,
Are ill-disposed and steal away from court.
OTTOCAR: If I had the letter, I'd know the traitors' names;
And then I'd crush the spawn beneath my heel.
But now there's not a man I don't mistrust;
And I must watch them all, each mother's son.
Suspicion, blood-hound of the devil's pack!
For shame! Do you lure *kings* to join your chase?
(While Ottocar *is speaking,* Zavish Rosenberg, *as winner of the
tournament, has entered with an escort and stands before the*
King*)*
OTTOCAR: What is it?— Yes, you won the tournament.
I've found you still a brave and able man;
Go where you see the Queen and get your prize.
Oh, Fuellenstein!
FUELLENSTEIN: My gracious lord and master!
OTTOCAR: You'll take armed men and post them at all doors
That lead out of the castle, front and back;
And when our guests are leaving to go home,
Arrest the men whose names I give to you,
And hold them in close guard as hostages.
Him, now! I don't trust him.— And Lichtenstein,
Ulrich, he's smooth, too smooth.—
FUELLENSTEIN: And Henry, too?
OTTOCAR: Don't shout like that! Come! Listen, and don't talk.
(withdraws somewhat with Fuellenstein *and whispers to him.
Whenever he listens to what* Fuellenstein *has to say,* Ottocar *turns*

his eyes toward where Zavish *and* Cunigunda *are talking together.*
Zavish *stands before the queen who sits with fixed gaze, lost in
thought)*
LADY-IN-WAITING *(tries to get the* Queen's *attention):* Illustrious
Lady!
CUNIGUNDA *(notices that* Zavish *is standing in front of her):* How
bold and rash! Here too?
(springs to her feet)
LADY-IN-WAITING *(points to the richly embroidered sash which a
page is holding on a cushion):* The reward!
*(*Cunigunda *takes the sash and the page puts the cushion on the
floor at her feet)*
ZAVISH *(to the* lady-in-waiting*):* Mistress, let me have the paper
I gave to you a little time ago;
It was meant for other hands.
LADY-IN-WAITING: Sir! Other hands?
ZAVISH: Give it to me!
(holds out his hands)
LADY-IN-WAITING: I'm sorry!
ZAVISH *(still holds his hands out):* It's not for you!
LADY-IN-WAITING: I—haven't it!
ZAVISH: The words I wished to hear!
It found the hand that I would have it find.
(throws himself on the cushion before the Queen; ardently)
O Queen and Lady, a thousand, thousand thanks!
(slowly)
Thanks for the prize that you are soon to give.
OTTOCAR *(breaks off his conversation):* Why don't you give the
prize now, Cunigunda?
CUNIGUNDA *(offended):* I was about to! You did not have to tell me!
(approaches Zavish *with the sash)*
Sir Knight!
ZAVISH: You make me very glad. My Queen!
My head will humbly bow in vassalage.
(whispers)
Oh hand of snow
And yet so hot!
CUNIGUNDA *(whispers):* Be still, or else—

ZAVISH (*aloud*): I'll throw aside my arms
And armor; and girt alone with this dear pledge,
I'll make my way across the wide, wide world
And there proclaim your glory and my King's;
Proclaim them and defend them everywhere.
My life is yours and his.
(*whispers rapidly as* Cunigunda *bends over to put the sash around his neck*)
                    Old men like him,
They ought to woo and wed old women. Youth
Belongs with youth.
                    (Cunigunda *throws the sash on the floor*)
OTTOCAR (*calls to her*): Haven't you finished yet?
ZAVISH (*whispers*): This head falls to the axe if you so wish!
OTTOCAR: What is it?
ZAVISH: The sash slipped from her hand.
CUNIGUNDA (*to the* lady-in-waiting): The sash!
No patience is so great but it has limits;
Then let presumption also stay in bounds.
Here is the sash. Take it and fare you well.
(*she puts the sash around his neck; as she is bending over him,*
Zavish *seizes the ribbon on her sleeve. It falls to the ground and
he stoops quickly to pick it up*)
CUNIGUNDA: My husband, listen!
                    (Ottocar *turns toward her*)
ZAVISH (*rises and withdraws toward the center*): The Queen, Sire,
craves your ear.
OTTOCAR: What do you wish? What is it, Cunigunda?
(*Pause. During it* Cunigunda *looks at* Zavish *who stands quietly
with his eyes fixed straight ahead of him; she gives him one more
glance; then*)
CUNIGUNDA: You go today to Ribnik[11] for the hunt?
OTTOCAR: I do. Today. Why do you ask me that?
You look so ill at ease, besides. What happened?
Awarding prizes is so hard a task
I won't require it of you in the future.
                    (*turns away from her*)
CUNIGUNDA (*whispers to the* lady-in-waiting): He must give back
my ribbon. Go tell him so.

*(Ottocar has moved to the center of the hall. The assembly forms
a half-circle: the Queen is at the left end, Zavish at the right where
he has come to the front in his efforts to avoid the lady-in-waiting)*

OTTOCAR: Gentlemen, which one of you will free me from
  A care that burdens me past all endurance?
  The Lord of Merenberg, in Styria,
  He has most wantonly turned traitor to me;
  To me, and to his land that I now rule.
  He sent his son to Frankfort secretly
  With letters to the Archbishop of Mainz,
  No doubt to hurt and hinder Our election
  As German Emperor, now going on;
  And bring about unrest and black sedition.
  His son slipped through my hands; the father, though,
  He will not fail to pay the penalty,
  Nor his accomplices escape detection.
  This felon, now, has fled to his strong castle
  Where he is safe from all attack by force.
  The one who brings him, brings him to me alive,
  As his reward shall have the traitor's lands,
  All his possessions forfeit by his treason.
  Ortolf of Windischgraetz, you seem prepared?

FUELLENSTEIN: Then let me be the second, gracious Lord.

OTTOCAR: I'll give you men, the best I have, to help;
  Him here, and him—
         (points out certain armed men at the rear)

LADY-IN-WAITING *(reaches Zavish's side after passing behind the
others)*: The Queen is very angry.
  She sends you word you must return her ribbon.

ZAVISH: The ribbon? Now and nevermore, my lass!
  I won it in fair fight and I'll give up
  My life, this head of mine, but not the ribbon.
         (takes the ribbon out of his doublet)
  Just see! How pretty! Red as your sweet lips
  And white as the bright silver of your shoulders.
         (touches her shoulder with his finger)
  No, this I'll keep and one day on my tomb
  With shield and helmet it shall proudly lie.
  Did I not stake my good red blood to get it?

You, blood-red ribbon, I shall keep for mine!
> *(holds the ribbon aloft)*

CUNIGUNDA *(at the other side of the stage):* He's mad; he is sheer
    mad! What if the King—

LADY-IN-WAITING *(to Zavish):* I see the Queen make signs. Put that
    away.

    Here is the King

OTTOCAR: What have you, Rosenberg?

ZAVISH *(puts the ribbon in his doublet):* Naught, Majesty.

OTTOCAR: What? Nothing?

ZAVISH: Sire, there are things
    One rightly hides and even from the King.

OTTOCAR: A love-token?

ZAVISH: A token, Sire, one loves.

OTTOCAR *(looks at the queen attentively; pause):* Who was it
    helped the Queen to dress today?

LADY-IN-WAITING: I, Majesty.

OTTOCAR: Are you so careless, wench,
    That you put bows upon one arm and leave
    The other plain?

LADY-IN-WAITING: Surely, it came undone.

ZAVISH *(bends over as if to look for it):* I'll look for it.

OTTOCAR: No need of that, Lord Zavish;
    Once the assembly's done it will be easy.
    By evening though I shall expect to see it.
    Whoever finds it, give this ring to him
> *(takes a ring from his finger and gives it to Zavish)*
    In the Queen's name, his lady and my consort;
    For queens make gifts of diamonds, but not
    Of ribbons from their bodice.— And you, my Queen,
    I pray you henceforth to take better care
    Not only of your dress, but my good name.
> *(to Zavish)*
    Do not forget your errand with the finder.

CUNIGUNDA: But in my name, sir, I would have you say
    That he may keep the thing that he has found.
    For what I give, a ribbon or a jewel,
    Changes its nature when it's I who give it,
    And is the Queen's gift then, and nothing else.

And let him also understand, I have
The right to give what pleases me, though it
Were more than ribbons, more than gold and jewels.
(exit)

OTTOCAR (walks up and down once or twice and then halts in front of Rosenberg): What happened, Rosenberg?

ZAVISH (sinks on one knee): Is my King angry?

OTTOCAR (looks at him steadily): You can't be fool enough to draw my wrath,
The wrath of Ottocar, down on your head
Just for a whim, just for a merest nothing?
Why, who are you that you should take that risk?
I breathe and Rosenberg has never been.
But I know you're too wise. Get off your knees!

ZAVISH: Not if you're angry.

OTTOCAR: I say, get off your knees!
(Zavish rises)

OTTOCAR: (to a servant who obeys): But you, go find my wife and say to her
That we have guests and she must not deprive
Them longer of their pleasure and her presence.—
You, Ortolf, I can trust to do for me
The thing you promised. And your reward is sure.
I'll teach these men to call the Empire in!
(strikes his breast)
The Empire's here!

SERVANT (comes back): The Queen is indisposed.

OTTOCAR: Oh, such a sickness is not hard to cure.
Just go again and beg her to come here.
(Exit servant)

OTTOCAR: Now, gentlemen, come with me to the hall,
And there let dance and feasting be your pleasure
And revelry hold sway till morning dawns.
(to Fuellenstein)
Do not forget my orders.

FUELLENSTEIN: Never fear.
(Enter servant)

OTTOCAR: Well, is the Queen coming?

SERVANT: She will not come, Sire.

OTTOCAR: She will not? Will not? When I say she shall?
Tell her— But no. She'll see it for herself.
Women have whims that we do well to humor.
I pray you, gentlemen—
FIRST AMBASSADOR: My Lord and King!
OTTOCAR: Why now, Ambassador! Are you still here?
FIRST AMBASSADOR: Still waiting for what answer you may give
To those who sent me, to the Prince-Electors
Of the Holy Roman Empire.
OTTOCAR: Sir, the answer
To such a question is not an easy matter.
I am a king, have charge of many lands,
Almost too many for one lone man's strength.
Now you would have me add another care,
The burden of new lands; of lands, besides,
That would help rule, and sit in council with me.
But I am used, when I have once said *Yes*
To have it cost the head of who says *No*.
Apart from toil, what can you give your Prince?
Your revenues from lands and customs, all
Are pledged. And what the Emperor had, this one
And that have seized with thieving hands, and shared.
This interregnum has endured too long.
Am I to risk the lifeblood of my rich
Inheritance in such a treacherous game?
You'd be well pleased, my lords, to help yourselves
In your crying bitter need, with my possessions.
But I prefer to stay in my own lands
And laugh at a poor German Emperor
To being a poor German Emperor myself.
Meanwhile, I'll not disdain the chance to crown
The highest power with highest name and title,
And sit, a second Charles, upon the throne
Of Charlemagne and wield the Empire's power.
But they must bring the crown to me themselves
And lay it there before me on its cushion;
And then I shall decide what's to be done.
I sent my chancellor of late to Frankfort

That he might learn what steps the Diet took,
And, see, he writes me
                    (produces the letter)
                         that the choice will soon
Be made, for they've agreed that Lewis, Count
Of the Rhine Palatinate, shall cast the vote.
He's not my friend, it's true; he and that bishop
In Mainz, they're hatching plots, my chancellor writes.
Only, these German princes will not dare
To risk a frown upon the brow of Ottocar.
The crown is mine—that is, if I accept it.
But it must first be here; then I'll decide.
SERVANT *(enters):* The Chancellor, Sire, Lord Braun of Olmuetz.
OTTOCAR: You see? He's back.
SERVANT: And with him is a knight
In shining armor such as Princes wear;
Two heralds, too, in black and red and gold,
An eagle on their coats, and blowing trumpets.
                    (Sound of trumpets outside)
ZAVISH: Permit us, Sire, our King and Emperor,
To be the first of your new servitors—
        (The whole assemblage starts to move toward Ottocar)
OTTOCAR: Keep back? Why, would you show the Diet's agent
He brings a pleasure that we'd dared not hope for?
And you don't know that I'll accept election.
            (to the Ambassadors as they start to withdraw)
Where are you going? I have not given you leave!
Nothing has happened to turn Us from Our thought.
That bishop, then, in Mainz, he'd best beware!
When I go to the Rhine, and that is soon,
In pay for all his insolent plots and moves
I'll come and oust him from his bishop's palace.
(The Chancellor *has entered during these lines and all surround
him with questioning gestures. He remains far back, wringing his
hands)*
OTTOCAR *(as before):* The Rhenish Palsgrave, too,—I like him not;
I'll give his office to his brother, Henry.
And there's much else I'll see to in your land;

And every man whose name is in this letter—

ZAVISH (*at rear: excitedly, but not too loudly*): What? Ottocar was
   not made Emperor?

   (*The* Chancellor, *his hands folded, shakes his head*)

ZAVISH: Who was elected?

CHANCELLOR: Rudolph, Count of Hapsburg.

OTTOCAR (*meanwhile has been showing the* Ambassador *the letter,
   pointing to several passages*): They all must go. He too—
   (*At the* Chancellor's *first speech he listens in keenest suspense but
   without changing his position, to what is being said behind him.
   When the* Chancellor *pronounces the name of* Hapsburg, Ottocar
   starts up suddenly; the hand with which he had been pointing to
   the letter, begins to tremble; he stammers a few further words*)

OTTOCAR: And he—must go—
   (*The hand which holds the letter sinks; he stands with trembling
   knees for a moment longer, then pulls himself together and walks
   with firm tread to his chamber*)

ZAVISH: Chancellor, tell me; is it really true?

CHANCELLOR: It's true, too true. Hapsburg is Emperor.

ZAVISH: How did it happen?

CHANCELLOR: Thus. All still went well,
   The Princes mostly voting for the King.
   Then suddenly appeared the Chancellor
   Of the Archbishop Mainz—he had been here—
   With him one Wolkersdorf, an Austrian,
   And Hartneid Wildon, who comes from Styria,
   Bringing complaints—But hush, the King returns.

OTTOCAR (*enters from his chamber*): Inform the Queen to hold
   herself prepared;
   I'm riding to the hunt while it's still light.
                (*walks up and down with heavy tread*)

CHANCELLOR (*after a pause*): Your Majesty!

OTTOCAR (*startled*): Who's that? You? Were you here
   A moment since?

CHANCELLOR: Ah, yes.

OTTOCAR: And did you speak?

CHANCELLOR: I did, Sir.

OTTOCAR: Hell's fire consume you!

(throws his glove in the Chancellor's *face; then leads him by the hand to the front of the stage)*
What did you prattle

Of Diet and election?

CHANCELLOR: Hear for yourself!

(Enter the Burgrave of Nuremberg *preceded by two heralds and followed by his retinue)*

OTTOCAR *(advances with heavy step as far as the center of the hall to meet him):* Who are you, sir?

BURGRAVE: Frederick of Zollern is my name,
Burgrave of Nuremberg, sent by the Empire.

OTTOCAR: Good luck!

(turns his back on him and comes forward again)

BURGRAVE: Rudolph, by God's grace Emperor—

OTTOCAR: Sir, the Empire would make sport of me, I think.
There stand the very envoys who came hither
To offer me the crown, and you elect
Another man before I answer?

BURGRAVE: Sir,
The Chancellor of the Archbishop of Mainz
Brought us report with what insulting words
You turned your back upon both crown and realm.

OTTOCAR: Why, they've broken faith, these insolent German barons!

BURGRAVE: You think those German Princes broke their faith?
You had best know what turned their choice from you!
We sought a ruler who'd be just and gracious,
And offered you the throne as such a man.
Then came the word—yes, then came witnesses
Who loudly cried in the Electors' ears
How you had hurt and wronged Queen Margaret
Who was your lady, but you cast her off;
How you curtail the rights of all those lands
That you withhold unrightfully from the realm;
How to displease you is to merit death,
And men are punished who have not been judged.
That's not our way in Swabia and Rhenish lands.
The Prince we choose must be a gracious man;

Before all else, though, we would have him just.
With this in mind, they moved to cast their votes—
LICHTENSTEIN *(behind the scenes)*: We are betrayed!
OTTOCAR: Who calls?
                    (Murmurs among the assembled company)
                                        That's Lichtenstein?
LICHTENSTEIN *(enters and comes forward)*: Let every Austrian that's
    here, beware.
    Outside the gate's a pack of castle bailiffs
    Who stop each one that's not Bohemian.
FUELLENSTEIN *(enters after him with drawn sword)*: Give yourself
    up!
OTTOCAR *(comes forward)*: Give me your weapons, Henry.
    You, Ulrich Lichtenstein, Count Bernhard Pfannberg,
    Chol Seldenhoven, Wolfing Stubenberg,
    You'll give your swords and selves in custody.
LICHTENSTEIN: What have we done?
OTTOCAR: Lest, friend, you may do something,
    I'll keep you fast locked up. Lest you take flight
    To the new Majesty, like Wolkersdorf
    And Hartneid Wildon, the two shameless traitors,
    And Merenberg—
                    (stamps his foot)
                            Who'll get me Merenberg?
    Once he's been haled here from his craggy nest,
    The judges shall confront you, each with all;
    And lucky he who feels his conscience clear.
                    (turning to Zollern*)*
    And now let us proceed with our affair.
                    (The hostages are led off)
BURGRAVE: This scene spares me the task of explanation
    Why the Electors, sir, did not choose you.
    Now to my message, King of Bohemia!
    Rudolph, by God's grace German Emperor,
    Summons you to meet with him at Nuremberg
    And take your place as cupbearer before him—
    Your office as Elector of the Empire—
    And there receive investment with the fiefs
    Bohemia and Moravia, rightly yours.
OTTOCAR: Just them? No more? And Austria, Styria?

BURGRAVE: And Austria, Styria, Carnten, Carniola,
 With Eger, Portenau, the Windish March,
 You will give back into the Emperor's hands
 As lands now wrongfully held in your possession.
OTTOCAR: Ha, ha, ha, ha! A merry tale indeed!
 Does the new Emperor ask nothing else?
BURGRAVE: Just what's the Empire's
OTTOCAR: But, sir, they are mine!
 Styria I won from Hungary in battle,
 With good Bohemian blood, mine and my subjects';
 Carnten I hold as heritage from my uncle
 By wills we made each in the other's favor;
 And Austria was brought to me as dowry
 When Margaret became my queen and wife.
BURGRAVE: But where is Margaret now?
OTTOCAR: Although we parted,
 She reaffirmed bestowal of her lands;
 And everything is mine that then was hers.
BURGRAVE: The fiefs of Austria and Styria,
 Pursuant to the Emperor Frederick's grant,
 May fall indeed to the last tenant's daughter,
 But not his sisters; and Margaret is sister
 Only to Frederick of Babenberg,
 Dead without issue to prolong his line.
 Imperial fiefs are not devised by will,
 Nor may a right to them be had through marriage;
 So give back to the Empire what's its own.
OTTOCAR: I can believe that he would be well pleased,
 Your new-made liege, if I should send these rich
 Domains to him in Swabia to mend
 His purse and fill his empty pauper hands.
 But I'll not do it! I'm old enough by now
 To know which side is loss and which is profit.
 So get you back and tell the German Empire,
 For there's no German Emperor I acknowledge,
 That many a crow shall fill his crop with flesh
 Before they get their hands on what is mine.
 He bids me come to him? Well then, I'll come;
 But I'll bring other guests to join the dance
 Whose stamping feet will shake the ground he stands on,

And far and wide clear to the River Rhine.
Now fare you well and tell your master that.
(Exit Burgrave)
ZAVISH: And we will meanwhile gird our arms about us
With life and limb to fight for our great King.
(exit; the others start to follow)
OTTOCAR: Halt, you! For what? For whom? Against what foe?
Throughout the land you are to carry on
As though deep peace prevailed. Then when it's time,
It's I who'll choose the guests to pay the visit.
Now come with me. Why, this new beggar-king,
He shall not save a single doe from death!
We'll ride to Ribnik to the hunt tomorrow.
You all are bidden. Merriment and joy!
Bring lights! It's growing dark. Bring out the torches!
Come follow me! The hunt is on! Away!
(exit, the rest following tumultuously.

It grows darker. A short pause. Then the notes of a zither are heard)
LADY-IN-WAITING *(enters through the door leading to the* Queen's *chamber)*: They've gone at last! Who plays the lute, I wonder?
CUNIGUNDA (enters): What's that? Who's playing?
LADY-IN-WAITING *(on the balcony)*: I can't tell who it is.
Hush! Words? "O hand like snow and yet so hot!"
It's Zavish, Lord of Rosenberg. He sings.
Shall I tell him he's to go?
CUNIGUNDA *(seated)*: Oh, don't disturb him.
It's pleasant, listening in the cool of evening.
(rests her head on her hand, lost in revery.

The curtain falls.)

Act 3

Hall in Merenberg's *castle in Styria.*

The elder Merenberg *stands at the open window, his cap in his folded hands.*

MERENBERG: The sun comes up. I give Thee thanks, O God,
An old man's thanks, who sees a new day dawn.
Thanks for the day, too, Thou hast given our land
When thou didst summon from the humble dark
Hapsburg's bright sun to shed its kindly light
And make our trampled meadows green again
And warm once more the harsh and icy air.
Oh, grant that we on Germany's outmost border
May likewise share the blessing it has brought;
That all who bear the name of Austrian,
Freed from an alien tyrant's harsh constraint,
Return like brothers to their parents' house,
Watched over by *one* father's kindly care.
Amen, so be it.— Yes! Who's there?
LADY MERENBERG *(outside):* I, father.
MERENBERG: It's you! Come in!
LADY MERENBERG *(enters with food and wine):* I bring you food
and drink.
MERENBERG: Just set it there. Who's talking down below?
LADY MERENBERG: Two horsemen, who wish to speak with you.
MERENBERG: They do?
Why weren't they brought to me?
LADY MERENBERG: I thought—
MERENBERG: Yes? What?
Am I at feud with any of my neighbors?
Am I not well beloved among the folk
That I should fear to bid two horsemen welcome?
Who knows, they may be bringing news of import;
News of my son, perhaps. Go bring them up.
                    (Exit Lady Merenberg*)*
I should, besides, seem to have grown suspicious
Were I to close my doors on guests and tidings;

Although the evil days we live in, urge
To caution and even justify distrust;
But I've got twenty sturdy guards below.
*(Herbott Fuellenstein and Ortolf Windischgraez enter, led by Lady
Merenberg. They are both fully armed and have their visors
closed)*

MERENBERG: Good morrow, gentlemen! Wife, bring more wine!
(Exit Lady Merenberg)
What brings you here? Before you tell me, though,
Be seated, pray, and share this food with me,
For that's our custom here in Styria.
(They sit down)
You would not like to put your helmets off?
(Both shake their heads)
A vow perhaps forbids?— But as you please.
You're on your way, no doubt, to serve the King?
King Ottocar?— His camp is by the Danube,
Far from here, at Tuln above Vienna,
On the northern side—or so I'm told, at least.
And Emperor Rudolph— Oh! Hapsburg, I mean to say—
He's on the right bank and lays siege to the city;
And neither thinks it wise to cross the stream.
But you keep silence? And you do not eat?

FUELLENSTEIN *and* WINDISCHGRAEZ *(rise to their feet):* We don't
break bread with traitors!

MERENBERG *(leaps up):* Take back that word!

FUELLENSTEIN *(draws his sword, takes his stand before the door,
and opens his visor):* You know me now?

MERENBERG: You're Herbott Fuellenstein.
(The other knight opens his visor)
And Ortolf Windischgraez! Why are you here?
(Ortolf steps to the window and sounds his horn)

FUELLENSTEIN: In the name of Ottocar, our King, I take
You into custody, charged with high treason.

MERENBERG: What treason?

FUELLENSTEIN: Did you not send your son to bring
Complaints before the Princes and the Empire?

MERENBERG: He's let himself be caught!—No, not complaints,
Only requests to help Queen Margaret

To hold what's lawfully hers by right of birth.
FUELLENSTEIN: But is your son not serving with the Emperor?
MERENBERG: I am undone!
FUELLENSTEIN: In very truth! Now follow!
MERENBERG: Where?
FUELLENSTEIN: There, where they will hold you tight and close
    Till you quite lose your taste for hatching plots.
SQUIRE *(outside):* Let me come in!
FUELLENSTEIN: Ortolf, guard the door!
SQUIRE *(outside):* Open the door! Be quick!
WINDISCHGRAEZ: Why, it's your squire,
    Young Bartosh, Fuellenstein!
FUELLENSTEIN: What can *he* want?
                (Windischgraez *opens the door)*
SQUIRE *(enters):* Sir, some Imperial troops are close at hand.
FUELLENSTEIN: Ill news, by God!
SQUIRE: They say they've taken Graz;
    They've captured Milota, the governor,
    And now are turning all the land to Rudolph.
FUELLENSTEIN: How can that be?
SQUIRE: Yes, and they say that Meinhard,
    The Count of Goerz, has joined the German side
    And now lays waste the land with fire and sword.
MERENBERG: Thank God for that!
FUELLENSTEIN: He'll not bring aid to you!
    Away with him! Put your two swords against
    His breast; and then if any in the courtyard
    Dare lift a finger, don't wait to strike him down.
    I know the way; I'll go ahead and guide you.
MERENBERG *(as he is led off):* My son is free, my Queen securely
    lives;
    My fate is naught; I'll bear what Heaven gives.
              (Exeunt all)

*   *   *

*Bohemian camp on the north bank of the Danube. The King's tent;
a table, with a map of the locality, in the foreground.*

Enter Ottocar, *the* Chancellor, *and several others.*

OTTOCAR *(as he enters, to his companions):* If he deserted, have
the rascal hanged.
It's nothing new to hang a thief. Hell's fire!
A coward, to my mind, is worse than any thief.
(comes forward, the Chancellor *following him)*
You dog my every footstep, Chancellor?

CHANCELLOR: Yes, every step you take, my King, my master,
Until you listen and grant me reply.
Sire, our case is evil!

OTTOCAR: *(paces up and down):* Our case is good!

CHANCELLOR: Is good!
With sickness, with a dearth of food in camp!

OTTOCAR: Fear is our sickness, courage what we lack—
Only a few of us, or so I hope;
And of that few there's one who hangs outside.
Have we the time for sickness? You say "hunger"?
I hunger but for one thing—victory!

CHANCELLOR: Five days we've had no word from Bohemia.
Perhaps—

OTTOCAR: Perhaps I'm just as ill served there
As here in camp.

CHANCELLOR: Here, Sire, you are well served;
Or here, at least,
(strikes his breast)
you are well served, my King.

OTTOCAR: May be, may be!

CHANCELLOR: Each night the Austrians,
The Styrians, desert your camp in crowds.

OTTOCAR *(halts):* I'll punish them! All this broad land you see
I'll make a waste where no man dwells, and only
The wolves and foxes have their lairs, such that
In years to come the idle traveller
Shall ask in vain where great Vienna stood.

CHANCELLOR: I have report that Rudolph's troops were seen
To the north of the Danube, on the side we hold.

OTTOCAR: Almost I think there's many a one would wish it!
But it's not so.

CHANCELLOR: The outposts, Sire, have seen it.

OTTOCAR: Send out brave men; they'll see no enemies.

CHANCELLOR: At Wolkersdorf—

OTTOCAR: I say you're wrong. I know.
They're my Moravian troops, if troops there are.
(stands by the table, looking at the map)
That was the plan. Moravians to the north,
Then Milota advancing from the south,
While we slip through the Danube like the eels,
And out of it like lions, once across; and then—
(strikes the table with his hand)
Like that, they're mine!
(resumes his pacing)
CHANCELLOR: Oh, God have mercy on us!
I think and think how we may save ourselves
And you talk of a victory.— I wonder
At the news that comes from Styria at times.
OTTOCAR: Aye, wonder all you will, good Chancellor.
Lord Milota is there, an able man;
No brains, but has a fist like stone and steel.
He'll hammer at one spot a score of times
And never ask you how.
CHANCELLOR: So be it, then,
I've entered protest. Once when I said before,
"Don't trust Bavaria, Sire," you trusted him;
And now he's let the Emperor cross his lands.
OTTOCAR: Fear's nose is very sharp at smelling fear;
You caught Bavaria's scent, I grant. None better.
CHANCELLOR: Don't think the Swabian Counts can lend you aid.
OTTOCAR: I don't believe they would have helped me much.
CHANCELLOR: To make the story short, Sire; Emperor Rudolph—
OTTOCAR: Emperor?
CHANCELLOR: Oh, I'll call him Hapsburg then—
He's not the man we have been wont to think him.
OTTOCAR: I should be sorry, were he less than that.
A soldier and a man, perhaps; no king.
CHANCELLOR: The thought of many a one who helped elect him.
The event has been quite different, quite unlooked for.
At Aix, when fiefs were just to be bestowed,
No one could find the scepter—they wished to plague him—
He turned aside, and walking to the altar,
Took down a crucifix—
OTTOCAR: To give the fiefs with?

The one who wants to give finds ready means.
If he would take, he'll need a stronger hand.
CHANCELLOR:
Throughout the German lands peace now prevails;
The robber barons punished; feuds allayed;
Through prudent marriages, by use of force,
The Princes are at one and leagued with him;
The Pope supports him; with one common voice
All praise and bless him who has saved their lives.
Just recently, when he sailed down the Danube
With all his troops amid much noisy clamor,
The sound of bells rang out from either shore;
On either shore the shouts of joyful praise
From crowds who came and gaped amazed and knelt,
Seeing the Emperor in his plain grey cloak
Who stood alone far forward in the boat
And bowed his head to them in friendly greeting.
Sire, called him Emperor, for he truly is one!
OTTOCAR: You speak so warmly for him?
CHANCELLOR: For you more warmly;
I swore no fealty to him, but you.—
But that two kings, so high and full of worth,
Should stand opposed when one word would suffice,
A single word, to bring them close together—
Yes, Sire, I've said it and won't take it back;
Though you be angry, I must tell you this:
The Emperor has sent a herald here
And bids you meet with him for sober counsel.
OTTOCAR: Be still!
CHANCELLOR: And he suggests the Isle of Kaumberg;[12]
For, since it's held by both of you alike,
You would not go to him, nor he to you;
And there on soil to which your claims are equal
You may agree on what will help us all.
OTTOCAR: My anger, sir,—
CHANCELLOR: Your anger shan't deter me;
I'll not keep still when duty bids me speak.
                    (*Enter* Zavish Rosenberg)
OTTOCAR: You come, and just in time. Silence this raven.

ZAVISH: What does he want?

OTTOCAR: He says to compromise.

ZAVISH: To compromise? The childish weak old man!
  A little time ago a troop of Kumans
  Approached the camp across a shallow ford,
  But I went out with my Bohemian men,
  And though they ran like mice, not one reached home.

OTTOCAR *(to the* Chancellor*)*: You see?

CHANCELLOR: One case! Luck fell his way, may be.

ZAVISH: Such luck as that will fell the foe at last.
  The axe is at the roots! We'll drive it home!

(to the Chancellor*)*

  You've never seen a force like ours, so full
  Of strength and courage, confidence and pride,
  Pride in itself and in the man who leads it.

CHANCELLOR: Zavish, you know too well that's not the truth.

ZAVISH *(goes on)*: And you can talk of compromise and peace?
  Though they are many, we are hardly less;
  Though they are brave, where will you find our match?
  An emperor leads them? The German Emperor stands here!
  This battle won, believe me, sir, he will be.

CHANCELLOR: Oh, Rosenberg, you play a treacherous game.
  I think you are not honest, Rosenberg.
  Our King, in other things just and gracious,
  Once did your house a wrong, in days long past.
  I fear that wrong took deep root in your heart
  And causes you to speak as you just spoke.
  Trust *me*, my King. My purposes are honest.

ZAVISH: The enemy's at a disadvantage, clearly.

OTTOCAR: Oh, no; *not* "clearly." The odds are in their favor.
  The sole advantage—but that will win the day—
  You're led by Ottocar and they by Hapsburg.

*(goes to the table and supporting himself on it with his right hand,
      studies the map spread out before him)*

ZAVISH: The day is ours, believe me, Chancellor.

CHANCELLOR: And if it is, what have we gained by that?
  Though you defeat the Emperor today,
  Next year he's down again with a new army.
  Your lands, once and for all, are discontented,

And ready for uprising and rebellion.
They'll call the Germans in, as quick as that!
And then, though Rudolph dies or falls in battle,
Another Emperor will claim what's due him,
And conflict with the Empire never cease.

ZAVISH: And then?

CHANCELLOR: And then?— You think it matters naught
To have our lands a prey to woe and horrors,
Our harvests ruined, homes and houses burned
And men and women slaughtered?—God have mercy!
Shame on you, Rosenberg, to say such things!
Was it for this our King risked gold and goods
To raise Bohemia to her prosperous state?
The ploughs are moving, weavers at their looms,
Spinners are busy, the mountains yield their wealth,
And you would have him wreck with his own hands
The very structure he himself has reared?
Let it be! You don't know what you say, Lord Zavish.
The King sees far more clearly than you think.

OTTOCAR (*to himself*): Was it not they who asked *me* for the
parley?

CHANCELLOR: Indeed it was!

OTTOCAR (*resumes his pacing*): What shame's in it, is theirs.

CHANCELLOR (*folds his hands in thanks*): He gives it thought!

OTTOCAR: It's weakness makes men friendly.
Why, Chancellor, to rule the whole wide world
I'd not have spoken the first word to him.

CHANCELLOR: Your honor is intact; your fame is doubled.

OTTOCAR: Forgive your foes! Good! When you've punished them!
It's weakness makes men friendly.

CHANCELLOR: My gracious master—

OTTOCAR: And truly, Zavish, I should like to see him!
How will he act, standing by Ottocar,
Poor simple Hapsburg in the Emperor's mantle?
What will he say when, using the same tone
I gave my orders in at Croissenbrunn—
"Count Hapsburg, on!"—I now demand my fiefs
And Austria and Styria from the Empire?

That way I'd triumph, without troops, alone!
ZAVISH: Suppose, though, by his cunning and deceit—
OTTOCAR: It's settled, Chancellor! Your offer's taken.
CHANCELLOR: A thousand thanks!
OTTOCAR: Don't thank me all too soon.
　I shall not go there just as you would have me.—
　When he stands there and finds no word to say
　And I tell him, "This mantle you have on
　I do not want. Just wear it undisturbed.
　But, sir, you're not to meddle with my lands!
　And so then, fare you well, and go in peace."
　The most I'll give him, is a bit of ground
　So he may boast of it at home and say,
　"This we have won and added to the Empire."
　I'll not grudge him that pleasure.—Now, Chancellor,
　Good luck! Our quest is peace and compromise.
　On that you lead the way; we'll follow *you*.
　And every soul in camp, both big and little,
　　(turns toward the entrance at which some men come in)
　Must be on hand in all his best array:
　Each coat of mail must glow with gold and jewels,
　And woe to any squire whose cloak does not
　Out-shine the Emperor's a hundred times.
　　　(exit, the others following him)

＊　＊　＊

*Isle of Kaumberg in the Danube. The Camp of the Imperial army.
In the background, elevated a few steps, a costly tent decorated
with the imperial eagle. Enter a* Captain; *after him, several armed
men who with crossed pikes try to hold back the on-crowding
populace*

CAPTAIN: Let them come in; those are the Emperor's orders.
　　　(Crowds of people come streaming in)
FIRST CITIZEN *(has made his way with a companion to the front of
　the* crowd*)*: We have a good place here, and here we'll stay.
SECOND CITIZEN: If he'll just come out once where we can see him!
A WOMAN *(to her little girl)*: Keep close to me; don't lose the pretty
　flowers!

SWISS SOLDIER: Where is our Rudy? I'm his countryman.
There's something I must ask the Emperor.
CAPTAIN: Be patient!— See! They're opening the tent.
*(The tent opens. Emperor Rudolph, clad in a leather shirt, is
seated beside a table. He holds a helmet in his hand and is busy
hammering out some dents in it. As he finishes his task, he looks
at it with satisfaction)*
RUDOLPH: There! That will serve me long, with careful use.
(looks around)
Some people here so early?— George! Lend me a hand!
(puts on his coat with the help of the servant)
FIRST CITIZEN *(well forward):* Just like a blacksmith, mark you,
the Emperor,
With a hammer in his hand! *Vivat Rudolphus!*
SECOND CITIZEN: Don't shout like that! He's coming out this way.
(The Emperor descends the steps)
SEYFRIED: *(kneels):* Most gracious Lord!
RUDOLPH: Ah! Merenberg? I'm right?
Don't worry longer; your father shall be freed,
I pledge my word to it. In the Western Realm
God's help has re-established peace and quiet;
And it will be no different here with you.
Bohemia's Prince comes to confer today,
And I shall speak of you before all else.
*(Seyfried retires; a little girl with a bouquet of flowers runs up to
the* Emperor*)*
RUDOLPH: Who's this? What is your name, my child?
A WOMAN: It's Kath'rine,
Katharine Fröhlich,[13] a Viennese burgher's daughter.
RUDOLPH: Don't stumble, Kath'rine. Such a pretty thing!
The look in her brown eyes is kind and good;
But roguish, too. And knows her charm, the minx!
What do you wish, good woman?
THE WOMAN: Alas, your Highness,
Bohemians burned down our home. My husband
Lies ill in bed with grief and shattered hopes.
RUDOLPH *(to one of his followers):* Write down her name and see
what can be done.
(to the woman)

As far as we can aid, you shall have help.
SWISS SOLDIER *(comes forward followed by three or four others):*
   By your leave, most high and gracious countryman!
RUDOLPH: Why, Walter Stuessi from Lucerne! What do you want?
                              (to the little girl)
   Run now and find your mother, Katharine;
   And tell her your father will be given help.
            (The little girl runs to her mother's side)
SWISS SOLDIER: Yes. I and the other men from Switzerland,
   We've come to ask you if you'd have the kindness
   And let us have some money?
RUDOLPH: Yes, money, friend!
   Money's a right good thing—if you but have some!
SWISS SOLDIER: You haven't any? I see.— And still make war?
RUDOLPH: Look you, my friend; you know from things at home
   That many a time a farmer lays up fruit
   And feed enough to last the winter through
   And on into the springtime. But the spring,
   Instead of coming late in March, holds off
   Till May, and snow lies where grain often stands.
   If then supplies run short, do you condemn
   The man as a poor farmer?
SWISS SOLDIER: God forbid!
   There's many a man's had that bad luck himself.
   And you? That's it!
                  (to the other Swiss)
                              You see? He is the farmer,
   And if the winter lasts,—the war, he means,—
   Supplies, that is the money, get used up.—
   Well, sir, we'll wait around a little while
   And meantime see what's in the peasant's larder.
RUDOLPH: If you don't wish to stay, go when you please.
   But any man who finds camp-fare too meager,
   And dares lay hand on any peasant's store,
   He'll hang, no matter who!
SWISS SOLDIER: Oh, well! It does
   No harm to ask and know just where we stand.
   We'll wait and see for three or four days more.
   Perhaps things may be better then.

RUDOLPH: So do!
    My greetings to the goodmen of Lucerne!
OTTOCAR OF HORNECK (*steps out of the crowd, forward*):
    Illustrious Sire and Emperor, hear my words!
RUDOLPH: Who are you?
OTTOCAR OF HORNECK: Ottocar of Horneck, liegeman
    Of the noble knight, Otto of Lichtenstein;
    Him whom with other knights King Ottocar
    Holds prisoner, unjustly, without trial.
    Oh, look upon him, look upon our land!
    He is a goodly liege; it is a goodly land,
    And worthy that a prince think of its weal.
    Where have you ever seen a land so fair?
    Look round about you! Where your eyes may rest,
    It laughs as when a bride goes to her bridegroom.
    Its meadows living green, its harvests gold,
    Broidered with flax and saffron blue and yellow,
    Sweet spiced with flowers and many a fragrant fruit,
    It sweeps beyond the verge in spacious valleys—
    A rich bouquet of blossoms everywhere,
    Tied with the Danube's bow of silver ribbon.
    Higher it climbs to hills all clad in vines
    Where up and up the golden clusters hang
    And swell and ripen in God's sparkling sunshine.
    While capping all, dark woods rejoice our hunters.
    And over it God's breath is mild and soft,
    Warming and ripening, making our pulses beat
    As never a pulse beats on the chilly plains.
    That's why the Austrian is blithe and frank
    And wears both faults and pleasures in the open.
    He envies none, preferring to be envied;
    And what he does is done with cheerful heart.
    May be, in Saxony or on the Rhine
    You can find men who have read more in books;
    But in what matters and what pleases God:
    A good clear eye, a sound and open mind,
    Therein the Austrian outdoes his brothers,
    Thinks not a little and leaves talk to others.

O goodly land, my country! 'Twixt the child
That's Italy and Germany the man
You stand, a gallant lad with warm red cheeks.
May God preserve the heart of youth in you;
May He make good what other have destroyed.

RUDOLPH: A worth-while man!

FIRST CITIZEN: Yes, sir; a scholar, also.
He's rhymed a chronicle, and you too, Sire,
Are mentioned in it.

RUDOLPH: I hope not without favor!
Your master, trust me, shall soon regain his freedom.
And you—in memory of this time—accept
The chain I give. Wear it where all may see:
Let knowledge and achievement have due praise.

(takes a chain from his neck and hangs it about Horneck *who has
knelt. To one of the knights standing near him)*
To you, sir, this seems much too high a favor?
Were I to touch this man here with my sword,
He would arise a knight, like many another.
What should I touch a man with, that on rising,
He'll write a rhyming chronicle like his?
But don't record this in your book, good friend,
Or I should seem to praise myself through you.

CAPTAIN *(enters):* Ottocar, King of Bohemia, draws near, Sire.

RUDOLPH: Almighty God, Thou hast brought me so far;
Complete the work that I began with Thee.

(A camp-stool is brought and set up, right front. The Emperor *sits
down and his retinue stands about him.*

Enter King Ottocar, *clad in splendid armor over which he wears a
richly embroidered mantel that reaches to his feet; he has a crown,
not a helmet, on his head. After him the* Chancellor, *and his
retinue)*

OTTOCAR *(as he makes his way forward):* I've long been looking,
both to right and left.
Where do you keep your Emperor, good sirs?
Ah, Merenberg! I come upon you here?
I plan to come upon you later elsewhere.

Well! Where is Rudolph? Oh!
      (catched sight of him and goes up to him)
                              Good morrow, Hapsburg!
RUDOLPH *(rises: to his retinue):* Why do you stand here with your
    heads uncovered?
    Ottocar's come to Hapsburg, man to man;
    Then Tom and Harry need not bare their heads:
    He's one of them, a man.— Put on your caps!
    But if a vassal comes to greet his liege,
    Bohemia to do homage to the Empire,
                  (steps among them)
    Then woe to him who fails to show respect.
                (walks firmly up to Ottocar*)*
    How are you, Ottocar? What brings you here?
OTTOCAR *(taken aback, retreats a step):* A meeting— I was asked
    to meet you here!
RUDOLPH: I see! You're here to talk about affairs?
    I thought you'd come to pay a friendly call.
    We'll waste no time, then. Prince of Bohemia,
    Why have you failed till now to heed my summons?
    Three times already I've set day and place,
    At Nuremberg, at Wurzburg and at Augsburg,
    That you do homage and receive your fiefs.
    You never came. Only, when last I called,
    The worthy Bishop Seckau came instead
    Whose actions were less worthy than his title.
OTTOCAR: I did homage for Bohemia to King Richard.
RUDOLPH: Richard of Cornwall. Aye! There was a time
    When one in Germany for good gold coin
    Could purchase more than merely lands and fiefs.
    But that time's past. I took a solemn pledge,
    I swore to my almighty, gracious God,
    That law and right and justice shall prevail
    In German lands. And they shall so prevail.
    You, an imperial prince and vassal, sir,
    Have done grave wrong to Emperor and Empire:
    You warred upon the Archbishop of Salzburg
    And harried all his land with fire and death;
    Your troops ran wild, and wrought such havoc there

As very heathen would turn from in horror.

OTTOCAR: He had fair notice that we were at feud.

RUDOLPH: Sir, we'll have no more feuds; we're to have peace!
The lands of Austria and Styria,
With Carnten and with Cran, the Windish March,
As fiefs illegally in your possession,
You will give back again into my hands.
Here is a pen and paper. It will be well
To draw and sign the deed without delay.

OTTOCAR: Why, by Almighty God! Who is this here?
Is this not Ottocar, and this his sword,
That any man dare speak in such a tone?
But, sir, what then, in case my sole reply
Is to return the broad path of the Danube
And ask more questions, at my army's head?

RUDOLPH: Even a year ago you'd have been welcome
If you'd thought fit to seek war's cruel verdict.
You are a prince well versed in war, who doubts it?
Your army, too, has long been wont to triumph,
Your treasury is tightly packed with gold,
While I lack much; or truth to say, lack all
And yet, sir, look! My spirit is so sure,
If all these men should go and leave me here,
My last remaining squire should quit my force,
I'd don my crown and take my sceptre up,
Go on alone to your rebellious camp
And call to you: "Sir, give what is the Empire's."
I am not he whom you knew on a time;
I am not Hapsburg, am not even Rudolph;
The blood of Germany flows in these veins,
The pulse of Germany beats in this heart.
All that was mortal I have taken off;
There's left the Emperor that never dies.
When I was called to take up this high office,
When, suddenly, I, who'd never dreamt such fortune,
Received upon my humble brow from Him
Who rules all worlds, the crown of this wide realm;
While still the oil was wet upon my brow,
I knew a miracle had come to pass,

And learned to put my trust in miracles.
No prince in all the realm so weak as I,
And now the Princes of the Realm obey me!
Disturbers of the peace fled at my voice;
It was not I that frightened them, but God.
Five shillings and no more lay in my purse
When I took ship in Ulm for this campaign.
Bavaria defied me, and he fell.
My troops were few when I marched on this land.
The land has furnished me with troops unasked;
They came to me, deserters from your ranks,
And Austria conquers Austria for me.
I swore that peace and justice should prevail;
And by the Triune God who sees all things,
Not so much, look you, not one little hair's breadth,
Will you retain of land that is not yours.
And so I come to you in sight of Heaven
Demanding: "Give back the Empire's lands you hold."

OTTOCAR: These lands are mine!

RUDOLPH: No; and they never were!

OTTOCAR: I have them from my wife, Queen Margaret.

RUDOLPH: But where is Margaret now?

OTTOCAR: No matter where,
    She gave her lands to me.

RUDOLPH: Shall I appeal
    To her to judge between us?—She's here in camp!

OTTOCAR: In your camp, here?

RUDOLPH *(in a different tone):* She whom you injured so,
    Whose rights and happiness you harshly stole,
    She came this morning, in kindliness of heart
    Pleading for mercy for the man who showed her none.

OTTOCAR: The woman could have spared herself the trouble;
    I'm Ottocar, and I need no one's pleading.

RUDOLPH *(sternly):* Aye, but you need it, Prince of Bohemia!
    If I but speak a word, you are undone.

OTTOCAR: Undone?

RUDOLPH: Undone. Cut off from Bohemia.

OTTOCAR: If you besiege Vienna, I'll come and free it.

RUDOLPH: Why, sir! Vienna's fallen.

OTTOCAR: Never!

RUDOLPH *(turns around):* Paltram Vatzo!
 Where is he? They asked for audience with me,
 The Mayor and the City Council of Vienna.

*(Enter Paltram Vatzo, Burgomaster of Vienna with members of the
    Council; they bear the keys of the city on a cushion)*

PALTRAM VATZO: In full submission, my Lord and Emperor,
 I bring you here the keys of our Vienna,
 Beseeching you not to be angry with me
 Because I've held the town until today
 In loyalty to the sovereign whom I served.
 I might have held it longer too—forgive me—
 Had not my burghers come and made me yield,
 Tired of the long blockade and sore privation.
                    (lays the keys at the Emperor's *feet)*
 Here with these keys I lay my office down,
 But you will find in me a loyal subject;
                    (rises)
 The country's liege is Paltram Vatzo's liege,
 Together with my land I give myself.
                    (retires)

OTTOCAR: By Heaven! O Viennese, unstable folk,
 Afraid you might not get your dainty foods!
 You'll rue the deed! I'll shut provisions off
 From Neuburg that's a fortress none can take.

RUDOLPH: Neuburg, the fortress, surrendered to me, too.
 You now hold nothing more south of the Danube.
 Frederick Pettau, come here.
                    (Pettau advances with down-cast eyes)

OTTOCAR: You shameless traitor!
 You let them have my fortress?

PETTAU: Not I, my king!
 A quick surprise attack, late yesterday—

OTTOCAR: No more! I know now I'm betrayed.
 But do not triumph! I'll laugh at you yet.
 An army's on the march from Styria
 With Milota, a leader tried and true.
 He'll strike your hireling squadrons from behind
 While like black thunder clouds I, Ottocar,

Sweep down the feeble straws that form your front
And there's no way to run but in the Danube.
RUDOLPH: I bid you say no more, hot-headed prince!
OTTOCAR: Do you see how far you're from your goal?
RUDOLPH: You should not base your hopes on Milota.
OTTOCAR: I'm on firm ground; it's rather you should tremble.
We'll meet in battle. Fare you well!
RUDOLPH: You leave us?
You won't give up the lands?
OTTOCAR *(as he turns to leave):* You think I'm mad?
RUDOLPH: Good! You shall learn from Milota yourself
If you do well to put such trust in him.
(Enter Milota *in chains)*
RUDOLPH: The men of Styria led him to me thus,
In chains, for he had cruelly oppressed them.
Remove his fetters from here.— Here is the banner
Of Styria, and here is Austria's banner.
*(The Estates of Austria and Styria come forward on the side of the
stage where the* Emperor *stands, carrying the banners and flags of
their lands)*
RUDOLPH: They came and begged protection from the Empire.
Be not so saddened, Prince of Bohemia.
Look round about you! The clouds have blown away
And everything lies clear for you to see.
Though Austria is lost—
OTTOCAR: Lost? No, not yet!
RUDOLPH: Do not delude yourelf! Your heart tells you
That it *is* lost! And lost to you forever.

You were a powerful prince and a great king
Before the chance of increase for your kingdom
Enflamed the passion for it in your breast.
And you will still be powerful, rich and great,
Though you have lost what you could not hold fast.
For God forbid that I should stir a finger
To take by force that which is yours by right.
Nor could I take it. You still have your great army
Trained and equipped for every kind of warfare,
And every battle's outcome is uncertain.

But do not use it. Recognize God's hand
That shows you here what is His holy will.

The futile lust for honors drove me on,
As it has driven you, when I was young.
My youthful arm essayed its hasty strength
On aliens, neighbors, friends and foes alike,
As though the world were just one broad arena
For Rudolph and his sword. Then I was outlawed.
I marched to war with you on heathen Prussia
And fought the hosts of Hungary at your side;
But in my heart I grumbled at the bounds
Which Church and Empire set with cautious fear
On dauntless courage, fit for larger tasks.
And then God seized me with relentless hand
And set me on the steps of yonder throne
That's built so high it rules a world, no less.
And like the pilgrim at the mountain's top
Who looks down on the broad expanse below
And on the walls that lately penned him in,
So my eyes for the first time clearly saw,
And all my sick ambition found its cure.
The world exists that all of us may live;
And none is great save only the one God.
The earth has dreamt its dreams of fiery youth.
And with the dragons and the race of giants
The age of titans and brute force passed by.
No more do nations sweep down on their neighbors
Like avalanches; the cloudy liquor clears;
Almost I'd say, unless all signs deceive,
We stand before the door of a new age.
The peasant walks behind his plough in peace,
While in the towns the workmen ply their trades
And industries and guilds lift up their heads.
Swiss towns, and Swabian, take thought of union,
The Hansa bravely sends its good swift ships
To North and East for commerce and for gain.—
Always you've labored for your people's good;
Give them the boon of peace, there is none better.

O Ottocar, that was a right good time
When we, but late returned from Prussia, sat
In the high hall of Prague's strong citadel
Talking of deeds we'd do in days to come.
And in those days Queen Margaret sat beside us—
Will you not see her? Not see Margaret?

OTTOCAR: Sir!

RUDOLPH: A Pity that you drove one from your side
Whose gentle counsel was of peace and concord,
Who knew the words to calm your hasty temper
And cared for all your needs like a kind sister.
With her you banished happiness and fortune.—
Your home brings you cold comfort, Ottocar.—
Would you see Margaret?—She's here in camp.

OTTOCAR: Not that, sir. But I'll do homage for my lands.

RUDOLPH: Bohemia and Moravia?

OTTOCAR: Yes, Liege and Emperor.

RUDOLPH: Restoring—

OTTOCAR: Austria and Styria,
All that's the Empire's; all that deserted me.
I have done much for them.— Ingratitude
And human baseness—how they sicken me!

RUDOLPH: Come to the tent.

OTTOCAR: Won't this place serve?

RUDOLPH: Vassals
Do homage to the Empire on their knees.

OTTOCAR: I kneel?

RUDOLPH: The tent will shield us from all eyes.
There you shall kneel before God and the Empire,
Not before any mortal man like me.

OTTOCAR: Lead on!

RUDOLPH: You're willing? Blessed be this hour!
Do you go first! I'll gladly follow you.
We *both* have won a noble victory.

(They enter the tent, the curtains close)

MILOTA *(crosses the stage and joins the Bohemians):* Thank God!
That makes me a free man again.
I'll not so soon forget the days just past.

(Enter Zavish Rosenberg)

ZAVISH: Where is the King?

MILOTA: He's in the Emperor's tent.
He does him homage.

ZAVISH: Oho! And hides away?
All who have loyal hearts must see that sight!

(draws his sword and at one stroke cuts the tent-cords so that the curtains fall to the ground. Ottocar *is seen kneeling before* Rudolph *who has just invested him with the fief of Bohemia)*

ZAVISH: The King is on his knees!

BOHEMIANS: On his knees!

OTTOCAR: Ha! Shame!
    (leaps to his feet and hurries to the front of the stage)

RUDOLPH *(follows him with the flag of Moravia in his hand)*:
Won't you do homage for Moravia too?
    (Ottocar sinks on one knee)

RUDOLPH *(gives him the flag of Moravia)*: I name you Margrave of
    Moravia,
Accepting for the Empire plight and pledge
In God's name and by my authority.
Arise, King Ottocar, and with this kiss
I welcome you as vassal and as brother.—
But all of you that are of Austria
And hold your lands in fief to Austria's sovereign
Come with us to Vienna and there take
Your oaths as loyal vassals at our hands.
You follow us, respected King and Monarch?
    (Ottocar bows his head)

RUDOLPH: Good! I await you at your gracious pleasure.—
Now wave your flags and let the trumpets blare
The happy bloodless triumph of sweet concord.
    (exit with his retinue

Ottocar *still stands with bowed head*

Seyfried Merenberg *has remained behind; after a little hesitation he advances to* Ottocar *with pleading gestures)*

SEYFRIED: Illustrious King, I come to ask—

OTTOCAR *(raises his head quickly and looks at him fiercely. With one hand he rips apart the buckle that fastens his mantle; the mantle slips to the ground. With the other hand he tears the crown from his head from behind and rushes off the stage exclaiming):* Away!

(As the others follow him, the curtain falls.)

Act 4

Before the castle at Prague. The great gateway with a portcullis, rear center, leads into it. Beside that, a small postern to which some steps ascend. It is closed. At the right, halfway forward, is the porter's house with a stone table and a bench. Before it is a bed of flowers. Enter Milota *and* Fuellenstein *at opposite sides*

MILOTA: Have you not seen the King?
FUELLENSTEIN: Not I.
MILOTA: Nor I.
FUELLENSTEIN: In Znaim[14] he slipped away from his retainers—
   One man who's missing may have gone with him—
   Since when he's wandered in Moravian lands
   And has been seen in little villages
   As he passed through; of late not far from Stip
   Where there's a fountain with prophetic waters
   That pilgrims seek from far and near for counsel.
   A miserable bath-hut stands far down
   Where no one lives and no one passes by,
   And there he hid away two weeks or more—
   A better place to die in than to live.
   And as the pilgrims there are wont to do,
   Who fix their thoughts on what they sorely lack
   And throw a cross of straw down in the pool
   To read the future as it floats or sinks,
   He did this days on end, and seemed depressed.
   As last the mayor of Hradech heard the story
   And went to Stip to bring the King away,
   But when he got there, found that he had left.
MILOTA: Where is he now? Have you no word of that?

FUELLENSTEIN: Some men report they've seen him on the way
  To Prague.
MILOTA: To here?— If so, I hope he'll stay.
  The wings he proudly spread are somewhat clipped;
  The land that always lured him off from home,
  He's given it back for good with solemn pledge.
  If he will rule here as his sires before him,
  If he'll drive out the Germans from his realm;
  And with us Czechish nobles at his side,
  Take thought for what will really aid his people,
  Perhaps I can forget the wrong he did
  To me and mine.— You'll see the Chancellor?
  Then take him word that an imperial herald
  Rode through the gates of Prague into the town
  Demanding that the treaty be complied with;
  That first of all the hostages be freed,
  The Austrians and Styrians who still
  Are wrongly kept as prisoners in this land.
  Tell him to do at once what is required
  Before the King comes, hindering this and that.
FUELLENSTEIN: But if the King should—
MILOTA: Do as I have said.
                    (Exit Fuellenstein*)*
MILOTA: If our whole land were not disgraced with him,
  I'd laugh at him as Zavish laughed that day.—
  We'll have all matters settled when he gets here;
  Then he can but approve—and go to sleep.
                    (exit into the castle)

                    *(Short pause. Enter one of the King's servants who looks
                    cautiously around and then calls off-stage)*
SERVANT: It's safe; there's no one here, my gracious master.
  *(Enter Ottocar, wrapped in a dark cloak and with his black cap,
  that has a black feather on it, pulled far down over his eyes)*
SERVANT: You wish the Chancellor?—Oh, good, kind master,
  Won't you consent to wait for him within?
                    (Ottocar shakes his head)
SERVANT: Two days now you've not eaten, you've not slept.
  Think of yourself, how much your life is worth.
                    (Ottocar laughs in bitter mockery)

SERVANT: I do beseech you, sir, to go inside.
      (Ottocar *impatiently stamps his foot*)
SERVANT: I'm going, sir. I pray you, do be seated.
      (exit into the castle)
OTTOCAR: How could I pass your doors, home of my fathers?
  Profane your threshold with these shame-shod feet?
  Victorious, amid triumphant crowds,
  I rode to you once through the cheering streets,
  Bringing you banners I had won in battle.
  Then you flung wide your gates to welcome me,
  And from your battlements my fathers watched.
  Your noble walls were built to shelter heroes;
  As yet none in disgrace has entered them.
  Here will I sit and act as my own gateman
  Lest shame should come and dwell within my house.
    (seats himself on the steps of the postern and covers his head
     Enter the Burgomaster *of Prague and several burghers)*
BURGOMASTER: Don't keep me back! I must get to the council.
  A herald from the Emperor's Majesty
  Has just arrived. In that case one must hurry,
  For now Bohemia is in the Empire;
  The King confirmed it with a solemn oath
  And pledged his loyalty upon his knees.
BURGHER: Upon his knees?
BURGOMASTER: Aye, at the Emperor's camp.
  He, down upon his knees; the Emperor, seated;
  The army all was there and watched amazed.
  What was that noise?
BURGHER: That fellow on the steps.
BURGOMASTER: Pride comes before a fall; I've said so, often.
  Just go see who the man is by the gate.
  Suspicious folk are roaming through the country.
  These paid-off soldiers should be closely watched.
BURGHER *(returns):* Oh, sir!
BURGOMASTER: What makes you tremble so?
BURGHER: The King!
BURGOMASTER: The man there on the steps? You must be mad!
BURGHER: He looked straight at me. See for yourself!
BURGOMASTER: It's he!

Can he have heard what I just said about him?
Should I get on my knees?— The best will be
To move away a little. He's lost in thought.
    (draws away from the burghers, *right front Enter* Benesh
        Rosenberg *and* Berta, *right rear)*

BENESH *(with a staff; leads* Berta): Just see how warm and fair the
    sun shines here.
You're better out of doors. Now, Berta, come.
The stuffy air inside is bad for you.
And talk a little, too; just to please me.
Please, Berta, please; just speak one single word.
Just "Yes" or "No," and make your father glad.
Why, come Midsummer's Day, it's been—how long
I don't just know—since you've looked up or spoken.
That grieves me, Berta. Won't you talk to me?
I'd rather hear your wandering feverish cries
Than not a single word the livelong day.
What's past, is past; we cannot change it now.
We'll think of it no more, then all is well.

BURGOMASTER: Hush!

BENESH: Ah, no need! She's silent as it is.
Day in day out her lips, sir, never open.

BURGOMASTER *(whispers):* The King sits yonder!

BENESH: Where?

BURGOMASTER: There on the steps.

BENESH: Oh, Berta, look! There sits the wicked king
Who brought you so much pain and grief, poor girl!
Now speak for once, berate him long and hard;
Tell him, "Poor man, I'm glad you're so unhappy.
It serves you right for wronging me and Father."

(Berta picks up a handful of earth and throws it straight in front
    of her like a child, failing to hit Ottocar)

BENESH: Yes, throw it at him! I wish it were a dagger!
Throw, Berta throw! An evil, wicked man.
But God himself avenged the wrongs he did us.
He had to kneel before his bitterest foe,
Before a man he'd thought was far beneath him.
He knelt to him in sight of all his troops.
Aye, toss your head! I'm not afraid of you.

There's someone higher has you in his power.—
Just make my daughter speak to me again;
Then have me killed, it's little I shall care.

   (Enter Cunigunda *with* Zavish *and servants)*

CUNIGUNDA: Who let that crazy girl come here again?
 Didn't I say to see she's kept indoors?
BENESH *(as he is led away):* Now, Berta, come. *His* lot is not light,
 either.

   (exit)

CUNIGUNDA: Away with all of you who've eyes to see!

   (Exeunt all but Cunigunda, Zavish, *and* Ottocar)

CUNIGUNDA: We're here alone, alone with our disgrace.
 Why don't you rise up in your pride, great King,
 And hold forth with great words, as was your way?

 See where he sits, the proud, the mighty one,
 Who felt the world too small for his great self;
 See where he sits, a beggar at the gate,
 And gets scant blessing, but the more contempt;
 This man who wore his crowns like wreaths of flowers,
 And when one faded, wove himself another
 Of fresh-cut blossoms culled in his neighbor's garden;
 Who held the lives of thousands in his hand
 And set them out, as for a game of chess,
 Upon a field marked off with blood and dust,
 And cried out "Check" as though they had been pieces
 Rude artisans had shaped from lifeless stones
 And then had nick-named *pawn* and *knight* in jest;—
 Who even sought to pick a quarrel with Nature,
 And when he rode one morning to the hunt
 And saw the sky was covered thick with clouds,
 He bade his company halt, called for the mason,
 And told him he need not hurry over much
 To finish the new church at Gueldenkron—[15]
 He sits there staring dully at the ground
 He used to stamp with that proud foot of his!
ZAVISH: Aye, Majesty, luck's round; and that's the truth.
CUNIGUNDA: What other men respect, he thought a game:
 He thrust his wife, Queen Margaret, aside—

My faith! Her years made her the one for him,
This Queen of Sorrows was a fitting mate—
And wooed a maid in far-off Hungary,
But never cared to ask if she perhaps
Had set her heart already on another,
Though at that very time one who ranked lower,
Yet was much greater, had asked her for her hand.
An unsubdued Kumanian prince counts more,
I'd think, than a dependent Czechish king!
But what cares he? He wants a wife and heirs,
Let break what must, and there's an end of it.
I came here with my free and valiant heart,
Quite worthy of a man of youth and strength,
And found— Why now, I found King Ottocar!
Not quite the sorry sight he crouches there,
Yet not much better, as God is my true witness!
He never let me share his plans or thoughts,
Treating me like a handmaid, not a queen;
For he must be the ruler, he alone.

ZAVISH: Ah, yes, my Queen; to rule's right sweet—well nigh
As sweet as to obey—and none will share it.

CUNIGUNDA: And he *did* rule; but now his rule is over,
Which, like a tawdry bubble, burst and vanished.

And he could talk, like a great man and sovereign,
And mouth loud words about the things he'd done!
What had not happened, what never came to pass,
Grew real upon his lips. When first he heard
The Emperor's message from the Count of Zollern,
How brave his talk, what royal airs he wore!
No single town, no house; no, not a clod
Would he release of Austria's broad domain.
And though the doctors swore a hundred times
The Emperor's sacred life was hanging on it,
He'd not concede them one small saffron leaf.
We have a beast on our Hungarian plains
Called donkey; and when he scents a wolf far off,
He loudly brays and kicks in all directions
And fills the air with flying dust and dirt;

But once the wolf comes close, he stands and shivers,
And dares not fight to keep from being fed on.
The King has done that very thing, well nigh.
He marched out on his foes with furious words,
Had half the world assembled in his army,
His camp a chorus, in ten different tongues,
Of Poles and Kumans, Tartars, Germans, Czechs,
So many Austria could not hold them all;
But when the time arrived to start the fray,
There was no heart behind these strong right arms.
And in his enemy's camp he— Rosenberg!

ZAVISH: Your Majesty?

CUNIGUNDA: Say, have you ever knelt?
Not before women—ever knelt to men,
For pay, for hire, from fear, knelt to your equal?

ZAVISH: Not I!

CUNIGUNDA: And never should?

ZAVISH: Not in my life!

CUNIGUNDA: But he, he did, knelt to his enemy,
Before the man whom he had once despised,
Who'd been his henchman, and when he said to him
"Come here!" he came, and when he told him "Go!"
He went and made some haste about his going.

ZAVISH: Your royal Highness, that was but a jest!
A jest among good friends. The Emperor, see,
He wished to show his strength to those who serve him,
And came and asked our King, and he consented.

CUNIGUNDA: But I'll not bear the name of bondsman's wife,
And share the lowly bed of a mean vassal,
And when the Emperor calls you to Vienna,
Help bear the train of his lowborn countess-housewife.
And I'll not kneel to Rudolph as you did.

                    (The King *leaps to his feet*)

CUNIGUNDA: Oh, don't jump up! Truly, I'm not afraid.
Would you have me the only person left
To shake in fear of Ottocar the King?
Give me an escort. I'll home to Hungary
Where kings can better keep their honor safe.
You, Rosenberg, your arm! And now no more

Of that disgrace which your eyes witnessed, too.
ZAVISH: Merely a jest. We all were much amused,
  Not only Rudolph; though he, of course, the most.
  And good it was to look at, I confess.
(Exeunt Zavish and Cunigunda)

OTTOCAR: Zavish!
ZAVISH *(returns):* What do you wish, sir?
OTTOCAR: Your sword!
ZAVISH *(gives it to him):* It's yours.
OTTOCAR *(draws back for the thrust):* You traitor!
CUNIGUNDA *(inside the gate):* Rosenberg!
OTTOCAR: Here, take your sword and go.
ZAVISH: Oh! Thanks so much! This is no place to loiter.
(exit in search of the Queen)

OTTOCAR *(stares at the ground for a considerable while):* Is that
  my shadow? Well, we are two kings!
(Trumpets off-stage)

OTTOCAR: They'll come and find me here! Where can I hide?
(wraps his cloak around him and steps to one side)

(Enter an Imperial Herald with two trumpeters; after him, the
Austrian hostages fresh from prison, Merenberg among them.
Jostling crowds follow; the Chancellor in argument with the
Herald)

CHANCELLOR: I enter protest here in the King's name.
HERALD *(holds the treaty in his hands):* Article three of the treaty
    that you signed
Declares all hostages shall be released.
Wherefore, with full authority given me,
I now claim instant freedom for these men
Of Austria and Styria, at this time
Leal vassals of the Emperor and the Empire.
And likewise I demand full execution
Of the terms of peace till now but half fulfilled.
Bohemian troops are still in garrison
In Austrian towns and districts, far and wide;
And Henry Kuenring, loyal to your cause,
Is harrying the land beyond the Danube,
Quietly helped by good friends in Moravia.

The Emperor sends word that that must cease.
And I have come to Prague to make an end.
CHANCELLOR: We cannot act before the King is told.
HERALD: Why not, indeed? The Emperor is sovereign.
    Such things are part of every vassal's oath.
CHANCELLOR: The Emperor, on his part, has not fulfilled
    The treaty in all the terms agreed upon:
    He still keeps soldiers in Moravia.
HERALD: They'll be withdrawn as soon as you comply.
CHANCELLOR: Why must Bohemia be the first to act?
HERALD: "To him that hath—" That law is of long standing.
CHANCELLOR: You call that *law?* I call it tyranny.
HERALD: Call it as suits you; but do as you're obliged.
CHANCELLOR: I can refuse you nothing, concede you nothing;
    The King, I'm told, is here in Prague. He only
    Can make decisions touching your demands.
HERALD: Then take me where he is.
CHANCELLOR: I cannot, now.
    We know he's here in Prague, but nothing else.
HERALD: Why, in that case, I'll have the trumpets blown
    Until their blare resounds throughout the city,
    Bearing the tidings to King Ottocar
    That messengers are here, sent by his sovereign.
        (Ottocar *steps out of the crowd. He has cast his cloak aside*)
OTTOCAR: Here is the King. What do you want from him?
HERALD: Sir; they refused to liberate these men!
OTTOCAR: Who has refused?
HERALD (*pointing to the* Chancellor): He!
CHANCELLOR: Only till you approved, Sire.
OTTOCAR: These men secured their country's debt to me.
    The debt is cancelled; take the garanty, too.
    But I see one face there among the rest
    That fairly makes me rue my given word.
    Hide yourself, Merenberg! You are no hostage,
    A traitor, you, traitor beyond dispute,
    The first, the leader of them all in crime.
    Out of my sight, I say! My hate is growing hot
    And craves to cool itself in your black blood.
        (Merenberg *retires behind two other hostages*)
OTTOCAR: What else?

HERALD: Remove your troops from Austria.
OTTOCAR: It has been done.
HERALD: Not all.
OTTOCAR: The rest shall go.
    The compact so provides; it shall be done.
HERALD *(makes proclamation):* Whoso has claims against
    Bohemia's crown
    For rights infringed or damages inflicted;
    Whoso owes homage to the German Empire,
    Is herewith bidden to the Council House.
    The Palsgrave there holds court and gives out fiefs.
    Vivat Rudolphus, Roman-German Emperor.
    (exit, the crowds following in a tumult; the Chancellor *alone*
        remains behind with the King*)*
OTTOCAR: They all go with him! They leave me here alone!
        (to the Chancellor*)*
    You're my whole retinue?— Ha, Ottocar!
    Held in contempt by the least of all my servants;
    Made mock of by my wife, and rightly so;
    Hounds at my heels, driven from house and bed—
    I cannot bear it, cannot live like this!
    My name is stricken from the roll of Princes;
    I'm now the vassal of the man I scorned;
    Scotfree, and laughing in my face, the knaves
    Who played me false, walk out my prison gates.
    Listen!
        (In the distance the herald can be heard repeating his
        proclamation)
OTTOCAR: *"Vivat Rudolphus!"* May he live in Hell!
    Call back the herald!
CHANCELLOR: My gracious liege and master!
OTTOCAR: Call back the herald or dread my anger, wretch!
        (Exit the Chancellor*)*
OTTOCAR: Better if I had sought my death in battle
    With my last swordsman fighting at my side.
    They basely tricked me, came on me by stealth.—
    A thick cloud lifts and leaves my eyesight clear.
    I have been dreaming; like cool morning airs
    Comes memory and wakens me again.

I took my troops and marched them to the Danube
And pitched my camp; so far my mind remembers.
From there all's dark! What happened next and further,
The way they lured me to the Emperor's tent
And there— By Death and Hell! I say I'll kill
Each living man who shared the sight!
Myself, too, if my mind cannot blot out
The image of that hour of black disgrace.

    (Re-enter the Herald, *with hostages; after them,* Milota)

HERALD: You sent one to recall me, sir. I've come.
OTTOCAR: First, you're to note that none makes proclamation
    In any name except in mine alone
    In Prague where I am King.
HERALD: But, sir—
OTTOCAR: Enough!
    Second, you'll have the hostages drawn up
    Before me. We must be sure that no one else,
    No one who's broken gaol, makes off with them.
HERALD: The Empire's guarantee should be enough.
    Still, sirs, I bid you fall in line before him.
OTTOCAR *(passes up the row):* I don't want you. Nor you.—How
    smart you look,
    Sir Ulrich Lichtenstein. You're glad, must be,
    To have got off! I don't grudge you your luck.
    You never cared for me, nor I for you.
    That makes us quits. So go, for all I care!
    But here is one with whom I'd speak a word.
    Good morrow, Merenberg, you knave and traitor!
CHANCELLOR: If he'll just hold his tongue, not contradict.
OTTOCAR: How does your son fare in the Emperor's service?
    A fine young man! A chip off the old block!
    You got him from the scene just in good time,
    Before things went awry with Ottocar.
    The last time I had speech with him, I promised
    He'd soon have news of me; and of you, too.
    How would it be if I wrote him a line,
    "That grey-haired knave, your father, lost his life?"

    (to the Herald)

He's not a hostage; he's guilty of high treason,

And can't go free with all those other men.
HERALD: He's just the one my lord, the Emperor—
OTTOCAR: He's just the very one his lord, the King—
        (to Merenberg*)*
  You were the first, you made the bad beginning,
  You showed the way that other traitors took.
  You wrote to Frankfort with complaints and charges;
  So they elected Hapsburg, who's my foe.
MERENBERG: I wrote no charges!
OTTOCAR: Not praise either, eh?
  No sooner did your son desert to Rudolph,
  Than all the other Austrians ran there, too;
  And that day by the Danube, played me false,
  Betrayed me; me, their rightful liege and lord.
  Perhaps you know where I last saw your son?
  It was in Tuln, at the imperial camp,
  There where King Ottocar— Death and damnation!—
  Before his foe—as slaves do—in the dust—
  May memory die out behind these brows
  And madness come and gather round my head
  And veil what happened there, in seething clouds!—
  There where King Ottocar—why not speak out
  When all the world looked on?—knelt to his enemy!
  And this man's son, he stood not far away
  And laughed.— And for that you must die! Aye you!
  The others may go free; he here, shall stay.
MERENBERG: O God in Heaven!
HERALD: Show him mercy, sir!
OTTOCAR: Rather, show you can hold your insolent tongue, sir!
  Or else, perhaps, before you speak again—
  No! Go in peace and let me have my way:
  I still am master here in my own lands!
MERENBERG: But Styria's vassal of the Empire now!
OTTOCAR *(to the* herald*):* He was my subject when he did me
    wrong;
  And as my subject I shall punish him.
  Into the dungeon with him! Whoso brings word
  That Merenberg is dead, shall be right welcome.
HERALD: The Emperor, though—

OTTOCAR: Sir, tell your Emperor
To rule in Germany as he likes and pleases.
I made a promise to him I have kept;
Although deceived, outwitted, aye, defrauded,
I've kept the promise, for I gave my word.
But tell him, too, there's that beats in my bosom
And ever cries: "Seize what they stole from you!
Look to your tarnished honor! A king's good name
Is priced above a thousand human lives.
Their wits were all too sharp for you at Tuln;
See if he also wins from you in battle."
Just tell him that, sir; and tell him this besides:
The treaty is complied with, he has the lands,
The hostages have gone; he has his due.
But in Bohemia he'd best beware
How he gives orders that I don't approve,
Or interferes in what is my concern;
Or there will come—no, rather say to him
To do just that, defy me openly,
Fall on my country with his army's strength,
So I can cool the hate, the hot red wrath
Of the blood that courses closest to my heart.
Tell him a lie! Say I spoke shame of him,
Called him a tyrant who'd usurped my rule
And stolen from me what was rightly mine;
Tell him I laughed the herald down he sent me;
Condemned the man he tried to save, to death.
HERALD: You can't do that!
OTTOCAR: I can; for it is done.
HERALD: The treaty's terms—
OTTOCAR: The treaty's terms! Great God!
You think to master me with terms and treaties?
I shall have swords; an army's at my back
Still undefeated; you vanquished me with tricks,
And I will tear these tricks as I now tear
The treaty that you filched from me by guile.
　　　　　(snatches the treaty from the herald)
See here!
　　　(as he is about to tear up the paper, he pauses suddenly)

CHANCELLOR: Oh, God! What will he do? Oh, good my lord!
OTTOCAR *(to a servant):* Go, you, and call my wife to me, the
  Queen.
(Exit the servant)
OTTOCAR: It was where all could see that I was shamed;
  Where all can see I'll wash my honor clean.
  She shot the poisonous shaft that irks me here
  Within my breast; and so let her look on
  When I withdraw it; or, in the attempt,
  Drive it deep down to the inmost seat of life.
(Enter the Queen*)*
CUNIGUNDA: What now?
OTTOCAR: You harshly chided me, and charged me
  With cowardice not long ago, with giving
  The Emperor my lands for fear of bloodshed.
CUNIGUNDA: I chide you still!
OTTOCAR: You see, here in my hand,
  The treaty that bound me to the Emperor.
  When I have torn it up, the bond is broken
  That holds me now, and I am free once more.
  Am I to tear it up?
CUNIGUNDA: A coward who doubts it!
OTTOCAR: Hear me. The demon, war, will rage again;
  Again the land will reek with fire and blood.
  One day, may be—there's naught to hinder it—
  They'll bring your husband to you on his shield.
CUNIGUNDA: And better far to stand beside your coffin
  Than lie by you with shame to cover us.
OTTOCAR: So hard? One drop of kindness would be sweet.
CUNIGUNDA: Nay, not until you're clean of your disgrace
  Shall you have entry to my room and couch.
(turns to go)
OTTOCAR: No, wait! See here! The treaty's torn in two
(tears the treaty into pieces)
  And honor's whole, the future's door unclosed.
  What comes of it—we both will share the burden.
  God grant you just a bit of what stirs here
(touches his breast)
  And give to me the strength that you display.

CUNIGUNDA: Now I can welcome you!
OTTOCAR: Not now! Not thus!
  For I see blood on those white hands of yours,
  Blood not yet shed.— I tell you, do not touch me!
  God shaped a woman out of softer clay
  And gave her mercy's name.— But what are you?
  And now my mind's awake and tells the tale
  Of how you met the King on his return
  And bade your husband welcome to his home—
  Be gone! I feel my eyesight growing dim!
  A sign that it's high time for you to leave.
  Begone! Begone! I say, begone!
               (Exit Cunigunda)
OTTOCAR *(to the* Chancellor *whom he has grasped for support):*
  Do I seem hard? She was not kind to me!
  Now one, and now the other! God strikes the balance.
             (to the herald*)*
  You, Herald, I will not delay here longer.
  Go tell your master what you've seen and heard.
          (turning toward Merenberg*)*
  To the tower with him! What would protect from treason
  Except prompt punishment of prior traitors?
  Before you sow, you root all foul growth up;
  Away with this tangling vine, this poison bracken!
MERENBERG: Hot-headed King, why do you call me traitor?
  Those are the traitors that stand next your throne,
  The Rosenbergs—
OTTOCAR: You're good at slander, too?
MERENBERG: This man whose hands will lead me off to prison,
  Oh, he deserves a prison more than I.
OTTOCAR: No Czech has ever yet betrayed his King!
  This proves your guilt to me beyond all doubt.
  To the tower with that liar!
MERENBERG *(as he is led away):* You'll rue this day too late!
OTTOCAR: To the tower!
MILOTA: And if he prattles, stop his mouth!
      (Merenberg *is led away; the* herald *follows)*
OTTOCAR *(steps out among the men):* No Czech has ever yet
  betrayed his King!

Despite that liar's words, I'm sure of that.
Now, on the threshold of a war to bring
New power and glory to our native land,
I put such trust in you as in myself.
Whoso's opposed and thinks my plan unwise,
He's free to hold aloof from our adventure.
He'll take no detriment, hear no reproach.
But whoso comes by choice, and thinks as I do,
I'll press him to my heart and call him brother.
The day I took the crown, I swore an oath
Beside my father's coffin. I swear anew.
True unto death! Do you the like!
The world is full of wicked knavish men;
Renew your oaths here on your sovereign's sword.
*(takes a sword from one of the bystanders; the men in the front
row kneel)*
Don't kneel! Stand up! I cannot watch men kneel!
And swear no oath! A man can kneel and swear
And still not keep the promise that he gave.
I'll trust you as you stand, without an oath.

Now to our work!—You, go to Breslau and invite
Duke Henry, him and Prinik, Duke of Glogau,
To Prague to join me in this enterprise.—
You, ride to Germany; in Dresden, Meissen,
From Magdeburg, Otto of Brandenburg,
Bespeak such strong support as they will lend.
(to the Chancellor)
You will address the other lords and princes.
We'll gather such a force of men about us
The Emperor will have good cause to marvel.
I still am Ottocar, as all shall see.
And all of you must lend me your strong arms.
The castles you have lost, your other holdings,
The lands I forced you to assign the Crown,
I'll give them back and give you more besides.
The Rosenbergs shall have their old demain,
Burg Falkenstein to boot; Lar goes to Neuhaus;

To Zierotin and Krushina, their old estates!
Receive your lands again! Rejoice in them!
And one at heart, we'll fight an honest fight!—
Moravia is Milota's to guard.
You're a good, able soldier. You'll keep it safe.
(Enter Zavish Rosenberg)
OTTOCAR: Look there! Lord Rosenberg! A happy meeting!
I think you'll follow us to battle, too?
You are among the first men of my realm;
I count on you more than on many another.
ZAVISH: That which my brothers do, I shall do likewise.
I pledge myself to serve the common need.
(exit)
OTTOCAR *(follows him with his eyes: with a gesture):* He hides
behind a mask; and I don't trust him.
You, Milota, you are my man: bluff, straight.
I have no doubt you too can hate a man,
But not deceive. I'll trust myself to you.
Chancellor, are you done?
CHANCELLOR *(where he sits writing):* I am, my King.
OTTOCAR: We have lost much by rashness and by haste.
Now we shall see what good will come of caution.
That suits you to a T no doubt, old man?
CHANCELLOR: O King, come on me with rash haste, as you were
wont;
I'd rather hear it than these gentle tones.
OTTOCAR: Write to the Captain of the Town of Znaim
To send a thousand men— But that's too many!
The fortress would be stripped of guards meantime.
Tell him to put five hundred on the border—
And yet five hundred are too few.
(turns toward Milota)
That's right?

He'd better send to Iglau—[16] That won't do!
My mind's a blur. Two nights I've had no sleep
Nothing to eat.—

Lend me that bench of yours;
I'll see if I can rest a while.
CHANCELLOR: Oh, Sire,

If you would go inside—
OTTOCAR: No, no, no, no!
  But you may bring my wife. She left in anger.
  I wish she'd sit beside me, talk to me,
  Until sleep comes upon my heavy lids.
                 (to a servant*)*
  My friend, do me this favor. Bring her here.
             (Exit the servant*)*
OTTOCAR: How good it is to stretch these weary limbs!
  God, I am tired! Go look to Merenberg;
  The old man has a hard couch there in gaol.
  Though he's a knave, they're not to torture him;
  Tell them to treat him as befits a knight.
        (Exit Fuellenstein; *the* servant *returns)*
OTTOCAR: Well, is the Queen coming?
SERVANT: She will not come, Sire.
OTTOCAR: Then let her go! Come *you,* old Chancellor,
  Lend me your knees today to lay my head on.
  When I wake up—you'll see at once—
  I'm still the Ottocar I used to be.
              (sleeps
        Enter Fuellenstein*)*
CHANCELLOR: The King's asleep!
FUELLENSTEIN: Old Merenberg soon, too.
  He would not hush and kept up talk of traitors
  Until some chieftain threw him down the steps.
  Small chance, they think, he'll ever rise again.
OTTOCAR *(sits up):* Ha, Merenberg! Is it you?
CHANCELLOR: He is not here.
OTTOCAR: I seemed to see him standing there.— Sleep, sleep!
(sinks back asleep. The Chancellor, *commanding silence, lays his finger on his lips. The curtain falls.)*

Act 5

The churchyard at Goetzendorf. Three quarters of the mid-stage is closed in by the sexton's house on which there is a bell tower. Vanguard of the Bohemian army. A bivouac fire with soldiers lying around it. Ottocar *sits back of it on an elevation, his chin in his two hands which are supported on the hilt of his sword. Right forward,* Milota *and* Fuellenstein *lying on the ground. Before daybreak. Darkness. Enter a* messenger

MESSENGER: Is the King here?
MILOTA: Yes. What now?
MESSENGER: Parties of Kumans
    And Huns from the Emperor's forces are moving up
    The River March in strength behind our lines.
    They've come as far as Droesing and were seen there.
    Should I inform the King?
MILOTA: No need to tell him.
    The King is in an evil mood already.
    Besides, the Poles are there; and my troops, too.
    They'll teach them how to find their way back home.
MESSENGER: Well, if you think—
MILOTA: Be off! I'll come at once.
                  (Exit the messenger*)*
FUELLENSTEIN *(in a low voice):* This endless waiting, endless talk
    and planning!
    And always we retreat. God's curses on it!
    The King has changed his nature root and branch.
    Affairs were going ill enough before;
    But when the Queen ran off, that broke his spirit.
    I'd long ago have left for other scenes
    If soldiering weren't the life I really love.
    First he lays two weeks' siege to Drosendorf
    And leaves the Emperor time to gather strength;
    And then, just as we think we'll start the fighting,
    As we stand armed and ready at Marchegg,
    Come orders to retreat. And we retreat.
    And every town and village that we held,
    And every stream and river that was ours,
    He gives them up and hardly strikes a blow.
MILOTA: Things will be soon decided, never fear.
FUELLENSTEIN: He calls it caution. I'd call it cowardice.
    Not like the other days when we would fight.
    We're craven now.

MILOTA: Be still! The King's awake.

FUELLENSTEIN: It's time!

OTTOCAR: Bad luck pursued us yesterday.
The enemy gains ground. Suppose he does;
I still hold Drosendorf. Our rear is safe.

FUELLENSTEIN *(loudly):* The rear is safer, almost, than the front.

OTTOCAR: This doesn't suit you, Fuellenstein?

FUELLENSTEIN: No, sir;
I won't deny it. It's not the way we did.

OTTOCAR: You'd have attacked them at Marchegg, no doubt?

FUELLENSTEIN: I should have, sir; and you'd have done it, too,
Two years ago. When we fought Hungary
At that same place, you weren't so long in doubt.
Swords out and at the foe! That brought success.

OTTOCAR: It brought success, for luck was on our side.
Oh, I was rash in those days, and a fool;
As you still are. Time ripens men at last.

FUELLENSTEIN: Sir, when the Emperor waited at Marchegg,
He had a thousand men and not one more.
Now he has thirty thousand, foot and horse.

OTTOCAR: God only could foresee it.— What's the hour?

SERVANT: Three hours past midnight.

OTTOCAR: The battle must be fought.
We've met the enemy. Today decides.
How is this place called?

SERVANT: Goetzendorf, my King.

OTTOCAR: The stream?

SERVANT: The Sulz.

OTTOCAR: I thought I was in Stillfried.

SERVANT: We passed through Stillfried in the dark last night.
The Emperor holds it now.

OTTOCAR: Well, as God wills.

SERVANT: You ought to go inside, your Majesty.

OTTOCAR: And see that none attacks till I give orders.
I've lured him here into this mountain pass
Deluding him with my pretended flight;
And he'll pass on; my center will retreat;
My wings move in—then, Emperor, "Adieu!"
I've got him like a cornered mouse. Ha, ha!

(breaks out into a hoarse laugh that turns into a fit of coughing; rubs his hands)

It's cold. Who has a cloak to wrap around me?
The wind is sharpest just before the sun comes.
(as a cloak is put around him)
Is this a summer night? The grain's not cut
And yet it's cold. The summer should be warm,
The winter icy. But they've exchanged their duties.
The times have gone awry and we with them.
Is there no news to tell us where the Queen
Has gone?

SERVANT: As yet there is no word, my King.

OTTOCAR: And Zavish keeps with her?

SERVANT: Yes, Sire, he does.

OTTOCAR: I think to come upon them in due course.—
Is it not yet dawn?

SERVANT: Beyond the March
The sky is gray; day must soon break.

OTTOCAR *(leaps to his feet)*: I hail thee, sun, on this portentous
Morning!
Ere thou hast gone to rest, we'll know our doom,
If it be peace in arms, or in the tomb.
(throws the cloak aside)
Put out the fires and let the bugles sound.
Make ready for the fray. It's now, or never!

MESSENGER *(enters)*: Sir, Drosing is in flames!

OTTOCAR: Behind my lines?
That's where your men are stationed, Milota.

MILOTA: A casual troop of Kumans, sir, if true.
I don't believe it, though.

OTTOCAR: Is there no height
Where you can see just what it is that burns?

SERVANT: The chapel tower.

OTTOCAR: Climb to the top. Be quick!
(Several men go and pound on the door)

OTTOCAR: How come Hungarians in Drosing? Hell's fire!
Whoso's to blame, shall hang.—Is it done?

SERVANT: Master,
They would not let us in.

OTTOCAR: They? Who are they?

SERVANT: There are women in the tower.

OTTOCAR: Women? You're mad!

SEXTON *(comes out of his house):* The retinue of the Queen of Bohemia, sir.

OTTOCAR *(seizes him):* Bohemia's queen, you say? Her retinue? She too, no doubt?—You knave!—And Zavish also? I shall be better when I've cooled my wrath.

SEXTON: Consider, Sire.

OTTOCAR: Aside!

SEXTON: Oh, sir!

OTTOCAR: Make way!

> *(forces his way into the house, the* sexton *after him)*

MILOTA: If he finds Zavish, it's the end of him!— I'll rescue him though the King's self must pay. Withdraw a little, and then, if I should call, Force your way in and do what I command. The King's not master of himself in anger.

> *(goes into the house; the others withdraw)*

* * *

A shallow room: at the back, a Gothic arch before which a dark curtain falls to the floor. Ottocar *rushes in;* Lady Elizabeth *steps in his path*

OTTOCAR: Out of my way, you bawd! Where are your clients?

ELIZABETH: Oh, Sire, I pray you, grant her peace at last.

OTTOCAR: The curtain there! The secret's hid behind it? Come, little dove! I'll fling the curtain wide!

> *(tears the curtain open and recoils. On an elevation, with candles at her head and feet, lies* Queen Margaret *dead in her coffin, the arms of Austria at her feet)*

OTTOCAR *(at front; dully):* That is not she, the Queen of Bohemia!

ELIZABETH: She was!

OTTOCAR: It's Margaret of Austria, Once my wife; my cousin in the fourth degree, So we were parted by the Church by law. God grant her rest eternal.

ELIZABETH: Amen, amen!

OTTOCAR: When did she die?

ELIZABETH: Yesterday, good my lord.

OTTOCAR: How came she here?

ELIZABETH: Driven from home at Krems[17]
  By roving bands of soldiers from your army,
  She tried to reach the Emperor at Marchegg;
  But Death caught up with her.

OTTOCAR: Why the Emperor?

ELIZABETH: She did not tell me, sir.
  I think she wanted to make peace between you.

OTTOCAR: She *was* a peace-maker.— What caused her death?

ELIZABETH: They call it commonly, a broken heart.
  She'd weep by day and night—

OTTOCAR: Enough, enough.
  And now where will you go?

ELIZABETH: We think to wait
  Until the war is ended, thus or so.

OTTOCAR: Yes, thus or so!

ELIZABETH: And then to Lilienfeld
  To bury her in her ancestral tomb
  Where lies Duke Leopold who was her father;
  And he, the last male heir of Babenberg,
  Her brother Frederick they call the Fighter.

OTTOCAR: That do; this ring—

MILOTA *(enters):* The enemy draws near!

OTTOCAR: I'll come at once. Just go.
                    (Exit Milota*)*

OTTOCAR: This ring I give,
  Pra lay it in the grave with her who's gone.

ELIZABETH: Oh, Sire!

OTTOCAR: And when the war has reached its end,
  If so be I survive, then come to Prague
  That I repay you all your loyal service.
  Now I must go.
               (moves toward the door)

ELIZABETH *(opens the door for him):* God bless you!

OTTOCAR *(halts at the door):* Margaret,
  You lie there dead and I'm still unforgiven.
                    (returns)

You went away, kind, loyal, virtuous soul,
Within your heart the sense of all my wrongs.
And now you stand before God's justice-seat
Accusing me, and call for vengeance on me.
Oh, do not do it, Margaret; do not that!
You *are* avenged. What I gave you, gave all for,
Is fallen from me like the autumn leaves.
Whatso I gathered, tempests strew and drive,
Heaven's blessing gone by which man's labors thrive;
And I stand lonely now, bowed down by grief,
With none to comfort me and none to hear me.
    (approaches the coffin)
They've evilly misused me, Margaret;
Ingratitude has raised his head against me;
Those who stood closest to me, played me false;
And those whom I raised up, have cast me down.
The woman that I sacrificed your worth for,
She cleft my heart in two within my breast,
She sold my honor to a serving man;
And when I came from battle, sore and bleeding,
She poured not balm but venom in my wounds.
She goaded me with mockery and contempt
Till I ran blindly in the fatal net
That soon will close around my helpless head.
    (kneels beside the coffin)
You often gave me comfort; comfort now.
Put out your cold dead hand and give your blessing.
I feel one thing is sure: that death draws on;
Before this sun shall set, my life is done;
So bless me now as you are blessed already.
    (lays his head on the cushions)
ELIZABETH: He must be praying. Thou, kind God above,
 Forgive him, too. And oh, how great a joy
 For my dear dead lady! I've told her many times
 That he'd return. And now they *are* together.
 You see?
    (looks upward)
VOICE *(from without):* Is the King there?
ELIZABETH *(at the door):* He would be alone.

He's not to be disturbed.
>   *(lets the curtain fall)*
>   Ah, strife and conflict!
For that a king like him can still find time;
But time for prayer may never come again.—
No peace or quiet! The heathen that they are!

(New alarms outside. Elizabeth *goes out the door with her finger on her lips, commanding silence)*

* * *

Place before the house as at the beginning of the act. Milota *leads a squire to the front of the stage. The rest remain at the rear. At intervals, the blare of trumpets and uproar outside*

MILOTA: Who? Zavish Rosenberg? He sent you here?
SQUIRE: Yes, sir.
MILOTA: He's at the Emperor's camp?
SQUIRE: He is.
MILOTA: Where is his letter?
SQUIRE: He did not give me any.
>   He told me only—it almost made me laugh—
>   He told me to remind you of the song:
>   "The winter comes again, the roses fade."
MILOTA: What can he mean now? Roses?— Rosenberg!
>   Tell him the roses shall not cease to bloom,
>   The snow will melt and winter not return.
>   *(Exit the* squire*)*
FUELLENSTEIN *(enters):* Where is the King?
MILOTA: Inside.
FUELLENSTEIN: What does he there?
>   The fighting's hot already.
KNIGHT *(enters hastily):* Is the King here?
>   They've forced the vanguard to give ground. Send aid!
MILOTA: He's not here yet.
FUELLENSTEIN: Look there! He's come at last.
>   *(Enter* Ottocar *with the* sexton *from the house;* Lady Elizabeth
>   *follows)*
OTTOCAR *(to the* Sexton*):* We'll spare your house in every way we can.

And now farewell. Include me in your prayers.—
Herbott, all's well!

FUELLENSTEIN: They're fighting hand to hand.

OTTOCAR: Give me my helmet.

FUELLENSTEIN: One of the Bishop's men,
Of Salzburg, his horse took fright and ran away
With him, and then the others galloped after.

OTTOCAR *(has his helmet on, draws his sword):* Well then, God
with us!

SEXTON: And may he bless you, Sire!

ELIZABETH: A thousand times; and grant you safe return.

OTTOCAR: Indeed, we'll hope as much.
(Trumpets outside)
                                        Yes, yes! We're coming.
Where are the horses?

FUELLENSTEIN: Just outside the gate.

OTTOCAR *(as he leaves):* Forward!

ELIZABETH *and* SEXTON: God bless your Highness!

SEXTON: Success and triumph!
(Exeunt all)

* * *

*Open field along the March: broad daylight. Enter Emperor Ru-
dolph with his two sons, accompanied by Austrian and other
Knights with banners*

RUDOLPH: The sun in splendor rises from the mists
A day of fairest promise. You, my son,[18]
Have never trod before on Austria's soil.
Look round you. You're standing in your land.
The plain encircling us is called Marchfeld,
A battle-field than which you'll find no better;
A field to give a harvest, too, praise God;
And that for you shall ever be its purpose.
There is the March; and where the mists still roll,
There lies Vienna. Nearby the Danube sparkles
That's broken everywhere by many an isle.
There you shall live, if God gives victory.
But there'll be fighting first which you shall share.
I give the flag to you for you to carry

Before me, rich in glory, through the fight.
(gives him the flag; to his younger son)
Your young arm is too weak to swing a sword;
Stay close by me that I may keep you safe.

You, Margrave Hochberg, bear the Empire's eagle;
And as the eagle strikes live prey alone,
Smite him who fights, but spare the one who flees.
(gives him the eagle)
You, Conrad Haslau, although gray with age,
I will entrust with Austria's fluttering banner
That you have borne with honor in twenty battles.
You, Henry, Lord of Lichtenstein, stay close
And guard the man and guard that which he bears.
They'll be well guarded. Did I need protectors
For this my head, I'd find no better men
Than them of Lichtenstein. And now, my lords,
Take up the banner, bear it before all,
The pure white noble stripe of Austria;
And as it, gleaming, crosses the red field,
I'll watch her army move in white-flagged rows
Between the blood-stained corpses of her foes.

Then on with God! *Christ* be our battle cry.
And as He died for us upon the cross,
So will we gladly die for right and justice
Though wrong should offer wealth to us, and life.
Reverend Lord of Basel, lead the way,
Strike up the battle song *Hail Mary, Maiden pure!*
SERVANT *(enters):* The Queen of Bohemia, Imperial Highness!
RUDOLPH: What can she wish of me?
(Enter Cunigunda *with* Zavish; Berta *is led in behind them;
attendants, who remain at rear)*
CUNIGUNDA: I'm here myself.
I've come here to your camp to seek protection.
RUDOLPH: Protection, madam, from your husband's foe?
CUNIGUNDA: No bitterer foe could be than that same husband.
He's crazed and turns upon those closest to him.

I fled, and barely got off with my life.
RUDOLPH: You put great confidence in me, good Queen.
  I know of women, nor do they lack in spirit,
  Who rather would lie dead at their husbands' hands
  Than flee to them who are their husbands' foes.
  However, you may wait within my tents;
  Perhaps the outcome will be one to please you.
      (to an attendant)
  See that her Majesty is brought to safety.
CUNIGUNDA: I thank Your Highness.— Zavish, come with me.
      (exit)
RUDOLPH: You, sir, why aren't you at your sovereign's side?
ZAVISH: The King did insult to me, deep and grave.
RUDOLPH: An insult, sir? And you can think of that
  When he perhaps goes out to meet his death?
  Thank God, sir, that you are no man of mine,
  Or I'd read you a lesson here and now.
  Follow your Queen, who's taken your King's place.
      (Exit Zavish)
RUDOLPH: And one thing more before the battle. I've learned
  That some of those whom I of late made knights
  And who because of some injustice suffered
  Are ill-disposed to Ottocar; and others,
  Most of them men from Austrian demains,
  Have sworn together to seek him out in battle,
  Agreeing the finder should slay him on the spot.
  As Emperor, I declare your oaths are void,
  And I forbid you all to lay your hands
  Upon King Ottocar this day except
  To save your lives from his attack.
      (to Seyfried Merenberg who stands next to him)
  You take me, sir? Then forward under God!
      (Enter a soldier running)
SOLDIER: The Czechs approach!
RUDOLPH: The Austrians have arrived.
  You do not think that we should be afraid?
  A single troop. Pray follow me, my lords.
      (Enter Fuellenstein with a troop, running)

FUELLENSTEIN: Where is the Emperor? I'll fight no other.
RUDOLPH: He's here, my friend!
FUELLENSTEIN: Soon we can say, he *was* here!
RUDOLPH: That's not so sure.— Just let him come, my lords,
Or else I'll soon forget my skill at fence.
Lay on, my friend!
FUELLENSTEIN: Follow, and slay them all.
(Exeunt all fighting)

* * *

Another part of the battle field. Left front, the slope of a little hill running down upon the stage. Close by, a tree. Enter Ottocar, *helped by a* servant; *two other servants and* Milota *follow*

OTTOCAR: Lord Milota, your men have not attacked.
What's keeping your Moravians? Hell's fire!
I fear that you're a knave, Lord Milota. And if you are, because I
trusted you
You are a knave ten times and a hundred fold.

They killed my horse beneath me as I rode.
My leg still pains where it was crushed beneath.
Go find a horse for me while I wait here.
(Exit the servant*)*
You, Milota, ride quickly to your troop—
No! Wait here, rather.
(to a servant*)*
Go tell the rear guard
To move to the attack or I will move on them!
(Exit the servant*)*
Look toward me, Milota! Straight in the face!
You look with hate. I hope it's for the foe.
If it's for me, then on your death-bed, sir,
There'd be a Milota to stand before you
And glare with hatred in your dying eyes.

Mount to the top of yonder hill and look
For Fuellenstein. See how the battle goes.
(Exit Milota*)*

OTTOCAR: And you, help me to reach that sturdy tree
   To hold me up until they bring a horse.
   Keep watch and warn me when a foe approaches.
   (stands beside the tree and supports himself on a low dry branch)
   The Czechs fight dully, as a man might fight
   For one he does not like: because he must.
   But Austria's soldiers, and the Styrians,
   Who never gave *me* more than grudging service,
   They seem transformed into avenging angels
   And every man's a hero, against me.
   The payment's due today and they are paying.

   My ways upon Thy earth have not been good,
   Great God. And like a whirlwind, like a tempest,
   I moved across Thy happy prosperous lands.
   But Thou alone canst ride upon the whirlwind,
   For Thou alone canst heal its harm, great God.
   And though my will and aim were never evil,
   Who was I, groveling worm, that I presumed
   To play the role of Him who rules all worlds
   And sought to find a path to good through evil?

   And man, whom Thou didst put here for his pleasure,
   An end, a being, a world within the world—
   Thou madest him a wonder of Thy hand,
   With noble brow, with proud and upright bearing;
   Didst robe him fair in beauty's festal robe
   And give him eyes to look out on the world,
   And set a ring of marvels all about him.
   He hears and sees and feels and knows delight.
   When he has taken nurture to his body,
   At once effective energies set in
   And work untiringly through veins and nerves
   To build his house for him; a royal palace
   Cannot compare with such a human body.
   But I threw them away by tens of thousands
   To satisfy a folly or a whim,
   As one would scatter rubbish out a door.
   Not one of them who lay dead on the field

But a fond mother bore him in her anguish
And suckled him with joy at her full breasts.
His father blessed him as his pride and pleasure
And cared for him and taught him what he knew,
And when he'd only hurt his finger-tip
They ran to him, and washed and bound the cut
And watched it to be sure it healed aright.
That was a finger-tip, a bit of skin!
But I, threw them on the field like straws
And for unyielding iron broke a path
To enter their warm flesh.— If Thou dost mean
To summon me before Thy judgment seat,
Then punish me; but spare my people, Lord.

My eyes were dazzled; so it was I sinned.
I never did a wrong with conscious purpose.
But once I did! And once again! O God,
I have done wrong and done it purposely.

Not from the fear of death do I speak thus;
And Thou to all hearts are opened,
Thou knowest whether fear disturbs this heart.
But if a *man's* repentance pleases Thee,
Who's frightened by no punishment, but by his sin,
Then look on me who kneel before Thy face,
(kneels)
And hear me when I pray as I now pray:
"Pronounce Thy sentence as a God of mercy."
(bows his head)

(Enter Seyfried Merenberg fully armed, at rear)
SEYFRIED: Ottocar!
OTTOCAR: Who calls?
SEYFRIED (halts just behind him): Where is my father?
OTTOCAR (arises): Who are you?— Merenberg!
SEYFRIED: Where is my father?
OTTOCAR (murmurs to himself): When God put Cain to question, he replied,
  "Didst Thou give him to me to be his keeper?"

SEYFRIED: I gave him to you, I myself, poor fool!
  And now I stand before you clad in steel,
  Demanding his return. Give me my father!
OTTOCAR: You well know where he is.
SEYFRIED: I well know. Dead.
OTTOCAR: He paid as traitors pay.
SEYFRIED: A traitor, he?
  Only too true to you, to me, to everyone.
  He did not know I'd joined the Emperor.
  The letter that he sent asked aid, naught else,
  For your rejected wife.
OTTOCAR: Then he's with God.
SEYFRIED: He is; to whom you'd best commend your soul!
                  (runs at him with drawn sword)
                      (Enter Emerberg*)*
EMERBERG: What are you doing, Seyfried?
SEYFRIED: A timely word!
  The Emperor forbade us all to slay you
  With weapons. So I will be a basilisk
  And slay you with my eyes, if that may be.
  Look toward me now and hear me: "Merenberg!"
  And hear anon Hell's echo: "Merenberg!"
OTTOCAR: Make way! I must go to my men.
SEYFRIED: Stay back!
  You were my teacher, model, an example;
  I honored you more than all other men.
  There is no glory, now your glory's dimmed;
  No happiness now my father's dead.
  Oh, give me back my confidence in man,
  Oh, give me back my father whom myself
  I left for you to seize. You slew in haste.
  Look at my features. They are Merenberg's.
  Come, slay him once again in slaying them.
OTTOCAR: Put down your vizor, then I'll grant you combat.
SEYFRIED: Not thus! No! King, come battle with the dead!
  How now, brave Ottocar! So soon afraid?
                  (Enter Ottocar's servant*)*
SERVANT: Lord Milota! Help! Help! The enemy!
SEYFRIED *(to* Emerberg*):* Hold that man back.— He must draw
  sword against me

That I may tell the Emperor, "Majesty,
I did not slay him. He was the first to strike.
You said we might strike back if he attacked."
(Emerberg fights with the servant)
SERVANT: Lord Milota!
EMERBERG: Give way!
SERVANT: God help me now!
(falls dead at the King's feet)
OTTOCAR *(takes the sword he had laid beside the tree):* So be it!
(Enter Milota)
OTTOCAR: Milota, come help your King.
SEYFRIED: Are you friend or foe?
MILOTA: No foe of yours, my lords!
This road will lead me homeward?
OTTOCAR: Milota!
MILOTA: My brother, Benesh, pays you his respects.
He died just now when he had lost his mind.
And now his daughter raves beside his coffin.
Make way, my lords. Good luck! I'll not disturb you.
(passes by them, wrapped in his cloak; exit)
OTTOCAR: You quit me thus and I cannot reproach you?
I was your sovereign, though. Then knave you are, forever.
SEYFRIED: Surrender!
OTTOCAR: You think to capture Ottocar!
First you must fight.
(stamps his wounded foot)
Support me, foot!
It's no time now to pain.— And you, make way!
EMERBERG: Look! You are lost. Your men have taken flight.
(Fleeing Bohemians fill the back of the stage)
OTTOCAR: You lie. No Czech would flee. I'll go to them.
SEYFRIED *and* EMERBERG *(hold him back with their swords):*
You'll stay!
*(Enter Henry of Lichtenstein, center, with a band in pursuit of the
Bohemians; he runs to the rear with the Austrian banner in his
hand)*
LICHTENSTEIN: Our foes are fleeing! Austria forever!
OTTOCAR: Halt, cowards; halt!— And you, make way!

SEYFRIED: When dead,
  Not else!
OTTOCAR *(fights):* Bohemia here!
SEYFRIED *(fights):* Here Austria!
OTTOCAR *(with a second blow):* Here Ottocar!
SEYFRIED: Here Merenberg and God!
                    (cuts him down)

*(Ottocar falls, quickly gets up again, strumbles a few steps and
          then falls dead beside the little hill)*
EMERBERG: What have you done? Transgressed the Emperor's
  order!
     (Seyfried stands motionless, his hands hanging at his side)
LICHTENSTEIN *(returns):* Triumph and victory! Hail Austria!
                (Enter Rudolph with his retinue)
RUDOLPH: An end of killing! Quarter to the conquered!
  What happened here? What turned you into ice?
  Ha! Ottocar! He's fallen; blood-stained; dead.
  You did it! Flee, like the first murderer,
  And never come before my eyes again!
                    (Exit Seyfried running)
RUDOLPH: Go tell the Czechs to turn their steps toward home.
  The one for whom they fought today, is dead.
ELIZABETH *(off-stage):* Help, help!
RUDOLPH: Who calls?
ELIZABETH: Oh, kind and gracious Lord,
  They're plundering in the house and setting fires.
  They cannot even leave the dead in peace.
  Protect us, Sire!
RUDOLPH: Go to their aid, at once!
  Who are you?
ELIZABETH: Lady-in-waiting to my Queen,
  Queen Margaret of Austria, now dead.
  Those men are bearers of my lady's body.
*(Four men, accompanied by women dressed in black, carry the
                    coffin in)*
RUDOLPH: Behold the body of your master!
ELIZABETH: Oh, God!
  So he is dead, just as he had grown kind!

My poor, poor master! Put the body down.
They lie there and are joined at last in death
(The coffin is set on the mound at Ottocar's *head.*

Enter Cunigunda *followed by* Zavish *and* Berta)
CUNIGUNDA: The King has been made prisoner, so they say.
RUDOLPH: Here, woman, here your husband lies!
*(*Cunigunda *sinks trembling to her knees with a cry;* Zavish *stands
with bowed head)*
RUDOLPH: At his wife's feet;
For that she was, she's given proof in death.
BERTA *(has taken her position on the mound behind the coffin and
leans on it with both elbows; she raps on the coffin and speaks):*
Come, open, Margaret. See, your husband's here!
(Enter the Chancellor *with several other prisoners; he throws
himself down beside* Ottocar)
CHANCELLOR: Oh, Sire! My valiant, my mistaken master!
(lays Ottocar's *head upon his knees)*
RUDOLPH: You lie here stripped of royal show, great King,
Your head supported on your servant's lap.
And now of all your splendid robes and riches
You've not a single scanty cover left
To use for shroud to wrap your body in.
The Imperial mantle you aspired to wear
See, I'll take off and spread it over you
(does so)
That you be buried like an emperor,
Who died a poor and lonely beggar's death.
Take him to Laa; there let him lie in state
Until they bear him where his fathers rest.
May God have mercy on him, and on us all.
(bares his head and prays silently; the others do likewise.
Cunigunda *wraps her veil about her face, and* Zavish *stares
straight in front of him. Pause)*
BERTA *(still leans on the cover of* Margaret's *coffin): Forgive us as*
we too forgive,
And lead us not into temptation.
RUDOLPH: Aye, lead us not into temptation, Lord!—
And now, my son, where this dead body lies,

The corpse of one who was a king in life,
I will invest you with the fief of Austria.
(at his signal, both his sons kneel; he addresses the older one
principally)
RUDOLPH: Be great and strong; increase your race and line
Until it dwells in lands both near and far
And Hapsburg's name shines glorious as a star.
You, stand in all things at your brother's side.[19]
But should you fall a prey to arrogance;
In pride, because you rule, raise up your head,
Then think of this strong man that here lies dead,
This very hour has answered God's stern call,
Of Ottocar, his rise, and of his fall.
Stand up! You, too! And never kneel again.
I hail you as the sovereign of this land.
Come everyone, come loud your welcome cry,
Until it rolls like thunder through the sky.
Hail! The first Hapsburg hail in Austria!
ALL: Hail! Hail!—Austria!—Hail!—Hapsburg forever!
(All kneel to do homage. Trumpets and cheers.

The curtain falls.)

Translated by Henry H. Stevens

THE TALISMAN

Farce with Song in Three Acts

Johann Nepomuk Nestroy

CHARACTERS

TITUS[1] FOXFIRE, *an unemployed journeyman barber*
LADY CYPRESSBURG, *a widow*
EMMA, *her daughter*
CONSTANCE, *her lady's maid, also a widow*
FLORA PRUNINGSHEARS, *head gardener, also a widow*
PUMPKINSEED, *assistant gardener*
M. MARQUIS, *hairdresser*
BUNG, *beer seller*
CHRISTOPH ⎫
HANS ⎬ *country boys*
SEPPEL ⎭
HANNA, *a country girl*
A GARDENER ⎫
GEORGE ⎬ *servants of Lady Cypressburg*
CONRAD ⎭
MR. FLATT
NOTARY FALK
SALOME GOBBLER, *goose girl*
GENTLEMEN, LADIES, COUNTRY BOYS, COUNTRY GIRLS, SERVANTS,
 GARDENERS
The action takes place on the estate of Lady Cypressburg, near a large city.

Act 1

The scene is a village square, Upstage center, a well flanked by two stone benches; to the left, a garden wall with a little gate standing ajar which opens into the manor garden.

Scene 1

Country Girls, *among them* Hanna, *enter from upstage left during the ritournelle of the following chorus.* Country Boys, *among them* Christoph, Seppel, *and* Hans.

CHORUS

GIRLS: The dancing starts early on the day of church-fair,
Now here come the boys who'll be taking us there.

BOYS *(entering stage right):* What's keeping them? No one's in sight, that's just grand!
On the dance floor they've already struck up the band.

GIRLS: We *are* ready, though.

BOYS: It's about time; let's go!

ALL: Let's each choose a partner, it's easily done;
The music is playing, today there'll be fun!

CHRISTOPH *(to a* Country Girl*):* We two will dance together!

HANS *(to another):* The two of us have been partners at ten church-fairs now.

HANNA *(to a* Boy*):* I'll dance with no one in the world but you.

CHRISTOPH *(looking upstage left):* Look! Here comes Salome.

HANNA: With the bass-fiddle-colored hair!²

CHRISTOPH: What does *she* want at the church-fair?

HANNA: To set your hearts on fire, that's what!

Scene 2

SALOME *(In poor country clothing, with red hair, enters downstage left):* There's a lot of fun going on here; has the dance already started?

CHRISTOPH *(coolly):* Possibly.

SALOME: You won't mind if I come along?

HANS: Well—why not? Anybody can come.

CHRISTOPH *(with reference to her hair):* But think of the fire hazard!

HANS *(likewise):* The constable will be there—

CHRISTOPH *(as before):* And he has grave suspicions about you. You drove your geese by a barn, and the day before yesterday it burned down.

HANNA: And it is believed you set it on fire with your hair-do.

SALOME: That's really mean, the way you always pick on me. But of course I'm the only girl in the village with hair like this. You won't admit I'm the prettiest, so you'll have me the ugliest.

GIRLS: Ah, that's priceless! She think's she's pretty!

CHRISTOPH *(to Salome):* Look to it that you find a partner.

SEPPEL *(a very ugly boy):* I'll dance with you; what have I got to lose?

CHRISTOPH: What's gotten into you? A fellow like you surely can find another partner.

SEPPEL: That's true. I mustn't throw myself away.

HANS: Onwards! No more dawdling around!

ALL: To the dance floor! Hurrah! To the dance!

(All exit upstage right)

Scene 3

SALOME: Well, I'm left behind again. And why? Because I am the red-headed Salome. And yet red is certainly a pretty color—the prettiest flowers are roses, and roses are red. The prettiest thing in nature is the morning, and it announces itself with the most brilliant red. Clouds are of course not a very pretty invention, and yet even the clouds are pretty when they stand there fiery red in the evening sun. That's why I say whoever has anything against the color red, doesn't know what pretty is. But what good does that do me? I don't have anyone to take me to the church-fair!—I could go there alone, but the girls would make fun of me, laugh and gaggle. I'll go back to my geese. They don't gaggle out of

meanness when they see me, and when I bring them feed, they look at my hands and not at my head.
(exits downstage right)

Scene 4

Flora *and* Pumpkinseed *enter upstage left.* Pumpkinseed *carries a heavily laden bag.*

FLORA *(annoyed):* Now this is really maddening! An hour and a quarter to come the little way out from the city. That post-chaise ought to be ashamed of itself.

PUMPKINSEED: How so? That's why it's called a post-chaise, because it never leaves the post.

FLORA: It's a pity, slow as you are, that you didn't become a post-chaise.

PUMPKINSEED: I'm not clever enough for that. A post-chaise is the cleverest thing in the world, because it lets everyone sit, regardless of standing.

FLORA: I believe you're having one of your witty days; you are even more unbearable than usual.

PUMPKINSEED: Stop fussing, don't take your spite out on me. It won't be much longer.

FLORA: Perhaps you want to leave her ladyship's service? That would be clever.

PUMPKINSEED: Oh no, you're sure to marry soon; then a new field will be open for your nagging and I'll no longer be the playground for your spleen.

FLORA: Stupid creature! I'll never marry again, but remain true to my dear departed.

PUMPKINSEED: Maybe he believes that, now that he is dead; when he was alive he never did.

FLORA: If I were her ladyship, I would have run you off long ago.

PUMPKINSEED *(pointedly):* If *I* were her ladyship, I'd have made some changes around the place too.

FLORA: Who knows, you may be about to be sacked! I've been given permission to take on a bright, able young fellow.

PUMPKINSEED: That's fine, then the work won't be quite so hard. I'll water the radishes, that's all the influence I need.

FLORA: Now go to Uncle Polz; he's to recommend a man for me.

PUMPKINSEED: Good. Perhaps some day your man will become your master.

FLORA: Not on your life! I'll leave them all holding the bag.

PUMPKINSEED: Unfortunately I feel you're right. But now you'll have to take it back if I'm to go see Uncle. *(hands her the bag)*

FLORA: Look lively now, you lazybones! *(exits through garden gate)*

PUMPKINSEED *(alone):* H'm, h'm! The garden isn't all that run down, yet how she carries on about getting a bright, able gardener—h'm, h'm. *(exits right)*

Scene 5

TITUS FOXFIRE *enters in a fury downstage right during the ritournelle of the following song.*

1

> He wasn't looking, the clown;
> I almost knocked him down.
> Yet even so, I swear
> He was making fun of my hair!
> Whose business is that, anyway?
> I hope at least that I may
> Be permitted to have my own hair.
> It's more than a body can bear!

Should red hair be a sign of a nature untrue?
Judging one by one's hair, what a dumb thing to do!
There are plenty of rounders with raven-black locks,
And whoever believes them will go on the rocks.
And many a blond lad is languid and mute
All day long—why? All night he's been out on a toot.
And those wise-looking gents with their hair of steel gray,
Why, they're often more hairbrained than young folks today.

> Yet they all have to go by the hair,
> Then afterwards catch it for fair.

2

(looking menacingly in the direction from which he has come)

> I shall never forget it—
> He'll live to regret it!
> He'll be in for a hard time, I swear,

When he finds he's got *me* in his hair!
 He'll lose his forelock
  When I run amok
 And yank it all out by the root;
 Then he'll go around bald as a coot.
They say red-headed girls lead men on, and it's true,
But how silly! That's something all shades of girls do.
Brunettes, it is said, are hot-blooded, I know,
And enticing, yet some are as dull as a froe.
Blondes are cuddly, you say? Oh, a blonde's a delight!
Yet I know of a blonde who will nag day and night.
But the gray-headed ones will be true, you suggest?
No, they give themselves rinses and no one else rest.—
 Yet they always must go by the hair,
 Then afterwards catch it for fair.

So wrongheadedly the world judges heads, and even if one were to stand on his, it would do no good. Prejudice is a brick wall, and those that run against it rebound with bloodied heads. I have taken the wide world for my home, and the wide world is much closer than you think. From the thorn bush of bitter experience I have carved myself a walking stick; I've put on my Seven League Boots, waved my traveling cap quietly, and with one step I've entered the wide world. "Enjoy and understand seldom go hand in hand." What I'd like now is to come across a really stupid fellow; I'd look on that as a good omen.

Scene 6

PUMPKINSEED: Another wasted trip!—*(catching sight of* Titus*)* But ho! A stranger takes shape before my eyes!

TITUS *(to himself):* Fortune, I think you were listening.

PUMPKINSEED *(sizing up* Titus*)*: According to the description Mister Polz gave me, this could be the very man he was expecting. Big frame, big mouth, very big eyes, ears in proportion—but that hair!—*(to* Titus*)* Is the gentleman seeking his daily bread?

TITUS: I'm seeking money; I'll figure out how to get the bread afterwards.

PUMPKINSEED *(to himself)*: He seeks money—and so suspicious looking—*(aloud)* Are you perhaps a treasure-seeker then?

TITUS: If the gentleman will show me where one is buried, I'll take lessons from a mole.

PUMPKINSEED: Or a robber?

TITUS: Not up to now, my talent is still in a developmental phase.

PUMPKINSEED: Do you know anything about gardening?

TITUS: I am qualified in all things.

PUMPKINSEED *(to himself)*: He's the one! *(to* Titus*)* Then you'd like to become our pretty young gardener-widow's helper?

TITUS: A widow's helper?—As I said, I'm qualified in all things.

PUMPKINSEED: She'd be helped by such a helper too—but she'd run me off if I brought her a Florian-noodle.[3]

TITUS *(furiously)*: Sir, that remark outrages me to the depth of my being.

PUMPKINSEED: Then I suppose you'll be moving on, carrot-top? *(Exits disdainfully through the garden gate.)*

Scene 7

Titus *alone, looking after* Pumpkinseed *in silent fury.*

TITUS: I am disarmed! The man is so decisive in his rudeness that it leaves one at a loss for words. People certainly are friendly, one might even say neighborly, when they meet me! But within me too misanthropy is already taking form—yes—I hate you, inhuman humanity, I'd like to flee you; let the wilderness receive me, give me complete solitude. Whoa there, bold spirit; such resolutions are appropriate to a full stomach; a hungry man can not carry them out. No, humanity, you won't lose me. Appetite is the tender bond linking me to what reminds me three or four times a day that I cannot get along without society. *(looking to the right)* Here comes an individual driving other individuals into a pen. Geese they are—geese!—Oh goose-girl, why don't you drive these geese before you roasted, I'd like to expropriate one.

Scene 8

Salome, *not observing* Titus, *enters from the right with a half loaf of bread and a knife in her hands.*

SALOME: I need a drink of water; something's pressing on my stomach. *(goes to the well and drinks)*

TITUS *(to himself):* Oh, if only I could share that blessed feeling!

SALOME *(catching sight of him, to herself):* A young stranger—and such beautiful hair, just like mine!

TITUS *(to himself):* Wonder if *she's* going to say "carrot-top?" *(aloud)* Hail, elective affinity![4]

SALOME: Your most obedient servant, fine sir!

TITUS *(half to himself):* She thinks me fine; she's the first of all—

SALOME: Oh stop it, I'm the last of all here in the village; I'm only the goose-girl, the poor Salome.

TITUS: Poor? I feel sorry for you, devoted governess of young geese! Your colleagues in the city are much better off, and yet they frequently spend years giving their charges only an imperfect upbringing. You, on the other hand, turn yours over to mankind every Martinmas[5] well crammed for their fine career.

SALOME: I don't understand you, but you talk so nicely—who is your father?

TITUS: He is at present a deceased schoolmaster.

SALOME: That's nice. And your mother.

TITUS: Was before her death the long-time connubial consort of her lawfully-wedded spouse.

SALOME: Ah, that's nice!

TITUS *(to himself):* She finds everything nice, no matter what kind of nonsense I talk.

SALOME: And may one know your name—at least your given name?

TITUS: I'm called Titus.

SALOME: That's a nice name.

TITUS: One fitting only for a man with a head on his shoulders.

SALOME: But what an odd name it is!

TITUS: Yes, and I hear it will soon be extinct altogether. Parents all fear they will be embarrassed in the future if they let their children be baptised Titus.

SALOME: And have you no living relatives?

TITUS: Oh yes! Aside from the aforementioned deceased there are definite traces on my family tree of a cousin—but he does nothing for me.

SALOME: Perhaps he has nothing.

TITUS: Don't be silly, child, he is a beer-distributor, they all have means. They're industrious fellows; not only do they turn beer into silver, they gild their own accounts as well.

SALOME: Did you perhaps do something to him to make him dislike you?

TITUS: Very much, I touched him on his tenderest spot. The eye is a person's most sensitive part, and I offend his eye every time he looks at me, for he can't abide red hair.

SALOME: The horrid thing!

TITUS: He concludes from my hair that I have a false, malicious character, and in light of this conclusion has closed his heart, and his bank account, to me.

SALOME: That's hateful.

TITUS: More stupid than hateful. Nature gives us here a gentle hint. If we take a look at the animal kingdom, we find that cattle hate the color red, and among them bulls manifest the most violent antipathy—in which gross defect man also indulges, in seeing red when he sees red!

SALOME: Oh, how cleverly you speak! One would never guess it to look at you.

TITUS: Flatterer! Let me tell you a bit more about my destiny. Rejection by my cousin was not the only bitter pill I had to swallow. I sought happiness also in the sanctuary of Love, but the Graces declared me in poor taste. I looked in at the Temple of Friendship, but my friends were all so clever, witticisms rained about my head until I retired permanently from that field as well. Without money, without love, without friendship, my situation became intolerable; therefore I cast off all human relationships, as one casts off a quilted jacket in hot weather, and here I stand before you in the shirtsleeves of liberty.

SALOME: And are you happy now?

TITUS: If only I had a mantle of provisions to protect me from the storm of famine . . .

SALOME: Oh, then it's a question of bread? Well, if you're looking for work, that's easily solved. My brother is apprenticed to the baker here; he has a big business and is in need of a helper.

TITUS: What? I become a flunky? I who have been a journeyman barber?

SALOME: A barber? We had one of those here, but he came to a bad end.

TITUS: How so?

SALOME: Because he was barbarous, the judge said.

TITUS: Oh, that cannot be. But to get back to your brother— (*pointing to the loaf of bread that* Salome *carries*) did he create this bread?

SALOME: Well, he was there when the loaf—as apprentice, of course—

TITUS: I'd like to see how far your brother has progressed in his breadological studies.

SALOME: Here, taste it! But it won't agree with you. (*she cuts off a very small slice of bread and gives it to him*)

TITUS (*eating*): H'm—it is—

SALOME: My geese like it, of course; animals have no sense.

TITUS (*to himself*): Oh, that smarts; I like it too.

SALOME: Well, what do you say? It's awful, isn't it?

TITUS: H'm. I don't want to condemn your brother prematurely; to judge a work, one must delve into it deeply. (*takes the loaf of bread and cuts off a very large piece*) I will give the matter careful consideration and notify you of my findings in due time. (*puts the piece of bread in his pocket*)

SALOME: So you'll be staying with us for a while? That's good; one must set aside pride when one has nothing. And you'll do just fine if the baker takes you on.

TITUS: All my hopes rest on the patronage of his apprentice.

SALOME: Everything will be all right. (*looking upstage, left, horrified*) Look! Look there!

TITUS (*looking*): The carriage?—The horse is running straight for the water—the devil, all is lost! (*exits, running, upstage left*)

Scene 9

SALOME: He's not going to—? He's running that way—oh don't let anything happen to him—he's grabbing the horse—it's pulling him down! *(screaming)* Ah! The horse has stopped—he stopped it—what a daredevil! A gentleman is getting out of the carriage—he's coming this way with him. I must tell the baker right away! When he hears about this, he's sure to hire him. *(exits right)*

Scene 10

MARQUIS: Ah! I'm still trembling in every limb!

TITUS: Would it please your honor to sit down for a little while?

MARQUIS *(sits down on a bench):* That damned jade, in all its life it has never run away!

TITUS: Would it please your honor perhaps to have a sprain?

MARQUIS: No, my friend.

TITUS: Or perhaps to have broken an arm?

MARQUIS: No, thank God!

TITUS: Or, if your honor pleases, to have suffered a little skull fracture?

MARQUIS: Not in the least. I am completely recovered now, and nothing remains but, as proof of my gratitude—

TITUS: Oh, I beg of you—!

MARQUIS: Three young men who know me were standing right there, screaming at the top of their voices, "Monsieur Marquis, Monsieur Marquis: the carriage is going into the water!"

TITUS: What? I have saved a marquis? That's really something!

MARQUIS *(continuing his discourse):* But not one of them lifted a hand to help me! Then you flew to my rescue—

TITUS: An ordinary humanitarian duty.

MARQUIS: And just in the nick of time—

TITUS: An extraordinary coincidence.

MARQUIS *(rising):* Your nobility of character places me in an awkward position. I don't know how to express my gratitude. One cannot reward such a deed with mere money.

TITUS: Well, I must say, money is a thing that—

MARQUIS: Can only insult a man of such high principle.

TITUS: Well, you see—that is—

MARQUIS: And it would only cheapen the value of your deed if one were to try to measure it in terms of money.

TITUS: Well, that depends—

MARQUIS: On *who* performs such a deed. Exactly! There was once a man— I don't know his name—who saved another's life—a prince it was—I don't know his name either. Anyway, he wanted to reward him with diamonds, but the rescuer replied: "Virtue is its own reward." I am certain you think no less nobly than what's-his-name.

TITUS: And yet there are circumstances in which nobility of character—

MARQUIS: Is offended by too many words, you say? Quite right. Words are inadequate to express true gratitude; therefore, nothing more will be said about the affair.

TITUS *(to himself)*: The marquis has delicate sensibilities—if he were a scoundrel, I'd have come off just the same.

MARQUIS *(looking intently at* Titus' *hair)*: But friend, I notice something here—h'm, h'm—that could prove a liability to you in many ways.

TITUS: It seems to me your honor takes exception to my head—it's the only one I have, I can buy no other for myself.

MARQUIS: Perhaps you can—I will—you must accept a small token of my—wait just a moment! *(exits running upstage left)*

Scene 11

TITUS *(alone)*: He came within an ace of saying "carrot-top" out of pure gratitude. What a fine marquis!—But what's he doing? *(looking offstage)* He's running to the carriage—he's looking for something—"a token," he said—maybe he'll give me an expensive present after all! What's that? He has taken out a hatbox—he's running this way with it. He's not going to reward me for saving his young life by giving me an old hat?

Scene 12

MARQUIS *(with a hat box)*: So, friend, take this, you will need it! A pleasing exterior can do much—almost anything—it won't let you down. Here is a talisman *(giving him the box)*; I shall rejoice if I become the author of your good fortune. Adieu, friend! Adieu! *(exits hurriedly downstage left)*

Scene 13

TITUS *(alone, holding the box in some bewilderment)*: Author of my good fortune?—Talisman?—I wonder what's in it? *(opens the box and takes out a black wig)* A wig!—Nothing but a coal-black wig! I think he was making fun of me! *(calling after him)* Wait, you human wig-stand! I'm fed up with always being the butt of jokes!—But wait! Isn't this what I have always wanted? Haven't I always been thwarted by the unattainable fifty gulden that these deceiving wigs cost?—Talisman, he said—he is right! When I put on this wig, Adonis will dwindle to a gipsy lad and Narcissus will be deleted from the books of mythology. My career goes forth, Fortune's gate yawns—*(noticing the garden gate standing ajar)* Why, the gate *is* standing open; who knows—? I'll risk it! Nothing can stand in the way of a good-looking fellow! *(exits through garden gate)*

Scene 14

SALOME *(Entering downstage right):* Oh, my dearest Master Titus, what a misfortune!

TITUS *(looking around):* Salome—! What has happened?

SALOME: The baker won't take you on. I can't help you; it makes me want to cry.

TITUS: And it makes me want to laugh. Is it then so hard to get a job as a servant around here?

SALOME: The baker said that on the one hand, he hasn't seen your credentials, and on the other, he gets so many recommendations that he is obliged to observe a certain protocol in allocating this position—

TITUS: Too bad he is not holding competitive examinations! My dear Salome, other opportunities have opened up for me. I have been summoned to the manor house.

SALOME: The manor house? That can't be. Oh, when her ladyship sees you, she'll chase you off right away. *(with reference to her hair)* I am not even permitted to come into her sight!

TITUS: Her ladyship's antipathies are immaterial, now that I have changed materially. I go to meet my destiny with bold confidence.

SALOME: Well, I wish your luck luck. It isn't right of me, but it hurts nonetheless, to think another hope of mine has been dashed.

TITUS: What kind of hope?

SALOME: Were you to stay here, looking like me, they'd have said, "There goes redheaded Titus and redheaded Salome, the wildest pair in the village!" And no girl would have looked twice at Titus, just as no boy ever looks at Salome.

TITUS: And then Titus, reduced to a single object, would have had to succumb, like it or not, to an inevitable passion.

SALOME: We would have had a very close friendship, of course—

TITUS: And the road from friendship to love is a path strewn with flowers, eh?

SALOME: Oh, I hadn't thought that far ahead.

TITUS: Why not? Thoughts are tax-free.

SALOME: Oh, no; there are thoughts which tax the peace of one's heart. My plans never work out.

TITUS: Ah, yes, man proposes, and— *(aside)* the wig disposes, that's what I say. Adieu then, Salome. *(starts to leave)*

SALOME: Don't be so proud, Master Titus; you could show a little friendship and take me by the hand and say in a friendly way, "God be with you, dear Salome!"

TITUS: All right. *(shakes her hand)* We part the best of friends.

SALOME *(shaking her head):* Farewell! Perhaps I'll see you again soon.

TITUS: That is most unlikely.

SALOME: Who knows? You go in through the gate so proudly that I can't help thinking I'll see you thrown out through the same gate.

TITUS: You are prophesying a convenient catastrophe.

SALOME *(indicating the stone bench):* I'll sit here every day and watch the gate—

TITUS: And wait until I'm thrown into your arms. Fine, enjoy your private fantasies. Goodbye! My destiny calls: "Please come in!" I'll follow its summons, and bring myself along in the bargain. *(exits through garden gate)*

Scene 15

SALOME *(alone):* There he goes, and I don't know—I have never had any luck at all, and now it seems as though he has taken even some of that away. If only I could get him off my mind! But how? By what means? If I were a man, I would know what to do—but as it is . . . Oh, men really have it over us in all sorts of ways.

Song

1

When a man doesn't know right away that we care,
What's a person to do? It's not easy, I swear!
For a man it is simple, he chases her so,
In two weeks, if not sooner, she can't help but know.
Then he plays the despondent, bangs his head on the wall,
With his hand in between, so there's no pain at all,
And the girl must give in, lest he damage the wood—
Ah yes, men have it good, have it good, have it good!

2

If somebody hurts us, we have no reply
Save to go to our bedroom and have a good cry.
If we hurt a man, though, it's almost a joke!
He goes to a tavern, sits down, has a smoke,
And while we think he's moping, he's eating a cheese,
Drinking wine, having fun with the waitress. If he sees,
On his way home, another as pretty, he would—
Ah yes, men have it good, have it good, have it good!

3

Let a girl have a second or third love affair,
It's all over, she's tarnished. But if we compare
How a man fares in matters like this, he's a king.
Though he ruin fifty girls, it's a trivial thing.
Girls in fact are attracted to such a Don Juan,
And if not out of love, out of envy they're drawn
To compete for his favor with all womanhood—
Ah yes, men have it good, have it good, have it good!

(exits)

Change of scene: *a room in the head gardener's quarters with a door in the center, a door to the right, and a window to the left.*

Scene 16

FLORA *(entering alone):* The weeds of gall and discontent grow all too thick in my garden patch; I can no longer uproot them alone. My dearly departed told me, shortly before his departure, that I should remain a widow—how could a late lamented have such a lamentable idea? The servants do not fear me, they show me no respect; I must have a husband to be their master. My dearly departed is going to shake his head in the clouds, if indeed he doesn't come back as a ghost. In the night, when I hear a knock at the door— *(there is a knock at the door; she screams in terror)* — Agh! *(tottering, she clutches at the table for support)*

Scene 17

TITUS *(wearing the black hairpiece, rushes in through the center door):* Has there been an accident? Or do you always shriek like that instead of saying "Come in?"

FLORA *(collecting herself with difficulty):* No, I was terrified!

TITUS *(to himself):* Strange creature! She is terrified when someone knocks at the door. Usually women find it terrifying when no one knocks at the door any more.

FLORA: The gentleman must wonder at my weak nerves.

TITUS: Wonder at the commonplace? Oh no! Nerves of gossamer, hearts of wax, and heads of iron—the very blueprint of feminine architecture.

FLORA *(aside):* A most pleasant person—and such raven-black hair!—However, I must— *(aloud, in a rather forced manner)* Who are you, sir, and what do you want?

TITUS: Oh, please, the honor is altogether mine! I am your most obedient servant.

FLORA *(surprised, nods a cursory adieu to him, under the impression he is taking his leave, when he remains standing before her, she says, after a pause):* Well? . . . That phrase is ordinarily spoken when one wants to leave.

TITUS: I said it, however, because I want to stay. You are in need of a servant, and as such I am at your service.

FLORA: What? The gentleman is a servant?

TITUS: Available for gardening.

FLORA: As an assistant?

TITUS: Whether you call me assistant or gardener or—it's all the same to me. Even if—and I am only speaking hypothetically—as gardener I were to succeed in planting some feelings in your heart—speaking hypothetically, of course—and you were to grant me sole possession of that dear plantation—only hypothetically— even then, I should always remain your servant.

FLORA *(aside):* The man is well bred, but— *(aloud)* Your language is somewhat bold, somewhat forward, sir!

TITUS: May I humbly point out that when one says, "I am speaking only hypothetically," then one may say anything.

FLORA: Then you are—?

TITUS: An exotic species, not indigenous to this soil, but uprooted by circumstance and transplanted by chance in the amiable parterre of your home, where, warmed in the sun of your graciousness, the tender plant hopes to find nourishment.

FLORA: The question is, first of all, do you know anything about gardening?

TITUS: I know the ways of men, consequently also the ways of plants.

FLORA: How does that follow?

TITUS: Quite naturally. Whoever knows men also knows vegetables, because very few men live, while many, untold numbers, vegetate. He who gets up early, goes to the office, then goes to eat, then goes to play cards, and then goes to bed, vegetates. He who goes to the shop early and then goes to the tax office and then goes to eat and then goes back to the shop, vegetates. He who gets up early, then studies a part, then goes to rehearsal, then goes to eat, then goes to a coffeehouse, then goes to perform a comedy, and continues to do so day in and day out, vegetates. In order to live one needs, at a modest estimate, a cool million, and even that is not all. Intellectual verve is also required, and the combination is most rare. At least, judging by what I know of millionaires, almost all of them, in their passion for profit, lead such a boring, dry, businessman's existence that it scarcely merits the flowery name of vegetation.

FLORA *(aside):* The man must have studied advanced gardening! *(aloud)* The interior of your head seems as bright as its exterior is dark.

TITUS: Perhaps you find dark hair objectionable.

FLORA: Objectionable? You rascal, you know only too well that a head of dark curls sets a man off best.

TITUS *(to himself)*: The wig is working!

FLORA: So you wish to work here? Very well, you are hired. But not as a laborer! You are a man of experience and quality; you present a favorable appearance—

TITUS *(to himself)*: Wig-power is winning out!

FLORA: You shall supervise the garden personnel. You are to give the orders to the others; after me, you shall be the first in the garden.

TITUS *(aside)*: The wig has won! *(aloud)* I am as ignorant of how to thank you as of how I came to be so fortunate.

FLORA *(studying his hair)*: My, how dark, quite Italian!

TITUS: Yes, it borders on the Sicilian. My mother was a southern gardener.

FLORA: You know, though, you are really a vain man. I'll bet you use a curling iron. *(tries to touch his locks)*

TITUS *(leaping back)*: Oh, please don't touch! My head is extremely ticklish.

FLORA: Silly man! Oh, by the way, I can't possibly present you to her ladyship in that suit.

TITUS: So you believe the saying, "Clothes make the man," the saying which makes us stoop before the tailor, and which is nevertheless so untrue! For many fine fellows go around in ragged coats.

FLORA: But the suit is nothing like what a gardener—

TITUS: Oh, the suit is altogether too gardenerish! It is oversown in patches, and it has come out at the elbows and elsewhere. It gets watered often, since I have no raincoat, and when it was in its bloom I frequently got a loan on it.

FLORA: What nonsense! *(pointing to the right hand door)* Go through that room into the bedroom. In the chest the pocket watch is on you'll find my late husband's wedding suit.

TITUS: I am to put on the wedding clothes of your dear departed? Listen— *(runs his fingers engagingly through his hair)* I cannot help it if certain feelings have been awakened which— *(gives her a meaningful look and exits through the right hand door)*

Scene 18

FLORA *(alone):* My, what a charming person!—Well, one never knows what might happen. Wouldn't it be fun if I were to remarry before her ladyship's maid, who always looks down her nose at me because she has a hairdresser for a beau. But he's taking his own sweet time marrying her. Things might go faster with me— what a triumph that would be!—First of all, though, I must call the help together. *(goes to the window)* Oh Pumpkinseed! *(calling)* Summon the help, a new gardener has been hired; in the future he will be giving the orders instead of me.

PUMPKINSEED *(from without):* That makes sense!

FLORA: But who is this?—her ladyship's maid! *(greeting her through the window)* Your obedient servant! *(moving away from the window)* She is coming to see me; what can this mean? Another complaint, no doubt. The help have made a mess of something, and I'll have to clean it up.

Scene 19

CONSTANCE *(entering by center door):* Mrs. Pruningshears—

FLORA *(with a curtsey):* At your service, ma'am. What is it you wish?

CONSTANCE: Her ladyship is expecting company from the city this afternoon and desires that no spoiled fruit be sent up to the manor house, as it was last time.

FLORA: I have some of the most beautiful—

CONSTANCE: Her ladyship is also most dissatisfied with the entire operation of the garden.

FLORA: It's not my fault. The help—But all that is going to change now. Her ladyship has given me leave to hire an able man, and as it happened, a very able man—

CONSTANCE: Good. I shall inform her ladyship of the news.

FLORA: I will take the liberty myself of presenting him to her ladyship.

CONSTANCE: What are you thinking of? Present him to her ladyship—a common lout?

FLORA: Oh, but I pray you, madam, you mustn't confuse this person with a common garden laborer; he is—it is even possible—almost certain, in fact, that I shall marry him.

CONSTANCE: So? This betrothal will be of as little interest to her ladyship as the man himself. As I have said, I find it entirely inappropriate that he should be presented to her ladyship.

Scene 20

TITUS *(enters through the right hand door, wearing a somewhat old-fashioned gardener's suit and carrying a bundle in his hand, he does not at first see* Constance): Well, here we are; I've bundled up my things here.

FLORA: You could have left them in there.

TITUS: Wearing this suit have I succeeded in conjuring up the faded picture in your soul?

CONSTANCE *(to herself):* I don't know when I've seen such a handsome black head of curls.

TITUS *(to Flora, pointing to the bundle):* And these things—where shall we put them?

FLORA *(pointing to a chest to the left):* As far as I am concerned, you may leave them there in the chest.

TITUS *(turning away):* Good. *(catching sight of* Constance) Oh! I wouldn't bleed a drop, not even if you severed an artery! *(bowing deeply before* Constance) I humbly beseech you— *(to Flora)* Why didn't you tell me—? *(to* Constance *with a deep bow)* —please do not be angry with me— *(to* Flora) —that her ladyship was here— *(to* Constance *with a deep bow)* —for not immediately showing the respect due your ladyship—! *(to* Flora) Oh, it's terrible, the situation you've put me in!

CONSTANCE: But I am not her ladyship.

FLORA *(to* Titus): What has gotten into you?

CONSTANCE: I am only—

TITUS: No, your ladyship only wishes to spare me the embarrassment.

FLORA: She is her ladyship's maid.

TITUS: Oh, go on!—This lofty carriage of forehead; this haughty batting of eye; this autocratic swing of elbow—

CONSTANCE *(flattered):* H'm . . . Nevertheless I am still only Lady Cypressburg's maid.

TITUS: Can it be?—I believe it only because I hear it from your own lips. Her ladyship's maid, then! My mother too was a lady's maid.

FLORA: But you said your mother was a gardener!

TITUS: She was a gardener first, then later she became a lady's maid.

CONSTANCE *(aside)*: Really, what an interesting, cultivated person!

FLORA *(to* Titus, *who is gazing fixedly at* Constance*)*: Just put your things in there!

TITUS *(still staring at* Constance*)*: Destiny really does not know what it is doing, placing such a one in the antechamber.

FLORA: Weren't you listening? There, in the chest!

TITUS: Yes, right away—*(gazing in admiration at* Constance*)* A figure of classic salon elegance! *(he goes, still looking at* Constance, *to the chest standing by the door)*

FLORA *(to herself)*: How she leads him on, the brazen hussy!

Scene 21

PUMPKINSEED *(entering by the center door)*: The help will be here right away.

TITUS *(noticing* Pumpkinseed, *turns away quickly)*: Damnation! If he should recognize me!— *(turns to* Constance *in order to keep his back to* Pumpkinseed*)*

PUMPKINSEED *(to* Flora*)*: So this is the new gardener! I must pay my respects to him. *(steps between* Titus *and* Constance*)*

TITUS *(turns to* Flora *in order to keep his back to* Pumpkinseed*)*: Send the fellow away! I am no friend to such ceremony.

FLORA: Don't be so shy.

PUMPKINSEED *(trying to get around in front of* Titus*)*: Sir, as the most deserving member of the staff—

TITUS *(much at a loss, dives into his pocket)*: Oh!—I must get a handkerchief in front of my face— *(instead of a handkerchief, he draws from his pocket a gray wig with a pigtail and buries his face in it)*

PUMPKINSEED: That's a strange handkerchief you have there.

TITUS: But what's this?

FLORA *(laughing)*: That's my late husband's wig.

TITUS: It does look somewhat *passé. (puts the wig in the bundle which he still holds in his hand)*

PUMPKINSEED: What the devil! This gardener looks strangely familiar!— *(to* Titus*)* Don't you have a brother with red hair?

CONSTANCE: What has gotten into him?

TITUS: I don't have a brother.

PUMPKINSEED: Oh? I guess he must have been somebody else's brother.

FLORA: What is the blockhead talking about?

PUMPKINSEED: Well, I saw this redheaded fellow . . . There's nothing wrong with that . . .

Scene 22

(*a pair of* Garden Laborers *enter through the center door, each carrying two baskets of fruit*)

FIRST LABORER: Here's the fruit!

FLORA: That should have been taken directly up to the manor house.

CONSTANCE: It would have been a fine how-do-you-do, sending up the fruit by the servants just like that.

FLORA: It has always been done that way.

CONSTANCE (*pointing to* Titus): The gardener will deliver the fruit. That will offer the most appropriate occasion to present him to her ladyship.

FLORA (*to* Constance): Present him? Why do you suddenly find it necessary to present him to her ladyship? You just said it was unseemly to bring such a lout into her ladyship's presence.

CONSTANCE (*nonplussed*): That was—that it to say—

TITUS: Lout?

FLORA (*in malicious exultation over* Constance's *embarrassment*): Yes, yes!

TITUS: That is really too much—

CONSTANCE (*very nonplussed*): I have—

TITUS: That is outrageous!

FLORA: Well, I think so—

TITUS: Incomprehensible (*to* Flora) that you could use the word "lout" to refer to me.

FLORA: Those were Madame Constance's very words!

TITUS (*to* Flora): If you will permit me, there are plenty of louts around beside me, and I am not such an egotist as to take everything personally.

CONSTANCE (*recovering from her embarrassment*): I only wanted—

TITUS *(indicating* Constance): If this lady actually let her lips form the word "lout," she no doubt had reference to a servant, perhaps one of these gentlemen here *(pointing to the two* Laborers), because she did not even know me at the time, and still knows far too little of me to pass judgment on my loutishness. *(to* Constance) Am I not right?

CONSTANCE: Entirely!

FLORA *(very upset and annoyed)*: So I am to be made a liar?

TITUS: No, merely a slanderer.

CONSTANCE *(to* Titus): Come along now.

FLORA: He is to go to the manor house? Why all the hurry? Her ladyship is out riding.

CONSTANCE: Well, would it not be more seemly for the gardener to wait on her ladyship than for her to wait on him?

TITUS: Clearly. *(to* Constance) She knows nothing of etiquette. At any rate, the most seemly thing is for me to wait with you until the appropriate moment arrives.

FLORA *(very annoyed, aside)*: I could tear her limb from limb, that person, that—!

TITUS: As gardener, however, I must observe the proper decorum— aha! Just what I need! *(rushes to the window and tears the flowers from the pots)*

FLORA: What's this? My flowers!

TITUS: They'll have to do for a bouquet. But we'll need a ribbon, too. *(hurrying to the table)* Ah, here's one. *(takes a wide satin band and wraps it around the flowers)*

FLORA: Here now, what do you think you're doing? The new ribbon I just bought in the city—

TITUS: For such a festive occasion even one's best is not good enough. *(to* Constance, *indicating* Flora) The good soul, she knows nothing of etiquette.

Scene 23

SEVERAL LABORERS *(entering center stage)*: We are here to pay our respects.

TITUS: Ah, my subordinates! You shall carry the fruit and follow me.

LABORERS: At your service.

CONSTANCE *(to* Titus): You must avail yourself of this opportunity to win the respect of the staff by showing your generosity—at least I think that it would not be out of place for you to do so.

TITUS: I too think it my place—however—*(exploring his waistcoat pocket)*—in another place I seem to find nothing.

CONSTANCE: It would give me pleasure if you would accept this— *(proffers him a purse)*

FLORA *(preventing her)*: If you don't mind, this is my affair. (to Titus) Here, sir, this! *(tries to give him money)*

CONSTANCE *(preventing Flora)*: Stop! I shall not tolerate this. This is a matter that touches the honor of the house, and consequently I must represent her ladyship.

FLORA: I can hand her ladyship the bill, too; but it is *my*—

TITUS: Permit me. This matter can be resolved without anyone getting hit over the head. If I may— *(taking the money from Constance)* Give me that! *(taking the money from Flora)* There! The important thing in such matters is that no one should be slighted. *(to the Laborers)* I'm treating everyone today.

LABORERS: Hurrah!

TITUS: Now onward, to the manor house!

CHORUS

The new gardener is off to a promising start;
Drink his health, he's a real man after our heart!

(Titus comes forward with Constance, the Laborers follow with the fruit baskets, Flora looks after them furiously, Pumpkinseed observes her with a meaningful smile; amid the general jubilation of the Garden Staff, the curtain falls)

Act 2

The scene depicts a part of the manor garden. Downstage right, the head gardener's quarters, with a usable entry. Downstage left, a table with several lawn chairs. In the background right one can see a wing of the manor house, with a window which can be opened.

Scene 1

Pumpkinseed *and several* Garden Laborers *sit around the table drinking.*

CHORUS
You'd never believe one could drink
A whole tankard of wine in a wink!
Though while working one loses one's temper,
While drinking there's nary a whimper,
For there'll never be to too much for one,
Nor does one ever long to be done.
Ah yes, drinking's a real delight
—To be continued tonight.

PUMPKINSEED: The work isn't pressing today; we've still got more than half the money left, and it's got to be drunk up; all this means we'll knock off early today!

FIRST LABORER: Nobody ever comes late for something like this.

PUMPKINSEED: Just remember, a gardener is the noblest of all plants and must be irrigated regularly, or else he'll dry up.

FIRST LABORER: But this new gardener is an unusual man, really a fine fellow.

ALL: That's right.

PUMPKINSEED: Oh shortsighted folk! He is a lazy rascal, believe me, I know! He won't get us out of any work, on the contrary, we'll have to wait on him, this stray mongrel. He'll stick his hands in his pockets and try to play His Lordship, the puffed-up deadbeat!

LABORERS: Wouldn't that be something!

FIRST LABORER: Well, if he does he'll—

PUMPKINSEED: Easy now— We'll have plenty of time this evening for such charges, and more like them. Then we can also make plans as to how to get rid of him.

ALL: Yes, we can do that.

PUMPKINSEED: So take it easy, everything in its own good time!

Scene 2

FLORA *(enters from her house with a basketfull of crockery and silver)*: Now I shall have to ask you to make an end of it. Take your tankards and go. I need this table now.

LABORERS: We were just going anyway.

PUMPKINSEED: All this is in honor of the new gardener.

FLORA (*to the* Laborers): Get back to work!

LABORERS (*leaving*): All right! (*exit upstage left*)

Scene 3

PUMPKINSEED: I don't see how you can have the heart to disturb these good people in their innocent pleasure.

FLORA (*takes the tablecloth from her basket and spreads it over the table*): Shut your mouth and help me set the table.

PUMPKINSEED: Right away! I never have to be told a second time to do this job. (*takes crockery and silver from the basket*) But this is only for two people!

FLORA: Of course! I don't know why there should be more.

PUMPKINSEED: Then the new gardener is going to eat in the manor house with her ladyship's maid?

FLORA: Idiot! He is eating here with me.

PUMPKINSEED: He, you, and I—but that makes three.

FLORA: You have eaten at my table because I found it boring to eat alone; now you have become superfluous. You have your food allowance; you may leave as soon as you have served us.

PUMPKINSEED (*piqued*): There was a time when I never left.

FLORA: Stop whining and go fetch the soup.

PUMPKINSEED (*maliciously*): So soon? It might get cold! Who knows when he'll be coming?

FLORA (*looking impatiently toward the manor house*): He will be here any minute now. (*half to herself*) Anyway, I can't understand what's keeping him so long.

PUMPKINSEED: Aha! I'm beginning to understand.

FLORA: Be quiet and do what you are told!

PUMPKINSEED (*leaving, as if talking to himself, but so that* Flora *cannot help but hear*): He must have made other arrangements in the manor house; otherwise I can't explain this long delay. (*exits into the gardener's quarters*)

Scene 4

FLORA (*alone*): That's the last time he'll go up there. The way that Madame Constance forces herself on men, it simply defies description!

TITUS (*appears at the manor house window with a napkin about his neck and the drumstick of a pheasant in his hand*): Ah, Mrs. Pruningshears, how good to see you. . . .

FLORA: Where have you been? I am waiting with the meal.

TITUS: Not I! I have already eaten.

FLORA: In the manor house?

TITUS: In the anteroom with her ladyship's maid. And very well, I might add. This was the first pheasant to whom I have done the last honors; with this drumstick his earthly shell is gathered into mine.

FLORA: But it is not proper for you to sponge up there! I forbid it.

TITUS: You can forbid *yourself* whatever you wish, but you can't forbid *me* anything! I no longer live beneath your tyranny, I have assumed a far, far better state.

FLORA (*greatly taken aback*): How's that?

TITUS: Wait a second! I want to give you something. (*withdraws*)

FLORA (*alone*): Madame Constance, I know you, this is your work! A widow who already has a beau of her own filches another's from her—that is a piece of widow's work without parallel!

Scene 5

PUMPKINSEED (*carrying the soup tureen*): Here's the soup.

TITUS (*reappearing in the manor house window*): And here are the old clothes that I no longer require. My compliments! (*hurls down the bundle of clothing so that it lands on* Pumpkinseed's *head, then withdraws*)

PUMPKINSEED: Bullseye! What's going on?

FLORA (*to* Pumpkinseed): Go to the devil!

PUMPKINSEED: Then you're not going to eat?

FLORA: No, I tell you. (*to herself*) Whoever wouldn't lose his appetite at this has none to lose.

PUMPKINSEED (*pointedly*): Am I to understand the dinner engagement is broken, for which I was superfluous?

FLORA: Out of my sight! (*to herself, leaving*) What a malicious rascal he is! (*exits to her quarters*)

PUMPKINSEED (*alone*): So he's not eating here, she's not eating at all, and I, the uninvited, will eat for the both of them! Oh, inscrutable Fortune! I wouldn't have thought you capable of such poetic justice. (*exits into the gardener's quarters*)

Change of scene: *The hall at the manor house, with a center door and two side doors.*

Scene 6

Titus *(alone, enters through the center door; he is dressed in an elegant forester's uniform):* She has done just what the other one did: offered me the late wardrobe of her former husband and wants me to become a forester. Well, if her ladyship demands no more of a forester than opening her little carriage door and hopping onto the footboard, that much forestry-science I can take care of. Oh, wig! I have much to thank you for! The food here is delectable, the drink exquisite—I really don't know whether it is my change of fortune or the Tokay that is making my head swim so.

Scene 7

Constance *(entering from the left):* Ah, I like that! That gardener's suit was so boorish; your exterior was made for the noble livery of the forester.

Titus: If only my exterior will elicit an equally ladylike response from her ladyship! I fear greatly that one unkind look from her may wrest the deer rifle from my hand and put back the shovel and hoe.

Constance: You credit me with little influence in this house. My late husband was forester here, and my mistress will certainly not expect me to remain a widow forever.

Titus: Certainly not! Such features were not shaped to wear a lifelong veil.

Constance: Assuming I were to remarry, can you doubt that her ladyship would find a place in her service for my husband?

Titus: To doubt would be blasphemy—

Constance: I do not say this, of course, with any designs on you—

Titus: Of course not, it never occurred to you—

Constance: I say this only that there be no misunderstanding, merely to show you it is within my power to secure anyone a position at the manor house.

Titus *(aside):* Oh raven-black crest, you work sky-blue wonders!

Constance: My sainted husband—

TITUS: Stop! Do not call that man sainted whom the conjurer Death has transported from your arms into the Great Beyond! No, sainted is rather he who in life still enjoys those embraces! Oh Constance!—We pay a very poor compliment indeed to wedlock when we call "sainted" only the dead, who have passed beyond it.

CONSTANCE: Then you are of the opinion that at my side one could—?

TITUS: Gaze proudly into the unknown and think to oneself: "Things can be good anywhere, but here they are best."

CONSTANCE: Flatterer!

TITUS *(aside):* Such are the new metaphysical gallantries that we've taken up lately. *(aloud)* I think I hear someone in the anteroom.

Scene 8

SALOME *(enters timidly through the center door):* With your permission—

TIUS *(startled, to himself):* Oh Lord, it's Salome! *(throws himself carelessly into a chair so that his face is turned away from her)*

CONSTANCE: How did you get in?

SALOME: There was no one outside, and I thought this must be the anteroom, but now I see— Oh, I beg you, Madame, please come outside for a moment; I am speechless in the presence of so much elegance.

CONSTANCE: Stop beating around the bush. What do you want? Quickly now!

SALOME: I am looking for someone, I have already looked for him at Mrs. Pruningshears', but I didn't find him there, so I came here.

CONSTANCE *(her suspicions aroused):* Who are you looking for?

SALOME: Well—that is—I'm looking for a man with red hair.

CONSTANCE *(relieved):* Well, you should be able to find him easily; he'll beam you a signal from a hundred paces.

TITUS *(to himself):* Oh rare new joke, how often have you delighted me!

CONSTANCE: You are wasting your efforts in the manor house, for neither her ladyship nor I would tolerate such a one here; we both have an antipathy for red hair.

SALOME: Still, if he should happen to come here, would you please tell him some people from the city were looking for him? They were asking me about him ever so suspiciously—

TITUS *(forgetting himself, leaps up startled):* And what did you tell these people?

SALOME *(recoiling):* What's that—?! *(recognizing* Titus) Oh! *(sways and falls into* Constance's *arms)*

CONSTANCE: What's wrong with the creature? *(to* Titus) Well, bring a chair over here. I can't just stand here holding her.

TITUS *(bringing a chair):* Put her here.

CONSTANCE *(lowering* Salome *into the chair):* She's not moving, she's utterly motionless. *(to* Titus) This is very odd. The sight of you had this effect on her.

TITUS *(nonplussed):* I don't see how that can be, I'm not ugly enough to make one faint, and as far as my good looks are concerned, they are not so great as to bowl one over, either.

CONSTANCE: But you can see for yourself, she isn't moving at all.

TITUS *(very nonplussed):* Yes, I can see that.

CONSTANCE: But now it seems to me—yes, she's moving!

TITUS: Yes. I can see that, too. I'll go fetch some fresh water. *(makes to leave)*

CONSTANCE: None of that; that will not be necessary. Or do you perhaps have a special reason for sneaking away?

TITUS: I wouldn't know why!—I don't know this person.

CONSTANCE: Then you needn't be afraid of her waking up.

TITUS: Not at all! Who says I am afraid?

SALOME *(regaining consciousness):* Ah, Madame—I'm better now—

CONSTANCE: What came over you?

SALOME: The gentleman—

CONSTANCE: Then you know him?

SALOME: No, I don't know him, certainly not! *(standing up)* But he spoke to me so sharply—

CONSTANCE: Was that the reason you—?

SALOME: It's a pity, isn't it—such city nerves in a country girl? *(to* Titus, *who stands by astonished)* Don't be angry, sir, and if you happen to see the man with the red hair, please tell him I meant well, I only wanted to warn him; and tell him, too, please, I'll never stand in the way of his good fortune! *(holding back her tears)* Tell him that, when you see the man with the red hair. *(to* Constance) Again, I beg you to forgive me for having fainted in these rooms that are not for the likes of me, and God bless both of you and— *(breaks into tears)* —now I am going to start crying—that is not the proper thing to do—I mean no harm—I am such a silly thing! *(exits by center door, crying)*

Scene 9

CONSTANCE *(looking after her in wonder):* H'm, —this creature—I must confess the whole thing strikes me as highly suspicious.

TITUS *(only gradually recovering his composure):* What?

CONSTANCE: She was so upset, so moved—

TITUS: About a red-haired man, you heard her.

CONSTANCE: She did speak of such a one, but it was *you* that she seemed so violently to—

TITUS: Now stop that! What has gotten into you?

CONSTANCE: You're not going to try to tell me she wasn't greatly moved?

TITUS: What is that to me? First you accused me because she was motionless, now you take me to task because she was moved. I really don't understand—

CONSTANCE: There's no need to lose your temper; I could be completely wrong—that you would have any connection with such a common person—that would be unthinkable.

TITUS: I should say so! I am a young man with a career to make! *(with emphasis)* My aspirations soar to the heights. . . .

CONSTANCE *(coquettishly):* Really? It was fortunate that this unpleasant scene took place in her ladyship's absence. . . . Her ladyship has an uncommon hatred of commoness; she interests herself only in intellectual pursuits, as do I. . . . She is herself an author.

TITUS: An author?

CONSTANCE: Should the conversation turn to letters—are you acquainted with such things?

TITUS: No.

CONSTANCE: That's too bad.

TITUS: Mere child's play! Though I may know nothing about writing, I know all the more about authors. I only need find her things divine, and she is bound to say: "Ah, this man understands . . . deep insight . . . solid background!"

CONSTANCE: You are a sly dog! *(to herself)* How unlike my hairdresser he is!

Scene 10

MARQUIS *(entering by center door)*: Most lovely Constance. . . .

TITUS *(to himself)*: It's the illustrious wig dispenser—if only he won't blab—! *(draws to one side)*

MARQUIS: I was very nearly deprived forever of the pleasure of pressing this charming hand to my lips. *(kisses her hand)*

TITUS *(to himself, shocked)*: Such condescension!—A marquis kissing her hand, the hand of an anteroom person—What a thing!

CONSTANCE: It is so late, I thought you were not coming today.

MARQUIS: As you must know, only an extraordinary incident—but what's this? *(catches sight of Titus, who seizes an antimacassar from a nearby chair and begins to dust the furniture furiously)* Has a new forester been taken on?

CONSTANCE: This very day. A man of many parts.

MARQUIS: How can you judge the parts of a forester? Did he make a hit? And anyway, why a forester in the household of a lady?

CONSTANCE: As you can see, he is very industrious, and makes himself useful in all sorts of ways.

MARQUIS *(tries to catch a glimpse of Titus' face, while the latter avoids him with comic bustle)*: Yes, yes, I can see that.

TITUS *(to himself)*: I mustn't show him my face at all costs.

CONSTANCE: But you are quite forgetting to tell me about the incident.

MARQUIS *(glancing frequently toward Titus)*: It was really more an accident, one that might easily have ended in a neck-breaking water fall, had not chance sent a man at the very moment that beastly animal, my fiery Fox—

TITUS *(taken aback)*: I thought he was about to call me by name.

CONSTANCE: Fox? I thought you still had that ugly sorrel.

TITUS *(to himself)*: Yet another veiled compliment!

MARQUIS: I traded him off because his appearance offended you so. At any rate, this man—*(looking intently at Titus)* my rescuer—*(whirling Titus around)* I was not mistaken!—This is he!

TITUS *(bowing deeply)*: Please, your honor, the marquis has taken me for another! *(makes to leave by center door)*

MARQUIS *(restraining him)*: Why deny it, noble sir? It is you,—that carriage, that voice, that hair color—

TITUS *(to himself, in alarmed embarrassment)*: Uh-oh, now he's coming to the hair!

CONSTANCE: Truly, whoever has seen this head of hair once, will never forget it. Such locks are indeed worthy of admiration.

MARQUIS *(feeling himself to have been complimented)*: Oh, please, you are too kind!

TITUS *(to Constance)*: The marquis thanks you on my behalf for the compliment; thus in my humility nothing remains to be done save to—

CONSTANCE *(to Marquis)*: You understand these things: have you ever seen such lustre, such waves—? *(gestures toward Titus' head, as if about to run her fingers through his hair)*

TITUS *(leaping back)*: Oh, don't touch! I am so ticklish there—

MARQUIS *(piqued, sotto voce to Constance)*: Incidentally, you seem to be taking a particular interest in the new domestic.

CONSTANCE *(somewhat embarrassed)*: I—? H'm—there is a kind of camaraderie, which—

MARQUIS *(as above)*: Which in my opinion does not exist between a forester and a lady's maid.

CONSTANCE *(to Marquis, sotto voce)*: Monsieur Marquis, I thank you for the explanation, but I am quite capable of judging what is proper and what is not.

MARQUIS *(to himself)*: Now I've offended her. *(to Constance in a soft tone)* Forgive me, most lovely Constance, I only wanted to—

CONSTANCE: You only wanted to comb out her ladyship's little blonde wig; you will find it in the dressing room *(pointing to the right)*, in the big wardrobe. Now go about your business!

TITUS *(astonished)*: What's this? A hairdresser! *(to Marquis)* I thought you were a marquis, a mixture of baron, duke, and knight of the realm.

MARQUIS: No, my name is Marquis, and I am a wig-maker.

TITUS: That's a horse of a different color. The vacant room of respect is now furnished with barbers' kits, and we can become friends without embarrassment. *(extends his hand)*

MARQUIS *(also extends his hand)*: I owe you a debt of thanks. *(softly)* But you also owe me one, and it will be very much in your best interest to see that we remain friends.

TITUS: Friends to the death!

CONSTANCE *(to herself):* Monsieur Titus must not learn of my relationship with Marquis; the hairdresser's jealous behavior could easily—I had better leave. *(aloud)* Gentlemen, important duties . . . I must leave you two friends alone now. *(exits center door)*

TITUS *(calling after her):* Adieu, dear lady of the chamber!

Scene 11

MARQUIS: Sir, why this gallantry? I tell you straight out, I forbid it! Madame Constance is my fiancée, and woe be unto you if you dare—

TITUS: What? Are you threatening me?

MARQUIS: Yes, my dear sir, at least I am warning you. Do not forget that your fate hangs by a hair, and—

TITUS: And you could be so ungrateful as to divulge the wig-connection.

MARQUIS: And that I could be so clever as to get rid of a rival that way.

TITUS: What? Thus speaks *this* man? This very man, to the man without whom this man would have been a dead man? Without which man this man would now be carp food?

MARQUIS: I owe you a debt of gratitude, but under no circumstances the relinquishment of my financée.

TITUS: Who says she is to be relinquished? I am no rival for her love, only for her patronage.

MARQUIS: Ah, now you are talking sense! If this is so, you may count on my gratitude and, above all, on my keeping the hair-secret. Be careful, though, to give me no cause for displeasure, or else—*(threateningly)* Just keep in mind that your head is in my hands! *(exits to the right)*

Scene 12

TITUS: What a damnable affair! Everything has come down about my head today! If only there weren't so much in it! But the Tokay vapors—and the fact that the lady's maid is also the hairdresser's financée, that too—*(pointing to his head)* makes it spin. *(flings himself into an armchair)* It really ought to be an affair of the heart, but the heart is silly and at the same time indiscreet. Every time a ticklish situation comes along, right away it's turned head over heels, even if it sees the head already has its hands full. I am so tired. *(yawns)* It could be another half hour before her ladyship returns— *(lets his head sink into his hands)* I could— *(yawning)* take a little nap—not really go to sleep—only a little nap—a little—nap—*(falls asleep)*

Scene 13

MARQUIS *(enters from the right after a short pause)*: There is a broken window in there. I can't stand draughts, so I closed the shutters. But now it is so dark in there that without light I can't possibly—the forester ought to—but where is he? Can he have sneaked away to my Constance after all? If so, he will— *(starts to run out the center door, then sees the sleeping* Titus *in the armchair)* On, no, I have wronged him—this jealousy—a foolish thing—I must get over it. How peacefully he lies there—no man in love sleeps like that, he surely has no thought for her. . . .

TITUS *(mumbling in his sleep)*: Con-sta-sta-stance—

MARQUIS: The devil! What was that? *(tiptoes nearer)*

TITUS *(as above)*: Char-ming—figure—Con-Constance—

MARQUIS: He is dreaming of her! The scoundrel has the nerve to dream of her!

TITUS *(as above)*: Only—another—kiss-kiss—

MARQUIS: Hell and damnation! I'll not tolerate such dreams! *(starts to seize him by the shirtfront, then reconsiders)* Wait!—it is better so. Let's see whether she'll give a redhead a kiss-kiss! *(approaches the chair from the back and very carefully grasps the wig)*

TITUS *(as above)*: Let go—Stan-stance—I'm ticklish—on my head—

MARQUIS *(takes the wig away)*: Now try your luck, you redheaded Adonis! Never again shall you have the talisman! *(puts the wig in his pocket and hurries out through the center door)*

Scene 14

TITUS *(Talking in his sleep)*: Oh—delicate—little hand!— *(one hears from without the sound of a carriage entering the court-yard, shortly thereafter a loud ring at the door* Titus *wakes with a start)* What was that? I believe— *(runs to the center door)* A servant is dashing out—her ladyship is coming home—now I shall be presented. *(straightens his suit)* My suit is all rumpled—my tie wrinkled—quick, where's a mirror? *(runs to a mirror which hangs on the left-hand wall, looks into it, then leaps back)* Good heavens, the wig is gone!—It must have fallen off while I was asleep— *(runs to the armchair and searches for it)* No, it's gone, lost, stolen! Who could be so malicious? There is jealousy at play here! Othello of a hairdresser! Pomaded monster! This is your work! You have committed this foul wignapping! Now, at my most critical, auspicious moment, I stand here like a windlantern[6] on the bier of my budding career! But wait!—He's in there combing out her ladyship's wig—he'll not get away from me! You shall give my wig back or tremble for your life, Knight of the Combs! I'll shake your hair-powder soul till there's not a grain left in your body! *(rushes out enraged through the side door)*

Scene 15

LADY CYPRESSBURG: I must say, I find it most high-handed, almost impertinent of Constance, that she should take it upon herself to hire domestics in my absence without my authorization.

EMMA: Don't upset yourself over it, mother dear; after all, she took on a forester, and it has long been my wish that we should have a forester. He will look so much better than our two bowlegged footmen in their old Franconian[7] livery.

LADY CYPRESSBURG: But why should ladies have need of a forester?

EMMA: And he is supposed to be quite a soldierly-looking, dark-haired fellow, according to Constance, though he doesn't have a moustache; you must get him to grow one, mama, and also fine black sideburns, so that one can't see anything of his face except for two black, glowing eyes! Such a thing would look marvelous on the back of the carriage.

LADY CYPRESSBURG *(not paying much attention to* Emma's *last speech):* Hush! I shall send the person away, and that's that! But where is he? Didn't she say his name was Titus? Hallo! Titus!

Scene 16

TITUS *(enters from the right, wearing a blonde wig):* Here I am; I grovel in the dust before your higheness, whom I am to serve in the future.

EMMA *(astonished, aside):* What's this! He is no brunette!

LADY CYPRESSBURG *(to herself, though loudly):* What a well-behaved towhead!

TITUS *(having heard the last word, to himself):* What? Did she say "towhead?"

LADY CYPRESSBURG *(to Titus):* My maid offered you the post of forester, and I have no objections— *(turning to Emma)* Emma—! *(begins to speak with Emma in dumb show)*

TITUS *(to himself):* Towhead, she said! But I have— *(looks around in confusion and catches sight of himself in a mirror hanging on the right hand wall, in great surprise)* By my soul, I *am* blonde! I must have picked up a blonde wig there in the dark. If only her ladyship's maid doesn't come in now!

LADY CYPRESSBURG *(continuing her conversation with Emma):* And tell Constance—

TITUS *(alarmed, to himself):* Uh-oh, she is sending for her now!

LADY CYPRESSBURG *(continuing):* She is to get my dress ready for the soirée this evening.

TITUS *(with a sigh of relief, to himself):* Thank God! That'll keep her busy for a while.

EMMA: At once! *(to herself, leaving)* That silly Constance was putting me on! Pretending a blonde is a brunette! *(exits by center door)*

Scene 17

TITUS *(to himself):* Now I stand before an author. Everyday words won't do; every speech must be clothed in one's Sunday best.

LADY CYPRESSBURG: And now to you, my friend.

TITUS *(making a deep bow):* This is the moment I have longed for and feared in equal degree, the moment which I contemplate with timorous valor and courageous trembling, so to speak.

LADY CYPRESSBURG: You have no cause for alarm. You have a good carriage, an agreeable manner, and if you behave yourself . . . Where have you served previously?

TITUS: Nowhere; it is the first fruit of my forestry that I lay at your ladyship's feet, and the livery which I now inhabit encloses an individuality which, though dedicated to service, has up to now never been in it.

LADY CYPRESSBURG: Is your father also a forester?

TITUS: No, he plies a quiet, retiring trade, whose only stock is that of peace. Though bound to a Higher Authority, he is nevertheless quite independent, and free to mold himself—in short, he's dead.

LADY CYPRESSBURG *(to herself)*: How prodigally he uses twenty elevated words to express what one could say in a syllable! The person obviously has an aptitude for literature. *(aloud)* What then was your father?

TITUS: He was a master of scholars; book, slate, and ferrule were the elements of his existence.

LADY CYPRESSBURG: And what sort of literary training did he give you?

TITUS: A kind of pedagogical potpourri. I have had a smattering of geography, a glimmering of history, a notion of philosophy, a hint of law, an inkling of surgery, and a foretaste of medicine.

LADY CYPRESSBURG: How charming! You have studied much, but nothing thoroughly! That way lies genius.

TITUS *(to himself)*: That's the first time I ever heard that! Now I see why there are so many geniuses about.

LADY CYPRESSBURG: Your blonde curls indicate an Apollonian temper. Was it your father or your mother who was blonde?

TITUS: Neither of them. It is by sheer accident that I am blonde.

LADY CYPRESSBURG: The more I observe you, the longer I listen to you speak, the more I am convinced that livery is not suitable for you. Under no circumstances shall you be my domestic servant.

TITUS: Then am I to be rejected, broken, crushed?

LADY CYPRESSBURG: By no means. As an author, I require some-one—not an ordinary copyist, more a consultant or a secretary—to stand at my side during my intellectual endeavors; it is to this position that I intend to appoint you.

TITUS *(happily surprised)*: Me?—Your ladyship believes me capable of serving as an intellectual sidekick?

LADY CYPRESSBURG: No doubt of it. I am also pleased to say that the position is at present vacant. I have just dismissed a man who was recommended to me, a man of great scholarship and learning. But he had red hair, and that to me is an abomination. I told him right off, "No, no, my friend, it's no use, adieu!" And I was glad to see him leave.

TITUS *(to himself):* I must really be on my guard, or else my career will fly right out the door.

LADY CYPRESSBURG: Now get out of that livery at once; I am expecting company in an hour, to whom I wish to present you as my new secretary.

TITUS: My lady, even if I set aside this forester's livery, my other suit is also a livery of sorts, that is to say, the livery of poverty: a coat of patches with ragged lapels.

LADY CYPRESSBURG: That is easily remedied. Go in there *(pointing to the right),* through the billiard room into the corner closet; there you will find my late husband's wardrobe. He was just your size. Choose what you like and come directly back here.

TITUS *(to himself):* Yet another suit from a late lamented. *(bowing)* I'm off! *(to himself, leaving)* I'll have had a whole lamentable flea market on my back before the day is out.

Scene 18

LADY CYPRESSBURG *(alone):* The heights to which I have raised the young man have made his head swim! How will he feel when I lead him into otherworldly regions through the recitation of my verse?

CONSTANCE *(excited, enters by center door):* Mean, that's what I call mean.

LADY CYPRESSBURG: What's the matter?

CONSTANCE: I really must complain about Miss Emma's behavior. I find it very mean to carry a joke to such extremes. She scolded me for having lied about the forester's hair. At first I thought she was joking, but she wound up calling me a silly goose.

LADY CYPRESSBURG: I shall reprimand her for that. By the way, the man is no longer a forester. I have made him my secretary, and as such he will be shown the respect due his position.

CONSTANCE: Secretary? I am delighted that he has met with your approval. The black secretarial suit will go nicely with his black hair.

LADY CYPRESSBURG: What did you say?

CONSTANCE: His black hair, I said.

LADY CYPRESSBURG: You must be mad. I have never seen a more beautiful golden head of hair.

CONSTANCE: Your ladyship is jesting!

LADY CYPRESSBURG: It seldom occurs to me to jest with my subordinates.

CONSTANCE: But my lady, with my own eyes I have seen—

LADY CYPRESSBURG: My eyes are no less my own than yours are yours.

CONSTANCE *(very puzzled)*: And your ladyship calls that blonde?

LADY CYPRESSBURG: What else?

CONSTANCE: If your ladyship will forgive me, that would require a very singular pair of eyes! I would call it the blackest black that ever existed.

LADY CYPRESSBURG: Laughable creature, make your little jokes with someone else.

CONSTANCE: Oh, this is enough to drive one mad!

LADY CYPRESSBURG *(looking to the right)*: Here he comes now—well? Is that blonde hair or not?

Scene 19

TITUS *(enters from the right, wearing a black tail coat, knee breeches, silk stockings and shoes)*: Here I am, most gracious mistress! *(startled at the sight of* Constance, *to himself)* Uh-oh, it's Constance!

CONSTANCE *(much surprised)*: What's this?

LADY CYPRESSBURG *(to* Constance*)*: In the future I shall not tolerate this sort of—

CONSTANCE: But my lady, I have—

LADY CYPRESSBURG: Not another word!

TITUS *(to* Lady Cypressburg*)*: Your ladyship seems upset. What is it?—

LADY CYPRESSBURG: Can you imagine, this fool here insists that you have black hair.

TITUS: That is a black lie!

CONSTANCE: I am going to lose my mind!

LADY CYPRESSBURG: A trifling loss—more importantly, I am liable to lose my patience! Go now and prepare my toilet!

CONSTANCE: Again, I can only assure you—

LADY CYPRESSBURG *(angrily):* And for the last time I am telling you to go.

CONSTANCE *(regaining her composure with great difficulty and leaving):* This is beyond all comprehension! *(exits by center door)*

Scene 20

LADY CYPRESSBURG: What an insolent person!

TITUS *(to himself):* My position here in this house is like the timber of a shipwrecked sailor; I must push the others under or go under myself. *(aloud)* Oh my lady, there is more to this female than meets the eye.

LADY CYPRESSBURG: Has she perhaps been discourteous to you?

TITUS: Oh, no, not that, she has been only too courteous! It may seem strange that I should discuss such a matter, but I find it offensive. This person constantly makes eyes at me, as if—and talks incessantly, as though—and invariably acts, as it were—and I simply don't care for it.

LADY CYPRESSBURG: She shall go this very day!

TITUS: Then too there is the behavior of your ladyship's hairdresser. He is carrying on shamelessly with your ladyship's maid, which naturally touches the honor of the house—

LADY CYPRESSBURG: I'll tell him goodbye, too.

TITUS: All this flirting, these amorous liaisons, trouble me, I don't like to stand by and see this sort of thing going on— *(aside)* I'd much rather be doing it myself.

LADY CYPRESSBURG: What delicate, noble sentiments! *(aloud)* Marquis has done my hair for the last time.

TITUS: And then there is the head gardener—No, I'll not say anything more—

LADY CYPRESSBURG: Speak up, I demand it!

TITUS: She halfway proposed marriage to me.

LADY CYPRESSBURG: The impertinence!

TITUS: A formal halfway proposal of marriage it was.

LADY CYPRESSBURG: She must leave my house this day!

TITUS *(to himself):* Once they're all gone, I'll remain the fairhaired boy! *(aloud)* I am sorry if I—

LADY CYPRESSBURG: Write letters of dismissal to all three of them immediately.

TITUS: No, that I cannot do. My first act as secretary must not be such a cruel one.

LADY CYPRESSBURG: My, what a noble heart the young man has!

Scene 21

EMMA *(enters from the left side door):* Mama, I have come to complain about Constance. Because of the way she behaved, she forced me to call her a silly goose.

TITUS *(aside):* They always have to peck away at one another!

LADY CYPRESSBURG: You shall dismiss her forthwith, Constance orally, and Mrs. Pruningshears and the hairdresser in writing.

EMMA: All right, mama dear!

TITUS *(feigning amazement):* Mama?

LADY CYPRESSBURG: Yes, this is my daughter.

TITUS: Ah!—No!—No!—Go on!—No, it cannot be!

LADY CYPRESSBURG: Why not?

TITUS: The years do not add up.

LADY CYPRESSBURG *(feels herself very flattered):* Oh but they do, my friend.

TITUS: Such a young lady—and this grown-up daughter? No, you may deceive someone else, but— She must be a younger sister, or perhaps a very distant relative of the house. If I am to believe your ladyship has a daughter then she could at most, at the very most, be only *so big*— *(indicates the height of a newborn infant)*

LADY CYPRESSBURG: Yet it is as I have said. One has conserved oneself well.

TITUS: Oh, I know what conservation can do, but no conservatory could have achieved this!

LADY CYPRESSBURG *(smiling benignly):* Silly man . . . But now I must make my toilet, or my guests will take me by surprise! You, Emma, come with me!— *(to Titus)* I shall see you by and by.

TITUS *(as though overcome by feeling):* Oh, let it be soon! *(pretending to be shocked at his own words, collects himself, makes a very deep bow, and adds in an obsequious tone)* Oh let there be soon some way for me to prove my eagerness to serve you!

LADY CYPRESSBURG *(leaving):* Adieu! *(exits with* Emma *by left side door)*

Scene 22

TITUS: Gracious lady! Gracious lady! For the time being that's all I'll say: Gracious lady! It's impossible to say how much fun it is when one has been despised, suddenly to become charming. When I think of this morning and then now, that's quite a change in the space of four or five hours. Yes, Time is the longsuffering tailor's apprentice who does the alterations in the workshop of eternity. Sometimes the work goes swiftly, sometimes slowly, but it always gets done, there's no denying it. Time changes all!

Song

1

This iron man would go dancing and work up a steam,
Then sit down in a draught with a bowl of ice cream;
At a gallop from mistress to mistress he sped,
Drank and played cards all night, never thinking of bed.
Ten years later he's hectic, his stomach's awry,
He must wear flannel nightshirts in the month of July,
And a warm quilted nightcap, *la grippe* to forestall—
Yes, time changes all.

2

This one spends the whole day with the girl he's to wed,
Leaving only when the servants are ready for bed,
Then sighs up at her window on high from below
And freezes his nose, standing there in the snow.
Six months after the wedding he's nowhere in sight,
Coming home, if at all, in the dead of the night.
When she's in Brühl,[8] he's in Naples, having a ball—
Yes, time changes all.

3

A singer once sang like the heavenly spheres,
When she belched, faery melodies rang in one's ears.

Her delivery was flawless, her tone so unique,
That the nightingales fled from their nests in sheer pique.
Silver bells were old dishpans compared with this crooner.
Six years later her voice was as cracked as a schooner.
Now she frets through a play in a theatrical squall—
Yes, time changes all.

4

What a well-behaved fellow, such a fine little man,
So handsome and modest, so spick and so span,
Though soft-spoken, he answers enquiries one makes him,
And redounds to one's honor wherever one takes him.
Men and women alike fawn over the boy.
Ten years later the lad's a great hobbledehoy,
A fool who butts in with remarks off the wall—
Yes, time changes all.

5

This great beauty turned down thirteen offers of marriage,
Eight of which were from owners of house, horse, and carriage.
Two strung themselves up at the door of the gal,
Three others were found in the Schanzel canal.[9]
In the Third Coffeehouse[10] four more shot themselves dead.
That was years ago. Now she would not turn a head,
If she stood on her own. What a terrible fall!
Yes, time changes all.

6

Once if someone said something of one held dear,
Then pow! One received a good clout on one's ear!
The boxing of ears led of course to a duel;
All year long bloody feuds such as this were the rule.
Lovers now at such forwardness take no offense,
But themselves make bad jokes at their sweethearts' expense,
Make their girls laughingstocks at the local beer hall—
Yes, time changes all.

(exits through right door)

Scene 23

(Mr. Flatt, *several* Gentlemen *and* Ladies *enter during the ritour-nelle of the following chorus*)

CHORUS

Nowhere else in the world is a party so nice
As this house, where one plays neither card games nor dice.
For when dear Lady Cypressburg holds a soirée,
One pays homage to naught but the Muse and the tea.

(during the chorus, Servants *bring in a large table spread for tea and place chairs about it)*

Scene 24

LADY CYPRESSBURG: Welcome, ladies and gentlemen!
GUESTS: We took the liberty—
LADY CYPRESSBURG: You are all well, I trust?
GENTLEMEN: Yes, thank you kindly.
LADIES *(among themselves):* Migraine, headaches, rheumatism—
LADY CYPRESSBURG: If you please (All *sit down to tea.*)
TITUS *(entering from the right side door):* Perhaps I come at an inopportune—?
LADY CYPRESSBURG: Not at all! *(presenting him to the company)* My new secretary.
ALL: How do you do?
LADY CYPRESSBURG *(to* Titus)*: Be seated. (*Titus *sits)* This gentleman will read you my latest memoirs at our next soirée.
ALL: How charming!
MR. FLATT: It's a pity your ladyship does not write for the theater.
LADY CYPRESSBURG: Who knows what may happen? Perhaps I shall try my hand at it soon.
TITUS: I understand it's fantastically easy to do, that it goes slick as a whistle.
MR. FLATT: I myself have long had a passion to write a farce.
TITUS *(to* Flatt)*: Then why don't you?

MR. FLATT: My wit is not so composed as to compose anything comical.

TITUS: Then write a sad farce. In a gloomy story even the dullest joke will stand out by contrast, just as the dullest needlework shows to good effect on black velvet.

MR. FLATT: But one cannot call something that is sad a farce!

TITUS: No. If there are three jokes in a play and other than that nothing but death, dying, corpses, graves, and gravediggers, nowadays that is called a slice of life.

MR. FLATT: I didn't know that.

TITUS: It is quite a new invention, and belongs to the school of House and Garden Poetry.

LADY CYPRESSBURG: Are you then no lover of sentiment?

TITUS: Oh yes, but only in a worthy cause, and one is not found very often. That is why a noble soul can make do for a long time with one handkerchief, while the common, good little garden-variety souls need a dozen hankies for a single comedy.

LADY CYPRESSBURG *(to her neighbor):* What do you think of my secretary?

Scene 25

FLORA *(enters crying through center door):* My lady, please forgive me—

ALL *(surprised):* The head gardener!

TITUS *(dismayed, aside):* Damnation!

FLORA *(to* Lady Cypressburg*):* I can't believe you have turned me out of service, I've done nothing!

LADY CYPRESSBURG: I owe you no explanation for the grounds which led to my decision. By the way—

FLORA *(catching sight of* Titus, *astonished):* What's this? He has blonde hair!

LADY CYPRESSBURG: What is the hair of my secretary to you? Out!

Scene 26

CONSTANCE *(enters, weeping, with* Emma *through center door):* No, it cannot be!

EMMA: I've only told you what mama told me to.

CONSTANCE: I've been dismissed?

ALL *(surprised, turning to* Lady Cypressburg*):* Really?

CONSTANCE: My lady, I would never have thought it of you! Without cause—

MY FLATT: What has she done?

CONSTANCE: It's all because of the secretary's hair.

LADY CYPRESSBURG: How ridiculous! That is not the reason at all. *(to the* Company*)* By the way, what do you think of this fool? She insists he has black hair! Now I ask you: is he blonde or not?

CONSTANCE: He is black-haired!

FLORA: That's what I say, too; he's a brunette!

Scene 27

MARQUIS *(entering by center door):* And I say he is neither!

ALL: What is he then, M. Marquis?

MARQUIS: He's redheaded!

ALL *(astonished):* Red?

TITUS *(to himself):* That does it! *(stands up and throws the blonde wig to the floor in the center of the stage)* Yes, I am redheaded!

ALL *(astonished, rising):* What's that?

LADY CYPRESSBURG: Fie!

CONSTANCE *(to Titus):* How revolting you look!

FLORA *(to Titus):* And this carrot-top wanted to marry me?

LADY CYPRESSBURG *to* Titus*):* You are a deceiver, and have maligned the most faithful members of my staff. Go, out with you, or my servants will—

TITUS *(to Lady Cypressburg):* No need of that. You are overcome with anger—I'm leaving—

ALL: Out!

TITUS: Such was Ottocar's rise and fall.[11] *(exits slowly with bowed head through center door)*

CHORUS

Now that was really too much!
Who ever heard of such?

(Lady Cypressburg pretends to faint, and the curtain falls amid general consternation)

Act 3

The scene is the same as the beginning of act 2: part of the garden with the gardener's quarters.

Scene 1

TITUS (*alone, enters in a melancholy mood from behind the wing of the manor house*): The proud edifice of my hopes has burned down uninsured; my fortune's stock has fallen by a hundred percent, and that brings my net worth to a good round sum, namely zero. Now I may call out boldly: "World, close your forests about me; Forests, set your robbers upon me; whoever now can make me a *kreuzer* poorer, him will I revere as a higher being!"—but wait! I did make a profit in this affair: destiny left me an excellent suit of clothes, though perhaps only as a mocking souvenir of a career thwarted and fallen on its face. Nonetheless, a boon—this black tail coat—

Scene 2

GEORGE (*who has quickly entered during* Titus' *last words, now interrupts him*): —Is to be returned to the manor house, together with the vest and stockings.

TITUS: Oh, dear envoy, do you know what an unpleasant mission you—?

GEORGE: Don't make any fuss, now!

TITUS: Have you considered, dear envoy, that I might already have skedaddled?

GEORGE: Oh, our constable catches every vagrant.

TITUS: Or have you reflected, dear envoy, that I might ignore the rights of man and knock you down and run away? Then what would you—?

GEORGE: Help! Help!

TITUS: Why are you yelling so? I was merely inquiring; surely questions are permitted?

GEORGE (*calling toward the gardener's quarters*): Pumpkinseed!

PUMPKINSEED (*from within*): What's up?

GEORGE (*opening the door and speaking inside*): He is to put on his old rags and leave the respectable clothing here.

PUMPKINSEED *(from within):* Fine!

TITUS *(to George):* You are too good.

GEORGE: No more of your compliments! In a quarter of an hour the clothes must be here and you must be God knows where! Understood? *(exits behind the manor house)*

Scene 3

TITUS *(alone):* Oh yes, I understand everything. Misfortune has visited me; I wanted to receive the visit in a black tail coat, but Misfortune said: "Don't go to any trouble for me, I'm an old friend, just put on any old rag—"

PUMPKINSEED *(from within):* Well, what's keeping you?

TITUS: Coming, coming! *(exits into the gardener's quarters)*

Scene 4

(Salome *and* Bung *enter from the left)*

SALOME: Then you really mean him no harm?

BUNG: I keep telling you, no! I'm only doing what the brewmaster told me to. He is the only man who has any spiritual influence over me.

SALOME: And what did he tell you?

BUNG: He said: "You had it coming, because you didn't look out for him when he was a boy! Now he has run away and may make your family a laughingstock in the world." That's why I have come after him.

SALOME: And do you want to have him jailed?

BUNG: Who, me? I'd give my life to! But the brewmaster said that that too would be a disgrace to the family.

SALOME: Oh, go on, how can you be so cross with your own nephew—?

BUNG: Even a nephew can be a thorn in one's side when he has red hair.

SALOME: Is that then a crime?

BUNG: Red hair aways indicates a foxy, scheming disposition—besides, he brings disgrace on the whole family. Of course they're all dead now except for me, but while they were in the family, we all had brown hair, all dark brown heads, not a fair head to be found in the whole family, and then this boy had the effrontery to come into the world redheaded!

SALOME: Still, that's no reason to let a relative go to ruin when one has means oneself.

BUNG: What I have I owe entirely to my own wits.

SALOME: And are you really a man of means?

BUNG: I should hope so! My parents didn't leave me a kreuzer. I was confined entirely to my own wits, and that's a pretty narrow confinement, I'll tell you!

SALOME: I can believe that, but—

BUNG: Then shortly afterwards a godmother died and left me ten thousand gulden. I thought to myself, if only a couple more relatives die, I may be able to make ends meet. And right away, four weeks later, an uncle died and left me thirty thousand gulden. The next summer another uncle came down with malaria and I got twenty thousand gulden; the following winter an aunt caught the fever and turned in her dinner pail, leaving me forty thousand gulden. A couple of years later another aunt, then another godmother—all just as I had planned! —Then too I won eighteen thousand gulden in the lottery.

SALOME: That too?

BUNG: Yes, one can't count on inheritances for everything; one must diversify. In short, I can say that all I have I owe to my wits.

SALOME: Well, Master Titus must be just as clever, since he'll inherit from you when you die.

BUNG: A wise man once told me I could not die—he didn't say why—he was probably only flattering me, but if I do, I will find myself some people to my taste to leave my money to. I can't have that redhead disgrace me by doing me the last honors.

SALOME: Then you aren't going to do anything for poor Master Titus, either now or after your death?

BUNG: I'll do what the brewmaster told me to. I'll buy him a shop in the city; that much I owe the dead relatives. Then I'll give him a couple of thousand gulden to set himself up as a respectable man; then I'll toss off a few well-chosen remarks about his red hair, and afterwards he is never to come into my sight again.

SALOME (*joyfully*): So you're going to make him rich and happy after all?

BUNG: I'm going to do what the brewmaster told me to.

SALOME (*sadly, to herself*): I'm glad to hear it, though when he's no longer poor, he'll be quite lost to me. *(sighing)* Oh well, he didn't want me anyway.

BUNG: What is he doing at the manor house?

SALOME: I don't know, but he is trimmed from head to toe with gold braid.

BUNG: He's in livery! Oh, blot on the family honor! The nephew of a beer distributor covered with gold braid! I'll bet the whole family have turned over in their graves! Oh unheard-of scandal! Quick, take me up there, I'll shake him out of that livery—hurry! I'll not rest until the stain is expunged and my family lie at peace in their graves again.

SALOME: But let me tell you—

BUNG *(highly agitated)*: Onward, I say! Lead on, torch bearer! *(drives her before him out behind the wing of the manor house)*

Scene 5

FLORA *(enters from the left)*: Hi! Pumpkinseed! Pumpkinseed!

PUMPKINSEED *(enters from the gardener's quarters)*: What do you want?

FLORA: That person has gone, I trust?

PUMPKINSEED: No, he's not quite ready.

FLORA: Tell him to hurry up!

PUMPKINSEED *(maliciously)*: Perhaps you would like a little farewell supper for two, at which I would be superfluous?

FLORA: Idiot!

PUMPKINSEED: I just thought you might like to, since you were so eager at lunchtime; now would be the perfect opportunity, her ladyship's maid won't snatch him away from you now.

FLORA: Shut up and send him away!

PUMPKINSEED *(calling into the gardener's quarters)*: Get a move on, sir!

TITUS *(from within)*: Right away!

Scene 6

TITUS *(in the shabby suit of clothes he wore at the beginning of the play, enters from the gardener's quarters)*: Here I am.

FLORA: Hardly the thing for a person who ought to have been gone by now.

TITUS: Oh, good Mrs. Pruningshears, who also found a hair in my hair! Would you perhaps care to give me something for the road?

FLORA: *Give* you something? For the impertinent hoax which you played on me? I'd better make sure you haven't *taken* anything. *(looking him up and down contemptuously, exits into her quarters)*

TITUS *(outraged)*: What?

PUMPKINSEED: Well, one never knows. *(also looks him up and down contemptuously)* Hairy snake in the grass! *(exits into gardener's quarters)*

Scene 7

TITUS *(alone)*: Impertinent folk! People certainly treat one kindly when one is down on his luck. Though actually, I had it coming. I didn't behave very generously when I was on top, either—but so much for that. Evening is coming on, evening in every sense of the word. The sun of my good fortune and the real sun have both set in the west—where turn now, where find shelter for the night without a *kreuzer* to my name?—that's the real Western Question.[12] *(looks toward the manor house and the gardener's quarters)* There are plenty of rooms there, but I seem to be a diet that these rooms cannot stomach.

GEORGE *(enters from behind the manor house and approaches* Titus *with great circumspection)*: Master Titus?

TITUS *(annonyed by his servility)*: I beg you, don't take me for a fool!

GEORGE: I know perfectly well what to take you for— *(aside)* thought I am not allowed to say it. *(aloud)* Would you be so good as to come up to the manor house?

TITUS *(astonished)*: I?

GEORGE: To her ladyship's maid.

TITUS: I? To Madame Constance?

GEORGE: And then perhaps to her ladyship. But not right away, in about half an hour. In the meantime you might like to take a turn about the garden.

TITUS *(to himself)*: Incredible!—but I'll do it. *(to* George) I shall wait here and then come as ordered. Would you be so kind as to tell the garden help over there *(pointing to the left)* that I am strolling here by her ladyship's leave. In light of the proverb, "Ingratitude is the worlds' reward,"[13] I have reason to suspect they may wish to show their gratitude to me for the way I treated them today by trying to toss me out on my ear.

GEORGE: Certainly, Master Titus. We shall see to the matter at once. *(making a courteous bow, exits)*

Scene 8

TITUS: This is what I make of it: her ladyship, in a fit of graciousness, must have realized she has treated me, poor devil that I am, too harshly, and in the end is coming forth with something for the road. Wait! *(struck by an idea)* Just to be doubly sure of success, I'll pay her a delicate compliment— *(reaching into his pocket)* I still have—since she can't abide red hair—I still have the late gardener's gray wig here in my pocket, *(pulls it out)* in which I'll make my farewell visit; she'll be bound to spring for something! I'll try my luck now with the gray. Black and blonde hair turn color all too soon—in my case both enjoyed but a brief moment of glory. Gray hair, on the other hand, never changes; perhaps my luck will hold with the gray. *(exits downstage left)*

Scene 9

FLORA *(from within)*: Didn't I tell you something like this would happen? *(enters angrily from her quarters)* Oh, I know people! *(to* Pumpkinseed) Run after him!

PUMPKINSEED: It's not worth the effort.

FLORA: But he stole my late husband's wig; it is invaluable to me when I want it.

PUMPKINSEED: Oh, go on, it's full of moths.

FLORA: Run after him and recover his loot!

PUMPKINSEED: He wont' get two groschen for it.

FLORA: Run after him, I say. Hurry!

PUMPKINSEED *(slowly making his way out behind the gardener's house)*: I'll see if I can catch him—but I don't think I will. *(exits)*

Scene 10

FLORA *(very angrily)*: What a pity it's already evening! The constable will be drunk by now, otherwise I'd have him arrested, that saucy rascal—I'd give him something to remember me by!

GEORGE *(enters downstage left)*: What's the matter, Mrs. Pruningshears? Why so angry?

FLORA: Oh, it's that good-for-nothing tramp!

GEORGE: Shh! Honor to whom honor is due! I too called him a vagabond earlier, but it seems he has a filthy rich uncle who has come to take care of him; he's going to buy him the best barbershop in the city, for he is a trained barber, and then he is going to give him thousands and thousands of gulden.

FLORA *(extremely surprised and taken aback)*: Oh, go on—!

GEORGE: It is as I say. I was just sent to ask Master Titus to come up to the manor house. He is not supposed to know anything yet, but I did call him "Master," because, as I said, honor to whom honor is due. *(exits behind the manor house)*

Scene 11

FLORA *(alone):* This news is enough to give one a headache—and to think of the rough way I treated him! Now everything must be altered and tailored to becoming the wife of a barber! It is a disaster only in the country, in the city one can make do with a redheaded husband. Here he comes now! *(looking to the left)* I'll pretend to regret what I did. What pretend? I'm out of my mind with regret!

QUODLIBET TRIO

FLORA:
Titus! Titus!

TITUS: *(enters from upstage left)*
Can the gardener be calling to *me?*

FLORA:
Master Titus, please listen to me!

TITUS:
Can the gardener be calling to *me?*

FLORA:

Master Titus, please listen to me!
I've lost all the peace I once knew.

TITUS:

Have your say, then; I'm listening to you.

FLORA:

It is never too early to rue!

TITUS:

Your farewell was unworthy of you.

FLORA:

I've lost all the peace I once knew!

TITUS:

Have your say, then; I'm listening to you.

} *together*

FLORA:

It is never too early to rue!

TITUS:

Your farewell was unworthy of you.

} *together*

FLORA:

It is never, no, never too early to rue!

TITUS:

Your farewell, though, was really unworthy of you!

} *together*

FLORA:

Don't turn your back on me, I pray,
Nor look vindictively my way,
I cannot bear it!

TITUS:

Well, what is it?

FLORA:

I am perishing—!

TITUS:

Sure you are!

FLORA:

Woe is me!

TITUS:

It never fails to smart,
It cuts one to the heart,
To be an object of disdain.
Far distant from your native weald

Shall other bonds of love be sealed;
In Switzerland, by cow-maid healed,
A man may seek surcease from pain.

FLORA:

If I seemed somewhat vexed when we parted,
Please forgive my ungovernable passion.
When avenging themselves, the greathearted
Always do so in greathearted fashion.

TITUS:

I am engulfed in a storm of vengeance
Called forth by Honor and Love—

FLORA:

Does that mean you're still going to leave?

TITUS:

Yes. I set forth, joyful and free,
Never thy temple to see.

FLORA:

Oh, you cannot conceive of the yearning,
Of the torments within this breast churning,
Of the fires of remorse ever burning,
In a heart that is bleeding and torn!
Yes, I call you my reason for living,
The one, ardent goal of my striving!
How *can* you be so unforgiving
As to answer my tears with scorn?

TITUS:

Something's wrong here, unless I mistake her.
To think I'd so quickly awake her
To passion. But so what? From the baker
You can buy kaiser rolls, but not me!
    It's no use, you see,
    I'm off for a year.
    You'll never have me,
    We'll not be a pair.
It's all for naught, you'll get nowhere.
It's all for naught, you'll get nowhere.

SALOME *(entering)*:

There's really no reason, I vow,

For my face to be smiling and gay.
Yet my mouth opens up even now
And breaks out in a laugh anyway.
It's so funny the way the fat man
Is behaving up there in the house;
Down here he plays the great Khan;
Up there he's as still as a mouse. —Hahaha!

FLORA:

What is *she* doing here?

TITUS:

It's Salome the goose-girl!
Shall she see me here as a churl?

SALOME (*catching sight of* Titus):

But what's this?—Now with *her?*
Yet another *malheur,*
That I happened upon them this way.
But I've made up my mind not to say
Another word more,
Nor to think heretofore
Of that which is never to be, ah no,
Of that which is never to be.

FLORA:

Titus! Don't be a boor!
We're alone here no more.   *all*
I shall try a soft-spoken refrain;   *three*
Thus I'm certainly sure to regain   *together*
The one I have lost,
The one I have lost,
The one who is all things to me, ah yes,
The one who is all men to me.

TITUS:

I'll at least seem to be
Full of sweet charity,
But don't let a soft-spoken refrain
Have you jumping for joy all in vain,
For I'm not won with ease,
And observe my words, please—
I only said "seem to be."

TITUS:

> Oh, to see her caught in the net—
> I confess with a touch of regret—
> Were the work of a moment, and yet
> I cannot, I cannot, I cannot!
> For I'm not deedidledeedum
> In love deedidledeedum
> With her dumdiddledeedum
>> At all, not at all!
>> Ah, to see her in the net—
>> I confess with regret—
>> Were so easy, and yet
>> I cannot! Her yearning
>> I mustn't be burning
> To think of returning, oh no!

ALL THREE:

> In airy hopes we often trust,
> And all we hope for turns to dust.

FLORA:

> *Mine* shan't be turned to dust, never fear;
> Luck holds us widows far too dear.

TITUS, SALOME: *together*

> Ours shall be turned to dust, we fear;
> Luck favors us but with a sneer.

ALL THREE:

> When one has luck beneath one's roof,
>> And thinks it's there to stay,
> It slips right out the window, poof!
>> And softly steals away.
> In airy hopes we often trust,
> And all we hope for turns to dust.

FLORA:

> *Mine* shan't be turned to dust, never fear;
> Luck holds me far too dear.

TITUS, SALOME: *together*

> Ours shall be turned to dust, we fear:
> Fate mocks us with a sneer.

SALOME:

> My brother the 'prentice sings thus:

"With the lasses it is really, really, really
    Always such a lot of fun;
Although in public they act silly, silly, silly,
    They're not deceiving anyone.
And I am such a handsome fool, fool, fool,
As straight and slender as a rule, rule, rule,
Among all men the very jewel, jewel, jewel,
    That's something no one can deny.
I've lots of gumption in my head, head, head;
I'm proud to say I've never plead, plead, plead,
For very long with a girl who said, said, said,
        She'd not get in the wagon bed, bed, bed,
        She'd not get into the wagon bed."

ALL THREE:
        Soon everything will change,
        Take courage on the road
        That leads us to our goal;
        March on till things look up.
            Fortune's round,
        O'er the earth it doth merrily bound;
            Without ground,
        Underneath it one often is found.

FLORA, SALOME:
        At any rate—
TITUS:
        We know our state—we're nothing great—
        We're pawns of Fate—
FLORA, SALOME:
        We're pawns of Fate, mere pawns of Fate.
FLORA:
        Though one may hate—
SALOME:
        To think of Fate—
TITUS:
        And have one's back to the wall—
ALL THREE:
        That's no reason to mope,
        With a glimmer of hope,
        We'll be able to cope after all.

FLORA, SALOME:
> Of this there's no question:
> With a healthy digestion,

TITUS:
> With a healthy digestion—

ALL THREE:
> One can stomach most everything,
> One can stomach everything.

(Flora *exits right,* Titus *behind the manor house,* Salome *downstage left*)

Change of scene: salon in the manor house with an arch and French windows in the background, opening onto a moonlit terrace and garden; side doors right and left, table lamps on either side of the room.

Scene 12

CONSTANCE *(enters from the right, alone):* Who would have thought it of the hairdresser! With a careless "Adieu, madame," he breaks off with me forever! Such a thing could cause an ordinary widow to lose her composure, but for me, thank God, it's only a moment before another suitor, Monsieur Titus, lies at my feet. If only her ladyship, who so kindly has made this affair her concern, can get the old walrus to make Titus his heir!

Scene 13

LADY CYPRESSBURG *(entering from the left):* Constance—
CONSTANCE *(hurrying to her):* My lady—?
LADY CYPRESSBURG: It's no use.
CONSTANCE: Is that possible?
LADY CYPRESSBURG: I have agonized over the man for the last half hour, but his waterproof leather soul is impervious to the dew of eloquence. He will set him up in business, nothing more—there is no hope for an inheritance.
CONSTANCE: H'mph! That would be fatal. And I thought it would be so easy; I even sent for the notary Falk, who has a summerhouse in the neighborhood. Let's try once more, my lady. Let us both set upon him together.

LADY CYPRESSBURG: If you like. Today in my haste I treated you very unjustly, and I wish to make amends through true motherly solicitude.

CONSTANCE *(kissing her hand):* You are so very kind—

LADY CYPRESSBURG *(existing with* Constance *by the left door):* I have very little hope, however; perhaps the sight of his nephew—

CONSTANCE: He should be here any moment now. *(both exit left)*

Scene 14

(Conrad *escorts* Titus *in through the french windows which open on the terrace,* Titus *is wearing the gray wig)*

TITUS *(Entering):* But at least tell me—

CONRAD: I am not authorized to say anything. *(ogling him in surprise)* What, what's that? You're wearing a gray wig.

TITUS: Is that your affair? I have been summoned here; announce me, and have done with it!

CONRAD: All right, all right! *(exits left)*

Scene 15

TITUS *(alone, pointing to his heart):* I admit it'll give me a bit of a pang here when I see Constance again. Just think how she said: "Oh, how revolting he looks!" Such a recollection is the universal remedy for chronic heartaches. She can remain a lady's chambermaid wherever she likes; but never again will she enter the chambers of my heart. Those rooms I shall let to a bachelor, whose name is Misogyny.

(Enter Conrad)

TITUS *(to him):* Well, have you announced me?

CONRAD: Not yet; her ladyship is in conversation, and is not to be interrupted.

TITUS: But I am—

CONRAD: Don't be impatient! Wait here, or *(pointing to the right)* in that room. In time I shall see whether it is time to announce you. *(exits right)*

Scene 16

TITUS: Off with you, you uniformed order-executing machine! He too is one of a uniform edition. Life is a collection of such editions that may be of great value, because they prompt even the most dissatisfied of us to make the sated remark, "I've had more than my fill!"

Song

1

Someone comes to your room; "Yes, what is it?" you say.
"Please help me, I beg you, I'm in a bad way.
I've been looking for work, but times are so hard,
And I've just spent ten weeks in a hospital ward!"
Yet it's not even noon, and he reeks like a still;
I've had more than my fill, oh yes, more than my fill!

2

"This affair is outrageous!" the husband cries out.
"You don't know," purrs the wife, "what you're talking about.
If to tender addresses the man seems inclined,
It is only because he's in awe of my mind.
What you take for love's ardor is merely good will—"
I've had more than my fill, oh yes, more than my fill!

3

In a cloak with red tassels the maiden is dressed,
And I'll bet she has cambric at home in her chest,
Her smoke-colored gown is the *crème de la crème;*
When she comes to a puddle, she lifts up her hem
And reveals just the merest suggestion of frill—
I've had more than my fill, oh yes, more than my fill!

4

I'm in love with a girl who is modest and bland,
So I go to her parents and ask for her hand.
"She is yours, you may marry tomorrow," they say,
"Though you'll have to look after us too, by the way,
And take in her ten brothers and sisters, if you will—"
I've had more than my fill, oh yes, more than my fill!

5

Two fräuleins are chatting on a neighboring bench,
I hear "oui" and "peut-être"—they are talking real French.
"Allez-vous aujourd'hui au théâtre, Marie?"
"Nous allons," says her friend, "au quatrième galerie,
Je vais toujours avec Maman au théâtre en ville—"
I've had more than my fill, oh yes, more than my fill!

6

"I shall go on the stage!" someone told me, inspired.
"What rôle would you like to play first?" I inquired.
"Well, Hamlet's not bad for a great virtuoso;
Then my Don Carlos will make all the others seem so-so.
There'll be no one like me on the whole Burg playbill—"[14]
I've had more than my fill, oh yes, more than my fill!

(exits through left side door)

Scene 17

LADY CYPRESSBURG: What can be taking him so long?

CONSTANCE: George told me that—

TITUS *(entering from the right):* Does your ladyship have reference to me?

LADY CYPRESSBURG: Ah, there you are.—You are in for a surprise!

CONSTANCE *(gazing in wonder at* Titus' *gray wig and calling* Lady Cypressburg's *attention to it):* My lady! Just look—

LADY CYPRESSBURG: What's that?

TITUS *(pointing to his wig):* This old wig was the only thing I could lay hands on. I used it to conceal the color which is so injurious to your nervous system.

LADY CYPRESSBURG: H'm, it's not all that bad. Sometimes I am a bit childish.

TITUS: Childish? Not even the most perceptive student of human behavior would find that quality in you.

CONSTANCE: Actually, red hair is not all that terrible on you.

TITUS *(astonished):* You say that, you who—?

LADY CYPRESSBURG: Now you must take off that wig at once, there is someone who—

CONSTANCE (*catches sight of* Bung, *who has entered from the left*): Too late, he's already here!

LADY CYPRESSBURG (*to* Bung): Here is your nephew, Mr. Bung. (*exits through left door*)

CONSTANCE (*to herself*): Now it is up to him to come to terms with him! (*follows* Lady Cypressburg *out*)

Scene 18

TITUS (*astonished*): Uncle? How did you get here?

BUNG: In a more respectable way than you did! Running off is not my way of doing things.

TITUS: Yes, of course, for one of your dimensions running cannot be very easy.

BUNG: You blot on the family, you! (*comes nearer and notices with surprise the gray hair*) But what's this? Gray hair?

TITUS (*to himself, startled*): Uh-oh!

BUNG: But you are redheaded!

TITUS (*quickly regaining his composure*): I used to be.

BUNG: And now?

TITUS: Now I am gray.

BUNG: But that's impossible!

TITUS: Actuality is always the best proof of possibility.

BUNG: But you are only twenty-six years old!

TITUS: So I was yesterday! But the anguish, the pain of being deserted by my own, my only uncle, and cast out into the world a helpless runaway, aged me a millennium. And I turned gray overnight.

BUNG (*amazed*): Overnight?

TITUS: It was seven on the dot when I left home; three quarters of an hour later I looked at myself in the mirror of unfortunates—that is, a puddle of water—and at that time it seemed to me my hair had been lightly dusted. Ascribing it to the poor light, I chose the Linigraben[15] as my mattress, wrapped myself in the night mists, and fell asleep. On the stroke of midnight I was awakened by two frogs in disputation on my necktie. This brought on an attack of desperation which in turn gave me the brillant idea to pull out a few handfuls of my hair. They were gray! I attributed this to the sickle moon's silvery reflection and fell asleep again. Then, all of a sudden, an ear-splitting chatter of milkmaids awoke me from deepest Linigraben slumber—it was broad daylight, and at my side a gypsy sat making his toilette. He looked at himself in a piece of broken glass that had once perhaps been a mirror; I followed suit, and an iron gray head stared back at me which I recognized as my own only because it was attached to my face.

BUNG: This is unheard of!

TITUS: Not at all. History offers us numerous examples: there was, for instance, a certain Belisarius;[16] no doubt you have heard of him?

BUNG: Belisarius? Was he a beer distributor?

TITUS: No, a Roman general. His wife got the senate to have his eyes gouged out.

BUNG: Wives usually take care of that sort of thing themselves.

TITUS: This one however did it with the help of the Justinian Code. Her husband took the matter much to heart and in three day's time was totally gray. Just think, Uncle, what took a Roman general three days, I accomplished overnight. And you, Uncle, are the cause of this historical phenomenon.

BUNG *(deeply moved)*: Titus, my boy, my kinsman—I don't know what's coming over me—I the uncle of a historical phenomenon! *(sobbing)* I haven't cried in nineteen years, this is all so unexpected. *(dries his eyes)*

TITUS: It's good to let the old beer out.

BUNG *(opening his arms)*: Come here, my silver-haired boy! *(embraces him)*

TITUS *(returning his embrace)*: Uncle Bung! *(leaps back suddenly from his arms)*

BUNG *(astonished)*: Why do you spring back like a wooden hoop?

TITUS *(to himself)*: He came within a hair of grabbing my pigtail! *(aloud)* You bruised me; it must have been your ring.

BUNG: Don't be so sensitive! Here, into your uncle's arms! *(embraces him vigorously)*

(TITUS *holds the pigtail up with his right hand during the embrace, in order to keep it out of the grasp of Bung.)*

BUNG *(releasing him)*: There!—By the way, so as not to bruise you with my ring any more— *(with some difficulty removes the heavy signet ring from his finger)*

TITUS *(in the meantime, aside):* If he sees the pigtail, that's it: I'll never be able to convince him I grew a pigtail in my grief.

BUNG *(giving him the ring):* There you are! I want you to know I'm here to take you back to the city and make you a successful man— I'm going to buy you a fine barbershop—I—

TITUS *(joyfully):* Uncle!

BUNG: But the way you look, that coat—I must present you to her ladyship as a relative of mine, and then there is someone else in there too—

TITUS *(taken aback):* The hairdresser, perhaps?

BUNG: Hairdresser! *(laughs with clumsy roguishness)* You young scamp, you can't put me on! I may have weak eyes, but I could see very well what that person had in mind. If it weren't for that coat—(Conrad *enters through right door and starts to leave through center door)*

BUNG *(to* Conrad): Hi, you—if you would—do you have a brush?

CONRAD: A brush? Yes, I think so. *(searching his pockets)* Right, I have one here in my pocket. *(hands* Bung *the brush)*

BUNG: Good. Give it here! You can go now. (Conrad *exits through center door)*

BUNG *(to* Titus): Now come here so I can clean you up a bit.

TITUS *(worriedly):* What are you going to do?

BUNG: Turn around—!

TITUS *(anxiously):* But an uncle can't serve as his nephew's clothes-cleaner!

BUNG: I'm not serving a nephew, I am brushing the coat of a natural wonder. I am removing dust from a world event, and that is no dishonor even to a beer distributor! Turn around.

TITUS *(in great anxiety, to himself):* Oh Lord! When he sees the pigtail—! *(aloud)* Start with the front!

BUNG: All right. *(begins to brush* Titus' *clothing)*

TITUS *(in great anxiety, to himself):* Fate, if you don't give me a pair of scissors, I'll run myself through with a knife!

BUNG *(brushing more vigorously):* It's awful how messy the boy is!

TITUS *(to himself):* Is there no escape? Then let lightning strike! *(as he stands looking toward the left door, it opens and* Constance's *hand appears with a pair of scissors)* Aha! A flash of cold steel strikes my eyes! An angel with a pair of English scissors![17]

BUNG: Turn around, I say!

TITUS: Let's go stand over there! *(without turning his back to* Bung *moves to the left side of the stage until he is standing near the door with his back to it)* The light is much better here! *(reaches back and takes the scissors from* Constance's *hand)*

BUNG: Now turn around!

TITUS: No, you can see there's still a lot more dust here on the front. *while* Bung *continues to brush his lapels, he quickly snips off the pigtail)*

BUNG: No, there's not! Come on, turn around! *(whirls him around)*

TITUS *(as* Bung *turns him around, carries the pigtail forward over his head with his left hand, so that* Bung, *who now begins to brush the back of the coat, has seen nothing. To himself)*: Thanks to you, Fate, the amputation was a success!

BUNG *(as he stops brushing)*: Now see here, Titus, you're a good lad, you came to grief because of a hard-hearted uncle. And why was I hard-hearted? Because you had red hair! But now you don't any more, so there's no reason why—I have no choice, my heart must soften. You are my only relative, you are—in a word, you are as good as a son to me, you shall be my sole heir!

TITUS *(astonished)*: What?

Scene 19

(Lady Cypressburg, Constance *and the* Notary *enter)*

LADY CYPRESSBURG: "Sole heir," those are the words we've been waiting to hear come from your heart!

CONSTANCE: We never doubted you for a moment; luckily the notary is right here, and he always has the proper forms at hand.

BUNG: Give them here!

(the Notary *takes out a sheet of paper and explains its salient points to* Bung *in dumb-show)*

TITUS *(to himself, with reference to* Constance)*: She's falling all over herself; she's going after my inheritance much more eagerly than I ever did myself.

LADY CYPRESSBURG: *(to* Titus) See how this good soul *(indicating* Constance) is looking out for your welfare? I know all about you two, and am pleased to give my consent to this union which love has sealed and which gratitude can only strengthen.

(Titus *bows without replying*)

BUNG (*to the* Notary): Good, everything's in perfect order! (Bung *is led to the table on which lie writing materials, sits down to sign*)

TITUS (*to himself*): I can let him buy me a barbershop; after all, he is a blood relation. But to become his sole heir through a trick, I can't have that! (*aloud to* Bung, *who is about to sign the document*) Wait, uncle! If you will permit me—

BUNG: What? Aren't you satisified yet?

Scene 20

FLORA (*entering by center door*): My lady, I have come—

LADY CYPRESSBURG: At an inopportune moment!

FLORA: To settle accounts—

LADY CYPRESSBURG: Did I not tell you that you may stay on?

FLORA: Yes, but—of course nothing's definite, but it may be that I'll marry in the city. . . . But why should I keep it a secret? Master Titus—

LADY CYPRESSBURG: What?

CONSTANCE (*simultaneously*): The effrontery!

BUNG: How many did you promise to marry out of desperation?

TITUS: Promise? None.

BUNG: Not that it matters; marry whoever you wish, you're still my sole heir!

Scene 21

SALOME (*hurrying in through center door*): Master Titus! Master Titus! (*startled at the sight of the company, without however noticing* Flora, *she remains standing in the doorway*)

LADY CYPRESSBURG, NOTARY *and* CONSTANCE: What's this?

SALOME (*shyly*): I beg your pardon—

LADY CYPRESSBURG: What can this person want here?

SALOME: Master Titus! Mrs. Pruningshears has ordered—

LADY CYPRESSBURG: But she's right here.

SALOME (*noticing* Flora): Right! Then she can say it herself.

LADY CYPRESSBURG: Say what?

SALOME: Nothing! She's making signs for me not to say anything.

LADY CYPRESSBURG: Out with it, now!

SALOME: I can't while the gardener over there keeps making signs at me.

LADY CYPRESSBURG (*to* Flora): Stop that! I won't have it! (*to* Salome) Now what is it?

SALOME (*embarrassed*): Mrs. Pruningshears told Pumpkinseed, and Pumpkinseed told me to—

LADY CYPRESSBURG (*impatiently*): What?

SALOME: Master Titus is to give back the wig.

(Lady Cypressburg *and* Constance in confusion)

BUNG: What wig?

TITUS (*taking off the gray wig*): This one!

BUNG (*infuriated, as he becomes aware of the deception*): What's that? You young whelp, you—

CONSTANCE (*to herself*): Damnation! Now all is lost!

LADY CYPRESSBURG: (*softly to* Constance) Stay calm! (*aloud to* Titus) You have played a rather silly joke on your worthy uncle. But surely you cannot believe he really let himself be taken in. He would have to be the most stupid man under the sun not to have seen through your clumsy deception at once. But as a man of intelligence and understanding—

TITUS: He saw through it right away, and let *me* be the butt of the joke.

LADY CYPRESSBURG (*to* Bung): Is that not so?

BUNG (*utterly dumbfounded*): Oh yes, sure, sure, I saw through the whole thing!

LADY CYPRESSBURG (*to* Titus): That this sensible man is not going to deprive you of your inheritance just because of your hair is something you can hope for with confidence. (*to* Bung) Isn't that so?

BUNG (*as above*): Oh, sure, sure.

TITUS (*to* Constance *and* Flora): But that I should freely renounce the inheritance, that is *not* something you hope for. My good uncle is going to buy me a shop—I can't ask for more than that. And for that I will be eternally grateful to him. I need no inheritance, I only wish he may live another three hundred years.

BUNG (*touched*): Ah, no beer distributor has ever lived that long! You're a good lad, in spite of your red hair.

TITUS (*with reference to* Flora *and* Constance): It is clear I cannot marry either of these ladies without an inheritance, for they find red hair pardonable only in a sole heir. Therefore I shall marry someone who cannot hold my red hair against me, someone who already has taken a bit of a fancy for a poor redheaded devil—as I believe is the case with this one! *(takes the astonished* Salome *in his arms)*

SALOME: What—? Master Titus—?

TITUS: Will be yours!

LADY CYPRESSBURG *(who has been speaking softly with* Constance, *aloud):* Adieu! *(exits haughtily through left door, followed by the* Notary)

CONSTANCE: Her ladyship washes her hands of the whole affair. *(follows her)*

FLORA *(to* Titus, *sarcastically):* I congratulate you on your excellent choice. As they say, "Birds of a feather flock together." *(exits center)*

BUNG *(to* Titus): You're acting as if I had no say in the matter at all!

TITUS *(with reference to* Salome): I know you don't like red hair, Uncle; most people don't. But why is that? Because it is an unfamiliar sight; if there were many redheads around, it would become popular, and you may rest assured, Uncle, that we'll make our contribution to the multiplication of our species. *(embraces* Salome)

(as the orchestra strikes a few chords, the curtain falls)

Translated by Robert Harrison and
Katharina Wilson

AGNES BERNAUER

Friedrich Hebbel

CHARACTERS

ERNEST, *reigning Duke of Bavaria.*
ALBRECHT, *his son.*
HANS VON PREISING, *his chancellor.*
MARSHAL VON PAPPENHEIM ⎫
IGNACE VON SEYBOLTSDORF ⎬ *Knights on the side of Duke*
WOLFRAM VON PIENZENAU ⎭ *Ernest.*
OTTO VON BERN
COUNT TÖRRING ⎫
NOTHAFT VON WERNBERG ⎬ *Knights on the side of*
ROLF VON FRAUENHOVEN ⎭ *Duke Albrecht.*
HANS VON LAUBELFING, *a knight of Ingolstadt.*
EMERAN ZU KALMPERG, *Judge of Straubing.*
KASPAR BERNAUER, *barber and surgeon of Augsburg.*
AGNES, *his daughter.*
THEOBALD, *his apprentice.*
KNIPPELDOLLINGER, *godfather to Agnes.*
HERMANN NORDLINGER, *Mayor of Augsburg.*
BARBARA ⎫
MARTHA ⎬ *Burghers' daughters.*
STACHUS, *a servant.*
A CHAMBERMAID *at Vohburg and Straubing, a* HERALD, *a* LEGATE
OF THE CHURCH, PEOPLE, KNIGHTS, TROOPS, *in great number.*
(*Place: Augsburg, Munich, Vohburg, Regensburg, Straubing.*
Time: Between 1420 and 1430)

Act 1

Scene 1

Augsburg. Barber shop, doors, windows, cupboards, tables, chairs.
THEOBALD *(alone, holding a bouquet):* I do not know what to do.
  (holds the flowers up) Trample you to pieces? Such lovely roses? It
  would be a pity; they are not to blame. Or shall I give them to her?
  No; most certainly I'll not. And I should have told Sir Fickleness
  so at once; he seems to think I have neither eyes nor heart nor
  blood. If—yes, that's what I'll do! I will just try her! There she
  comes, with her father's porridge! How that must taste! If she
  should ever cook anything for me, I—*(conceals the bouquet
  behind him)*
AGNES *(enters, bearing the porridge):* Good morning, Theobald!
THEOBALD: Many thanks, Miss Agnes, many thanks. Did you sleep
  well?
AGNES: I should ask *you* that! You are so often disturbed at night
  when there is a brawl—and bandages are needed.
THEOBALD: Have you noticed that? *(aside)* I'll give her the flowers,
  and the whole message. If she makes a face and rebukes me with:
  "You can stoop to such a thing?"—
AGNES: What are you hiding behind you?
THEOBALD *(shows the flowers):* Oh, yes, I nearly forgot.
AGNES: Oh, but they are lovely! Give them to me! *(she buries her
  face in the flowers)* If only we had a garden! Whose name day is it
  today? *(hands them back)*
THEOBALD: Oh, they are for you!

AGNES: For me? Oh, I thank you. But your uncle must be very feeble, then?

THEOBALD: My uncle?

AGNES: Yes, since he is beginning to give away his flowers. Gardeners do not usually do that. Surely you did not buy them!

THEOBALD: They are not from me.

AGNES: Not from you? From whom, then?

THEOBALD: Guess!

AGNES: From—No, it could not be Barbara. She'll not look at me anymore, though I do not know why.

THEOBALD: It is not "she" at all.

AGNES: It is *not?* Nor you? *(she lays the flowers on the table)*

THEOBALD: Thank heavens! She does not guess anyone else!

AGNES: But I must ask you—

THEOBALD: Scold me! I only wanted to know—

AGNES: What?

THEOBALD: If you had been flirting with him in church, or possibly pressed his hand while dancing!

AGNES: *Whom* do you mean?

THEOBALD: It is all right, if you cannot guess. *(he takes the bouquet)* I'll give them to our old Gertrude—she shall wear them on her shrunken bosom when she hobbles to market—and thank him with a curtsey when she passes the house. *(dances up and down)* Oh, I could—*(sings)*
> When two join hands together.
Oh, Miss Agnes, that is a merry song. *(sings on)*
> Who makes a good apprentice
> Becomes in time a master.
Oh, don't you think that is true?

AGNES: You are merry too early in the morning. It is better late in the evening.

THEOBALD: And yet the birds sing when they awake, not when they go to sleep! *(he takes her hand)*

AGNES *(draws her hand away):* What is it?

THEOBALD: I only wanted to see if— You *did* let me hold it once, didn't you?

AGNES: Oh, the time you had to bleed me!

THEOBALD: Of course. *(he takes her hand again)* Did my blade leave a scar? I did it so awkwardly!

AGNES: Do you always tremble the way you did that day?

THEOBALD: Oh, no; only I felt so faint, because I was going to hurt you. How red your blood was! *(to himself)* I would have gladly bound the wound together with my lips, if her father had not stood by.

(Knippeldollinger *appears at the window*)

KNIPPELDOLLINGER *(calls in at the window):* Good morning, goddaughter!

AGNES: Good morning, godfather!

THEOBALD *(aside):* That old simpleton, too!

KNIPPELDOLLINGER: I dreamed of you last night.

AGNES: Many thanks for the honor.

THEOBALD: You ought to have been dreaming of your funeral instead. That would have been more appropriate.

KNIPPELDOLLINGER: I gave you cherries, the large foreign ones, from the tree that grows by the wall.

AGNES: Are they ripe already?

KNIPPELDOLLINGER: Oh, yes! I'll take a whole basket of them to the dance hall tonight!

THEOBALD: You'll get a good price for them there!

KNIPPELDOLLINGER: And I dreamed that while you were eating them I was taking you for a stroll!

THEOBALD *(loud):* To the graveyard, surely; I was there, too.

KNIPPELDOLLINGER: That's funny. So you are here, too?

THEOBALD: You stepped on a skull, and it snapped at you. It belonged to your last wife.

AGNES: Oh, shame!

KNIPPELDOLLINGER: Never mind, goddaughter, never mind! A barber has to be a joker! Everyone wants to hear something jolly when he is having his beard trimmed or his hair clipped. Theobald is a good one for the business. Only he must not slash people's ears the way he did mine the other day. Well, are you going to let me go away unsatisfied today, too? Not even your little hand?

AGNES: I have the smallpox again!

KNIPPELDOLLINGER: Do not always make the same excuse! Well, I shall see you again today, for I am going to send old Ann for you, to take you to the tournament. I have secured seats for you. That is what I really came to tell you.

AGNES: Thank you! I do not know—

KNIPPELDOLLINGER: Oh, such a thing does not happen every day. Knights, counts, and barons come seldom enough to Augsburg; but the Duke of Bavaria himself! No one will be absent from the tournament but the executioner and his men—and they have good reasons for not mingling with honest Christians. *(exit)*

THEOBALD: There he hobbles along on his three legs! Has he mentioned you in his will? Well, he's right; things are going to be lively—and I am glad of it! *(something is thrown through the window)* What is it? It jingles.

AGNES: Keys!

(Barbara *enters through the middle door*)

BARBARA: May I get them again?

AGNES: Barbara?

BARBARA: Agnes!

AGNES: You have not been here for a long time.

BARBARA *(picks up the keys)* And now I am here to get something— do you see?

AGNES: We have always been such good friends. What have you against me now?

BARBARA: Oh, I am not the only one.

AGNES: Holy Mother! What are you saying?

BARBARA: You probably do not look at your old playmates anymore that you do not know how they look at you.

AGNES: It is true, my greeting is not always as cordially returned as I give it.

BARBARA: I can believe that.

AGNES: But, for goodness' sake, whenever that happened, I simply thought that the girl had slept badly, or had argued with her mother or lost her ring—

BARBARA: That made things very easy for you!

AGNES: But what should I do? Tell me.

BARBARA: Do? What should you do? If things had reached that point, we could settle the matter quickly enough!

AGNES: Barbara!

BARBARA: Just tell me why—*(pointing to* Theobald) Now, there stands another one in open-mouthed admiration! *(to* Theobald) I am not here, am I? *(to* Agnes) Are you going today? To the tournament, I mean? You are? Well, then, I'll tell them all, so that they can stay at home—myself first of all!

AGNES: That is too much. My father must know this.

BARBARA: Heaven forbid! Nobody says anything about you!

AGNES: And yet they shun me! Exclude me!

BARBARA: Agnes, just look at me!

AGNES: Well!

BARBARA: How would you feel, if—let us go to your room!

THEOBALD: I'll not interfere, if confessions are to be made! *(exit)*

BARBARA: Now, how would you feel, if you—how shall I say it? If you were fond of somebody, and he had eyes for nobody but me?

AGNES: How should I know?

BARBARA: Then I'll tell you! You would—but I'll not make myself ridiculous! You know very well yourself. And do you suppose the others fare any better? *(notices the bouquet)* Now where are these from?

AGNES: I do not know.

BARBARA: You don't? Do you get so many? If they came from my Wolfram, I— And it is quite possible, for he has these very flowers in his garden. Yesterday, the whole day long, I showed marked favor to his cousin—forced myself to cast loving glances at him— thinking Wolfram would be raging. But in the evening, on the way home, didn't he praise the fellow to the very skies? It has suited him perfectly—I had done him a favor!

AGNES: Poor girl!

BARBARA: You are to blame, no one but you! Until he knew you, he stuck to me like a burr. He would have bearded the lion in his own den, and brought my glove back to me! And now! Oh, shame!

AGNES: You are scolding me, and I do not even know what you are talking about!

BARBARA *(takes the bouquet):* I'll get at the bottom of this. I'll take it along.

AGNES: I do not care.

BARBARA: You ought to be ashamed of estranging every girl's sweetheart from her.

AGNES: Can you say that I even glance at a single youth?

BARBARA: That is just it. A nun, and still not one! A saint, but not yet in heaven! You have to snatch her away from the church, sparing no effort. Why aren't you like the rest of us? Just look up, and talk—and things will be different.

AGNES: If I did, you would still be provoked!

BARBARA: Then go the cloister, put on the veil that no one dares to lift. *I* ask your pardon? Never in all eternity!

AGNES: Who desires you to?

BARBARA: My confessor! Do you suppose I came of my own accord? Indeed no! I would rather kneel on peas! *(holds up the bouquet)* I'll give this to him! If he does not recognize it, I'll send you one twice as nice! *(exit)*

AGNES: I am sorry for her! But how am I to help her?

THEOBALD *(returns):* She robbed poor Gertrude of her flowers!

AGNES: I think she's lost her mind.

THEOBALD: I would not say that!

AGNES: Do you mean, she is right?

THEOBALD: I almost think so! Agnes, every morning I could—.

(Kaspar Bernauer enters, carrying a book wrapped in a red cloth)

BERNAUER *(to* Agnes*):* Yes, yes, yes—if I only do not have to go along! Run upstairs and put on your trinkets; the trumpets are signalling now!

AGNES: No, father, I am going to stay at home!

BERNAUER: What? Why have you been waiting for me, then? *(to* Theobald*)* Go to the stills; the fire surely needs tending. *(exit* Theobald*)* Well?

AGNES: All those eyes, father! It is just as if that many bees were stinging me! And you know they all do stare at me!

(Theobald returns)

BERNAUER: Just stare back at them! But then, if you prefer to say your rosary—I have no objection. *(looks round to* Theobald*)* No salves mixed up yet? Didn't the cock crow this morning? *(Theobald goes to work)*

AGNES: Barbara was here. They all hate me. She says I'll spoil the day for them, if I come.

BERNAUER: And for that reason you are going to stay away! That's nothing my child. Then the best knight could not go, either; for he will surely spoil the day for all the rest. And the next best, just as little; and so on down the line to the very last one! Utter foolishness! Go to your room and get ready. *(to* Theobald*)* Get down the lotion bottle.

(Agnes and Theobald *exeunt)*

BERNAUER *(alone):* The porridge is cold. I'll consider it eaten. *(places the book on a table)* His Reverence, the Bishop, is right. I can get little out of it, and especially the principal subjects—those from Hippocrates—for they are in Greek. I shall have to carry it back—unread—

(enter Knippeldollinger*)*

KNIPPELDOLLINGER: Good morning, Bernauer! You have a book there, haven't you?

BERNAUER: And you have a brand new doublet, haven't you?

KNIPPELDOLLINGER: Well, if old folks did not have any new clothes made, many a tailor would starve. *(opens the book)* Heaven help us, but that is a confused jumble! And can you read that as well as the Bishop?

(enter Theobald, *carrying bottle, and begins work)*

BERNAUER: What a question!

KNIPPELDOLLINGER: How old do you suppose that is?

BERNAUER: Since the crucifixion of our Lord and Saviour, Jesus Christ, one thousand four hundred and twenty-six years have passed; but the author of this book, that is, the compiler of it, the man who made it, had been dead more than four hundred years when the Lord appeared in the body upon earth.

KNIPPELDOLLINGER: That makes it nearly two thousand years! Is it possible there are people who can keep such books so long? If it were gold, now! But so perishable—and to think of all the conflagrations and floods, pests and plagues!

BERNAUER: There have always been learned men.

KNIPPELDOLLINGER: Oh, of course! Of course! What hasn't there been? When we think it over and carefully consider—yes, yes! Now, isn't it so? Just tell me yourself.

BERNAUER: I do not know what you mean.

KNIPPELDOLLINGER: Ho! Ho! Better than I. You cannot get out of it that way! Well, just as you wish. Where is my godchild? Old Ann is probably waiting.

BERNAUER: Oh, she was inclined not to go at all. *(to* Theobald*)* Just go up and call her. Bring down the surgical case with you; we shall need it today. *(exit* Theobald*)*

KNIPPELDOLLINGER: Aren't you going, too? There will be room for you with us.

BERNAUER: The only things that interest me in a tournament are bruises and wounds, and I have an opportunity to see those here, for they bring all the wounded to me.

KNIPPELDOLLINGER: But the Duke—the Duke of Bavaria!

BERNAUER: I do not crave his acquaintance, and I hope he will not have to seek mine, for only a broken rib could induce that. Tonight—that is a different matter.

KNIPPELDOLLINGER: Imagine, behind the old monastery wall, where my cousin lives, they found a dead man last night.

BERNAUER: That's no surprise. Something always happens when the soldiers come to town.

KNIPPELDOLLINGER: That's true. But this one was so mutilated that they could not recognize him.

BERNAUER: Then they should take three drops of his blood, mix it with some alcohol, and drop it on a piece of glowing charcoal at midnight. The dead man will then appear in the steam, just as if he were alive, but transparent like a bubble, with a dark red mark in the middle. That is his heart.

KNIPPELDOLLINGER: Well, well, do you have that alcohol?

BERNAUER: If you had it, you would let the town crier announce it.
    (Agnes *enters in holiday attire.* Theobald *follows*)

KNIPPELDOLLINGER: Just look! *(taking* Agnes' *hand)* Now I have it, after all!

BERNAUER *(to* Agnes*):* Shall I make you a new face with burnt cork, as I do for the masquerade, since you do not like to wear this old one?

AGNES: Come, godfather.

KNIPPELDOLLINGER *(leading* Agnes *away and turning at door):* Do you know, Old Syndikus is going to be married again? He is ten years older than I.

BERNAUER: You're wrong. It is only five. Much pleasure to you, few accidents.
                    (exeunt Knippeldollinger *and* Agnes*)*

BERNAUER *(to himself):* There is no fool like an old fool. Well, Kaspar, do not be superior. You have your weaknesses, too. *(to* Theobald*)* Go on to the Tournament now, but be back in time. You can see when they bear someone from the field *(exit* Theobald*)*

BERNAUER *(picks up the book again):* I will try it once more. I am

ashamed to take it back just as I borrowed it. Truly the town of
Babylon causes me a great deal more trouble than the fall of man,
for if it had not been for that, we would all speak but one tongue.
Even in my younger days that bothered me. How I did long to go
out into the world, in my apprentice days, to try to discover the
unicorn, or the Phoenix, or capture mandrake in Turkey, where I
am sure they hang many an innocent man! But then, I always
thought: "You could not understand the people anyway, nor they
you!" And so I stayed at home. *(exit)*

Scene 2

The Augsburg Hospice.
(Duke Albrecht, Count Törring, Nothaft von Wernberg, Sir
Frauenhoven, *coming from the lists, with squires and attendants.*
Mayor Hermann Nordlinger)

ALBRECHT: I thank you, Mayor. I thank you for your escort.

MAYOR: Your Grace, it is my pleasure to perform my duty. *(calls)*
Bring wine!

WERNBERG *(to the* Duke *aside):* You cannot dismiss him before we
drink his wine.

ALBRECHT: Frauenhoven!

FRAUENHOVEN: What is it?

ALBRECHT: Did you see the girl? But, of course, you did—of course,
you did.

FRAUENHOVEN: Which one do you mean?

ALBRECHT: Which one! I beg you, follow her! I would have dis-
mounted at once, if he had not—*(points to the* Mayor*)*

MAYOR *(with a goblet):* Your gracious Highness, the tournament
being gloriously ended, the Free City of Augsburg extends to you
a hearty welcome and offers you thanks for honoring her with
your cause.

ALBRECHT *(drinks):* Long may Augsburg prosper, as it deserves!
Oh, where such rare beauty beams—*(passes his hand over his
forehead)* Yes, the city merits it. *(turning aside)* What, Frauenhoven, are you still here?

FRAUENHOVEN: But—

MAYOR: I hope—accordingly—

ALBRECHT: This evening at the ball, of course. Nothing can keep me from it, provided she, too—Pardon my confusion—a message from my father—

MAYOR: Aside from extending the invitation to you, according to the privilege of my office, I must add—as a patrician—that not only the aristocracy are to be there, but also the guilds.

ALBRECHT: I would wish the whole town to be there.

MAYOR: I commend myself unto your Grace! *(exit)*

ALBRECHT *(to* Frauenhoven*):* And now, my dear heart's friend, quick, quick! Or, rather all of you—you down one street, you another, and you a third!

FRAUENHOVEN: But this morning you gave me orders to pursue Werdenberg. Have you forgotten that he has run away with your betrothed, the Countess of Würtemberg?

ALBRECHT: Do not mention her name to me!

WERNBERG: And I was to go to her father to demand the keys of Göppingen Castle, because her flight prevented the marriage agreed upon; and, therefore, the forfeit would have to be paid!

TÖRRING: And I was to bear the news to the court and your father in Munich.

ALBRECHT: That is all past. It is as if it had never happened. I rejoice that Elizabeth has severed a tie—which otherwise I would have been forced to tear asunder. I do not demand even a tile from the roof of Göppingen, nor one farthing's ransom—for I might as well demand payment for living or breathing as for my new freedom! As for my father, he owes me a favor; this he shall grant me—that he take the same stand in this matter that I do!

TÖRRING: This is a very sudden change.

WERNBERG: And costs Bavaria twenty-five thousand guldens.

ALBRECHT: I do not know you anymore! Squire, remove my armor! I am going myself, and in this attire I would drag after me a train of a hundred curious folk. *(a* squire *removes his coat of mail and other armor)* There lies the duke—do you see? *(unbuckles his sword)* And there, the knight. Bring me flowers, so that I may scatter them before her, wherever I may find her. *(putting on a cap)* Would anyone recognize me now?

TÖRRING: Without your sword? Everyone would believe himself mistaken.

ALBRECHT: Be patient with me, good friends. *(exit)*

TÖRRING: Do you comprehend that?

WERNBERG: Duke Ernest's eyes will open wide with surprise. He will hesitate somewhat longer about losing twenty-five thousand guldens.

FRAUENHOVEN: Brothers, judge not, that we be not judged. We all have the same thing behind or before us. If you did not understand before, you will now understand why, since the earliest times, woman has been held responsible for man's downfall. She affects him like an intoxicant; but this intoxication can be cured by indulgence, as the other by restraint. The deeper the drought, the quicker sobriety. Therefore, we must stand by him.

WERNBERG: But we will take note of his strange remarks. We may be able to make use of them again, if only to protect ourselves. "Have you any eyes?" "Bring me flowers." "I do not know you anymore." I'll store those up. You gather up whatever drops this evening, for without a doubt this new Adam will see his Eve at the ball. Perhaps she is the Angel of Augsburg.

TÖRRING: The Angel of Augsburg?

WERNBERG: That is what they call a barber's daughter here—Agnes Bernauer, whose beauty, they say, has driven half the town mad. Shall we hunt up her father's shop? We can have our beards trimmed and—who knows—we may have a chance to see this miracle of beauty.

FRAUENHOVEN: Agreed! *(exeunt omnes)*

Scene 3

Great ballroom, gaily adorned with the banners of the guilds and the coats-of-arms of the patricians.

(Mayor Hermann Nordlinger *and* Nothaft von Wernberg *enter. The guests rapidly assemble. The masters of the guilds receive*)

MAYOR: Yes, your lordship, ever since that miserable St. Katherine's eve, when we had to admit the rabble to our council, things are pretty well mixed here. Pearls and peas all in one sack. The duke will find difficulty in selecting them. I am surprised that he cares to come.

WERNBERG: You have not grown accustomed to the new order of things yet? That happened some time ago.

MAYOR: Not so long ago that the hope of a return to the good old times has wholly vanished. Just look at that portly person! Master of the bakers' guild, and doing the honors of the town! Whenever he greets a new arrival, he either elbows a man's chest or with his awkward bow knocks somebody's shins behind him. Didn't I tell you so? Just like a kicking horse! And that is what we have to grow accustomed to!

WERNBERG: You ought to have made stronger resistance.

MAYOR: We were taken by surprise. Empire and Emperor should have stood by us better in our need. Why was His Majesty obliged to affix his seal to the accursed charter of the guilds, which was forced upon us? We had all we could do to keep ourselves from being taken up by the butchers and glovemakers and having our old names exchanged for new ones, for that is what they desired.

(*enter* Frauenhoven *and* Törring)

FRAUENHOVEN: There is the mayor. He can tell us. (*approaches the* Mayor) Is it true what they tell in the empire: that there are no rats in Augsburg?

MAJOR: That is certainly true! You will never find such vermin here. It's been that way since Drusus' times.[1]

TÖRRING: Very strange!

(*trumpets*)

MAYOR: His Grace, the Duke! (*hastens to greet the entering* Duke)

ALBRECHT (*steps up to* Frauenhoven, Törring, *and* Wernberg): Here you are!

FRAUENHOVEN: We have been hunting all afternoon.

ALBRECHT: And found?

WERNBERG: Just now.

ALBRECHT: Oh, you mean me! A valuable find, that. Thanks.

FRAUENHOVEN: I wandered about alone—

ALBRECHT: You fared better than I? You found a trace of her!

FRAUENHOVEN: Yes.

ALBRECHT: Why didn't I meet you before?

FRAUENHOVEN: The ravishing creature! Oh, indeed you were right in asking if we had eyes.

ALBRECHT: You love her, too?

FRAUENHOVEN: Could I help it?

ALBRECHT: Frauenhoven,—that is a great misfortune. I believe you cannot help it. Indeed, it would be insanity for me to desire you to help it. Here your knight's allegiance to me is at an end—in fact, friendship's, too; for now begins the struggle for life and death—

now it is a question in whose veins a drop of blood is to be left. (Frauenhoven *smiles*)

ALBRECHT: You smile. Pray do not. If you do not feel as I do, you are not worthy to look at her.

FRAUENHOVEN: Those jetblack eyes! And how she holds her head! It makes you long to throw your arms about her neck! And then, her chestnut hair!

ALBRECHT: Are you drivelling? The curls are golden that play about her brow, and never was a head so humbly bowed—and her eyes cannot be black. No, no; they flashed like the phosphorescence of the waves which, strange and wonderful, suddenly darts from the deep, blue waters, then as suddenly vanishes.

FRAUENHOVEN: Your lordship, I know nothing of her. It was only a jest, which you must ascribe to this place of merry-making.

ALBRECHT: Then flee, all of you, that it may not become terrible earnest; for, I tell you, no one can look at her without the greatest danger!

(*enter* Agnes, *accompanied by her* Father *and* Knippeldollinger)

ALBRECHT: There she is!

WERNBERG AND FRAUENHOVEN *(simultaneously):* Wondrously fair, that is true!

TÖRRING: And true that she is the Angel of Augsburg. There is her father.

ALBRECHT: Do you know her?

TÖRRING: She is generally called the Angel of Augsburg. She is a barber's daughter, your lordship. We just had him trim our beards. See—the man is skillful, isn't he? It would not hurt yours to go to him, either. *(he steps up to the group)* Good evening, Master, here we meet again.

BERNAUER: For me—a great honor.

ALBRECHT (*follows. to* Agnes): Fair maiden, why did you not bestow the rewards upon the combatants in the jousts? What had passed through your hands would be more precious than gold—more rare than jewels—even if it were only a spray plucked from the nearest shrub.

BERNAUER: My daughter is not accustomed to such speeches, gracious sir. Catechize her on the chief articles of our most blessed faith, and she will be able to answer.

AGNES: Come, come, father; the Duke of Bavaria intends to address his betrothed thus, and is merely practicing on a burgher's daughter.

BERNAUER: Well said, my daughter; but you cannot answer—so thank his lordship, and come.

ALBRECHT: Why, you stubborn old man? I have not yet heard the tone of her voice, nor have all twenty-four letters of the alphabet crossed her lips! *(aside).* I could ask her: "Say this word, or that, or another, not for its meaning, only that I may learn with how much music your mouth endows it! *(to Kaspar Bernauer):* You are going? Then you must allow me to accompany you! Your shadow will desert you sooner than I.

BERNAUER: Your equals would be envious.

TÖRRING *(grasping* Bernauer's *arm)*: Bavaria's Duke has no equal here! *(leads him away)*

(Wernberg *joins* Knippeldollinger, *and both follow)*

ALBRECHT *(to Agnes, who likewise follows, endeavoring to reach her father's side)*: Fair maid, I was not mistaken—your eyes followed me this morning. Dare I claim the honor of the glance, or was it only my Venetian plume?

AGNES: I trembled for you, sir. You were looking toward me while you were riding to meet the enemy. I thought of the harm that might befall you.

ALBRECHT: And you were not indifferent to what might happen to me? *(they are lost in the crowd)*

BARBARA *(with* Martha *and the other girls)*: Ha, ha, ha! Now, I told you so, didn't I? That it would be better to stay at home? Be merry, if you can!

MARTHA: Why, things are going beautifully! If the Duke takes her with him, then she will not be in our way, any more than if she ascended into heaven.

BARBARA: Take her with him? What are you thinking of? He'll leave her here, you may be sure. But she'll be more superior than ever before, since the Duke, too, has succumbed to her charms. Just see how everyone is staring at them and whispering. (Barbara *and* Martha *pass on)*

(enter Wernberg, *with* Knippeldollinger)

MAYOR *(approaches with* Young Lady*)*: Sir, my cousin, Juliana Peutinger. When only four years old, she delivered an address of welcome in Latin to his Highness, the Emperor, in the name of the Council. I should like to introduce her to his Grace.

WERNBERG *(walking out with him):* Afterwards, Mayor, afterwards! *(in a low voice)* The Duke has been given such a warm welcome by the citizens that they have almost split their throats with cheering, and you see how grateful he appears. *(they pass on)*

ALBRECHT *(with* Agnes): Now, *you* must say something. What is your answer?

AGNES: It seems as if I heard the tones of one more violin, so sweet the sound, so fair the dream it brings!

ALBRECHT: But I am asking you if you can love me?

AGNES: You should ask a princess that—surely not me.

ALBRECHT: I implore you—an answer!

AGNES: Spare me, or make the request only as you would to a poor creature who is in danger of an overwhelming misfortune!

ALBRECHT: These words——

AGNES: Do not analyze them, I beseech you! Never snatch away the hand clasped for protection over one's heart!

BERNAUER *(who has been following, with* Törring, *and trying to approach* Agnes): Tomorrow, Count, tomorrow!

KNIPPELDOLLINGER *(who is walking along beside them, with* Wernberg, *to* Törring): I knew a man once who could cure by magic.

ALBRECHT: Agnes, you misjudge me. I *do* love you.

BERNAUER *(stepping between* Agnes *and* Albrecht): Come, my child! You, too, have an honorable name to save! *(starts to lead her away)*

ALBRECHT: I really do love her, but I never would have told her so, if I had not intended to add, I sue for her hand.

WERNBERG: Your Grace!

FRAUENHOVEN: Albrecht, remember your father!

TÖRRING: Think of the emperor and the empire! You are a Wittelsbach. That is only by way of reminder.

ALBRECHT: Now, my good man, are you still afraid of her losing her honor?

BERNAUER: No, your Grace. But fifty years ago she would not have dared to appear at a tournament without being flogged for it; for then such a privilege would never have been granted to the daughter of a man who set the knights' broken bones and dressed their wounds. That is only by way of reminder.

ALBRECHT: And fifty years hence every angel like her shall occupy a throne on earth, even if erected by someone who today must pay obeisance to you, for I shall set the example!

FRAUENHOVEN: He is insane! (*to* Albrecht) Do not proceed any further tonight. Everyone is now on the alert, and at all events the affair must be kept secret.

ALBRECHT (*to* Bernauer): May I come tomorrow?

BERNAUER: What good would it do for me to say, "No"?

ALBRECHT: Agnes?

AGNES: Who was telling me this very morning that I should enter the cloister? I think I see a finger plainly pointing that way.

ALBRECHT: You grow faint. Let me support you; and, if the whole world falls, you will be safe.

BERNAUER: Your Grace, we take our leave before she swoons. (*Exeunt* Bernauer, Agnes *and* Knippeldollinger)

ALBRECHT *(following):* Oh, I must—

FRAUENHOVEN: Not a step! For her sake, if not for your own.

ALBRECHT: Perhaps you are right.

FRAUENHOVEN: Talk with the other guests now—with all of them—a long time, I beseech you!

ALBRECHT: I should have loved so to hear my name, just once, upon her lips! But why wish to celebrate Christmas, Easter, and Whitsunday all at once? *(mingles with the guests)*

(Mayor approaches with Young Lady)

Act 2

Scene 1

Tavern in Augsburg. Early morning.
        (Wernberg, Törring *and* Frauenhoven)

WERNBERG: The matter is growing serious.

TÖRRING: Very serious. The line of succession depends upon a pair of eyes.

FRAUENHOVEN: Not that bad yet! You forget, Duke William also has a son who is a possible heir to Bavaria's throne.

TÖRRING: But who is weak and sickly, and only four years old. Have you ever seen the poor little lad? I know what I am talking about.

The Munich line depends practically on this pair of eyes, and if we do not succeed in interfering with Albrecht's mad project, he will be the father of children who do not even rank with yours and mine. What will happen then? Even now Bavaria is torn into three factions, like a cake that three starving wretches are fighting over. Shall it be completely ruined? And that will be the outcome if we cannot prevent this misfortune.

WERNBERG: Quite true. From all quarters of the country they would appear with their yellowed charters and moldy treaties; and, when they had quarreled and fought long enough over them, the Emperor would settle the matter in his own way. For, while the bears are tearing each other to pieces, the eagle always flies off with the booty!

TÖRRING: Well, then, let us take precautions.

FRAUENHOVEN: But how begin? Don't forget that he has as much Italian as German blood in him, and perhaps a few drops more. I am telling you, if you did not know it yet, the heritage of his mother is strong in him, and if you can't give him a pair of new eyes that see beauty as ugliness and ugliness as beauty, you won't get far with him. You ought to have heard him on the way home last night! And isn't every word he says true? For which one of us can boast of ever having seen such an angel of beauty before he came to Augsburg?

TÖRRING: Do you think I am a fool, who intends to conjure the fire? That is not my idea. Let it burn to ashes, for all I care. But I believe the fuel for *this* fire can be more cheaply bought than with crowns and thrones. Damn it, doesn't Albert deserve such a woman? Let me arrange it. I tell you they are good, sensible people. Didn't the old barber stand there yesterday as if the archangel Michael himself were asking to become his son-in-law? And the girl! She looked as if she had been invited to ascend into heaven, instead of to dance. Just pay heed. I shall settle things satisfactorily. *(exit)*

FRAUENHOVEN: He's mistaken—in the father and the daughter, as well as in the Duke.

WERNBERG: We must appeal to the Duke's conscience.

FRAUENHOVEN: And why? Simply to have done our duty, in case we should be called to account some day? Borrow Gabriel's trumpet, and see if you can make him listen. I am content if we can keep it secret for the present. Lazy Wenzel of Prague educated him; and the notions then put into his head to the sound of flute and violin, God himself will never be able to eradicate!

ALBRECHT *(entering):* Well, my friends, what do you think of this glorious morning that is turning everything to gold, as perfect as if made to order? But why are you all standing there like that, as if you were to enter the fray immediately and were still undecided about your last will and testament?

WERNBERG: I hope to look differently then; although I have not a father to pull me out, whenever I get into deep water as you have.

ALBRECHT: Yes, that's true. In that I have the advantage. I can jump boldly into the very jaws of death, like the lion and the mouse, and my sire would snatch me back to safety, even from the throat of a devouring monster.

WERNBERG: That was proved to you at your first battle at Alling. If he had not been there—

ALBRECHT: Then my first battle would have been my last one as well, and I should never have heard the sweet music of the victor's trumpet. But why mention that? I should never have beheld my Agnes.

WERNBERG: Your Agnes?

ALBRECHT: Oh, I owe an infinite debt of gratitude to him, greater than ever son to father before!

WERNBERG: You realize that?

ALBRECHT: Just since yesterday. This eye, which I would now close voluntarily, as the mouth closes when it has eaten a cherry, without him this eye would now be dead and covered with sand, a mirror broken before it could catch the image it was to have reflected, and this heart—Some day your hour will come, too, and you will understand better. Then I can say more. If you ever feel as if you had a million lips, all opening to draw in the deep breath of life; when you do not know whether it is joy or pain that puts your heart in a whirl; when your breast is bursting, and you tremble with heat and cold at the same time, crying out in doubt, "Surely, joy, joy, the supreme of joy!"—If, like me, you suddenly understand this mystic meaning, while groping dizzily for it between life and death with your last breath, then, then, not before!

WERNBERG: Your lordship, one request.

ALBRECHT: What is it?

WERNBERG: Just picture your father's amazement when he hears of this.

ALBRECHT: Well?

WERNBERG: But very vividly—with that expression which his face wears when he not only wishes to refuse a request, but to force it back into one's throat; so that, instead of asking for sugar plums, one begs for a beating!

ALBRECHT: Well and good!

WERNBERG: Can you see him plainly? Now ask yourself if you would care to repeat to him all that you have been ranting to us about intoxicating joy and pain and life and death!

ALBRECHT: To him? Most surely, for I had a mother. But to *you*, not for the whole world would I mention it again!

WERNBERG: Your mother, sir, was a princess of Milan.

ALBRECHT: And would she not have been my mother just the same, if she had not happened to be a princess of Milan? She was an ideal woman. Would not that have sufficed?

WERNBERG: I doubt it. But, if so, there would be nothing now to prevent your marrying the Angel of Augsburg, for you would have no claim to Bavaria's throne.

ALBRECHT: You think not, Sir Knight? Who can tell? Who knows what would happen if I should appeal to my people, saying, "Behold, they say I am not worthy to be your monarch, because my father lifted up one of your daughters to his level, one who could best tell him what your needs are! They say I am not worthy to be your ruler because my compassion for you was instilled in me through my mother's heritage, because I understand you even before you speak, because the desire to help you is in my blood. They say I am not worthy to be your ruler because I am your brother?" Who knows what they will do, these staunch old Bavarians, when one day my son shall summon them to assemble in a forest of oaks, as in the days of yore, and speak such words to them? Who knows whether the last peasant may not be turned into a knight, and whether the scythe may not clash against the sword, till the whole German empire begins to totter, and mighty Charlemagne in his tomb at Aachen reaches out for his crown in terror?

WERNBERG: Most gracioius lord, do not misjudge me. Nothaft von

Wernberg cannot advise you to leap over the precipice; but, when you do, he can jump after you!

ALBRECHT: That is nobly said, my friend. Come, then.

Scene 2

Augsburg. The barber shop.

(Agnes, Bernauer)

AGNES: Here, father?

BERNAUER: Here we shall see him. Nowhere else. How do you feel, my daughter? Not quite the same as other mornings when you awaken, do you? Well, that's perfectly natural. Girls are fond of hesitating on the threshold, from timidity or a love of teasing, even when they are eager to enter, knowing the bridegroom has long been waiting. But you, poor dear, do not even have time to make the bridal wreath!

AGNES: Your decision is settled, then?

BERNAUER: There is but one way; and, if you are ready, I can answer for him.

AGNES: You can?

BERNAUER: I know the symptoms, even if it was a long time ago that I suffered from the same fever. He's a good, faithful soul. *(takes something from pocket)* See this!

AGNES: My necklace! I thought I put that away last evening before going to bed.

BERNAUER: That's quite impossible, for Theobald found it in the street as he came along behind us.

AGNES: Theobald?

BERNAUER: Yes; you did not see him either, did you? Just imagine! Ever since the Duke and his nobles have been here, the foolish lad has been secretly following us every evening, upon our leaving the house, and has waited until we returned. He never let it be known, and I learned about it only because he found your necklace. He is a fellow!

AGNES: I am happy to see his devotion to you.

BERNAUER: I have concluded the best answer for this hot-headed Duke would be your marrying Theobald this very morning. You know, you owe him a finder's reward.

AGNES: What are you saying father?

BERNAUER: Then you two could go to meet the Duke together, while

I extend my hands in blessing over your heads, calling out to him, "Thus has heaven decreed, and what God has joined let no man put asunder!"

AGNES: Father!

BERNAUER: You do not have to be afraid of violence. This is red soil too; Augsburg is Westphalia, too, indeed—but, nevermind! What do you say? The bridgegroom is, I hope, ready and even the preacher is not far. Well, speak, my daughter! Shall it be?

AGNES: *Never!* Not in all eternity.

BERNAUER: Oh, you mean, not today?

AGNES *(blushing):* I mean—

BERNAUER *(interrupting):* Tomorrow, tomorrow, tomorrow.

THEOBALD (coming out from behind a cabinet): What's the use, master? I can stand it today as well as ever.

BERNAUER *(to* Agnes): There, now.

THEOBALD: Don't scold her. I myself am to blame. I ought not to have followed you—not this time, at any rate.

AGNES: Theobald, you are hurting me!

THEOBALD: I know it, Miss Agnes, I know it. I feel too that I—O God above, I must not even mention my unhappiness! You could never have been intended for me. I need only to look at you to realize it. Master, may I have a few moments for myself? I shall come back in an hour; there are not apt to be many patrons at this time of day. *(he seizes* Agnes' *hands)* Agnes, I wish I might transfer my love for you to someone worthier—not to relieve my own heart—O God, no! That would be the greatest sacrifice I could make, and I could only make it in the hope of giving you happiness; but, believe me, you would be happy if what is burning here— *(he beats his breast)* inflamed a worthier bosom! *(exit)*

BERNAUER: I can well believe that.

AGNES: Do not be angry, father. If I had dreamed—

BERNAUER: Not another word about it. Things are as they are. Who can go against the stars? But I shudder to think of your future, my daughter, for— *(pointing to his barber's bowl)* Such a thing and a coronet were never made to go together.

AGNES: You did not let me finish before. I could not give my hand to Theobald, nor to anyone else—

BERNAUER: And pray, why not?

AGNES: Because—Oh, I could not!

BERNAUER: Then he really does possess your heart? Curse the tournament!

AGNES: But I could flee to the Mother of Mercies—I could enter the cloister.

BERNAUER: And leave your Duke outside?

AGNES: No-o—

BERNAUER: What would you be doing in a cloister, then?

COUNT TÖRRING (*entering*): Good morning, Master Bernauer! You too, young lady. Your hand, good sir! We greatly enjoyed seeing you at the ball yesterday evening. Fair Agnes, if Törring's memory for the sweet poetry and compliments of Heinrich von Ofterdingen and Wolfram von Eschenbach were not so poor, he would now regale you with all that he remembered. But unfortunately he can only recall the nursery rhymes of his childhood. But I must tell you: You are truly worthy of winning a duke's favor.

AGNES: That is saying too much, sir.

TÖRRING: Heaven forbid! If Emperor Wenzel had an attendant like you, I can pardon him for believing for a time that he and she were quite alone in the world; but I cannot pardon him for carrying things too far and never coming to his senses again, for she had to pay the penalty, and he might have realized that beforehand. (*looks sharply at* Agnes) Poor Susanna! Fair young child! How pale you must have been when the stern, unrelenting Bohemians burned you at the stake, led by bishops and archbishops, as if it were a sacred rite! You were not an enchantress, either; unless this girl before me is one, too.

BERNAUER: Did that happen in the joyous land of song and dance?

TÖRRING: Oh, yes; and I suppose someone has turned the tale into a verse. People are fond of singing of such things when they are merry.

BERNAUER: What do you say to that, my daughter?

AGNES: Shame upon the emperor who let such a thing happen!

TÖRRING: He lay in a dungeon, and his angry nobles stood with drawn swords at the gate—executioner or rescuer, he knew not which would be the first to knock at his door.

AGNES: Then it was her fate, and she will probably find out why some day.

TÖRRING: Bernauer, a word in private with you.

BERNAUER: Leave us, Agnes. Put away your necklace now. *(exit Agnes)*

BERNAUER: We are alone now, sir.

TÖRRING: Well, my good man, what do you think? Tell me.

BERNAUER: I do not know what you are referring to.

TÖRRING: Oh, I'm thinking the Duke has probably arisen this morning in the same frame of mind that he went to bed last night.

BERNAUER: To be sure! Eight hours are only eight hours.

TÖRRING: That is my opinion, too. Therefore, we must come to an agreement in time. Accordingly— *(picks up a razor playfully)* Your sword, is it not?

BERNAUER: If you please—

TÖRRING: My own is somewhat longer. *(tapping his sword)* But what I intended to say was this: The Duke loves your daughter. *He loves her.* If every wife were so loved, this would be heaven on earth.

BERNAUER: Before a potion and after it are always two very different things, and must always be.

TÖRRING: You've been married—perhaps are still, and are making excuses for yourself; but I can assure you the Duke is burning like a crackling bonfire when a good wind is blowing. But— *(he picks up a shaving bowl)* Your helmet?

BERNAUER: Are all Bavarians so witty?

TÖRRING: But see here, see here, it would do. *(pretending to set the shaving bowl on Bernauer's head)* Did you never try that? I assure you the Duke is in such a flame that he can roast chestnuts by simply looking at them. But, as far as courting, marrying, are concerned— *(picks up the cupping instrument)* Snip, snap—you doubtless have this in your coat of arms? Or do you have a naked arm with a spurting vein, like the one I saw painted by the outer door?

BERNAUER: Neither, Sir Count.

TÖRRING: Neither one? Well, then, to come to the point (if it is of any use), the Duke's love springs from his heart; his courting— well, you saw that for yourself! It was intoxication; perhaps, indeed, for aught I know, the influence of wine.

BERNAUER: I am glad to hear it. But this message does not concern me alone. *(calls)* Agnes!

TÖRRING: You are glad? Then I was not wrong in my judgment of you. Give me your hand again!

BERNAUER *(withholding his hand):* You have already honored me sufficiently.

(enter Agnes)

TÖRRING: If we should settle on her a moderate fortune for life—just between ourselves—the Duke has splendid estates from his mother, you know.

BERNAUER: Listen carefully, my child *(to* Törring*)* Well?

TÖRRING: Oh, you called her! You can speak for yourself.

BERNAUER: Very well. *(to* Agnes) The Duke withdraws his suit.

TÖRRING: Oh, not by any means.

BERNAUER: He withdraws his suit for your hand. That he leaves to you. He is not without shame. As for the rest, he would like to keep you—for a time at least, I know not if forever. *(*Agnes *drops into a seat)* There is her answer. Now, hear mine. First of all! *(looks up with hands folded)* Thank you, Father in Heaven, that this happened. Whatever sorrow you can send me now, it cannot be worse than this terrible, double-faced fortune. *(to* Törring*)* You see how I feel, and that explains why I listened to you so calmly. You were a welcome messenger, for I know that my daughter would not consent to any shameful deed. Your offer gave her back to me, or else she would have been forever lost to me. And now to answer your question. You are asking about my sword. We citizens of the realm do indeed have swords, although they are usually hanging on the wall. In my younger days I used mine many times on a person's back not unlike your own.

TÖRRING: Bernauer!

AGNES *(jumps up and stands next to her father):* You are right, father, you are right.

BERNAUER: You have the advantage of a plumed helmet. Like all those of us who do not joust in tournaments but only fight when it is a matter of defending our property, I was always content with a simple helmet. But even that would have dulled a good sword when it was necessary. As far as my coat of arms is concerned: you have probably seen it already here and there early in the morning at the castle gates. Some members of my family have a rope and a dagger in a red field in their coat of arms, and they know how to get respect, even from the emperor and the empire.

TÖRRING: That is the sign of the vehme![2]

BERNAUER: Do you know it? It protects the virgins, too, and even if justice has to find its way underground, like the mole, in these sad times, it will always prevail at the right time!

AGNES: Father, I can defend myself. Last evening robbed me of speech and senses. This morning gives them back to me. You may tell the Duke, your lord, I would not have considered his first proposition possible; but, God knows, I would have believed the second one much less so!

(enter Albrecht)

BERNAUER: There he is himself.

ALBRECHT: Yes, here he is! *(to* Agnes*)* Was he expected? *(Agnes turns away)* If on my way to you a flaming chariot had come down to me from the skies above, with every wheel set with stars, I would not have ascended. And you?

AGNES: Gracious sir, yesterday I had not the courage to look at you. Today I should think you would scarcely be bold enough to look at me!

ALBRECHT: What have I done to you?

AGNES: Is that nothing, your lordship? You could never bestow so great an honor upon me, not even by placing a crown on my brow, that it would atone for this insult.

ALBRECHT: Insult?

AGNES: Is it not an insult? Is not that to me an insult which, offered to a highborn lady, would snatch every blade from its scabbard in the entire family, even to the tenth removed, to be pointed at you? Your lordship, I, too, am one of God's creatures!

ALBRECHT *(catching sight of* Törring*):* Törring, you here? What does this mean?

AGNES: I, too, am one of God's own creatures. He can make something nobler of me, if it is His holy will; of you, He may make something lowlier. For everything on earth is merely a trial, and high and low must exchange places, if they do not stand the test in His presence. Your lordship, never hurt anyone again as you have hurt me! As such a thing could never be expected of you, it must be doubly bitter. *(to her father)* Now, father, to the cloister! Now I shall take nothing from the world with me but a never ending horror.

ALBRECHT: Agnes, yesterday I asked for your hand; today I come for your answer, while my friends bring the priest who is to unite us. Is that an insult?

TÖRRING *(stepping forward):* The Duke knows nothing of this, upon my word of honor! I was only voicing my own ideas. I thought—well, to err is human, they say.

ALBRECHT: You offered her insult? To my betrothed? For *that*— *(draws his sword)*

TÖRRING: Now, my lord, for that! *(steps up to* Agnes *and kisses her hand)* You know I am not a coward, but it would not be well to lessen the number of her friends; and, now that I really know her, I am her friend, too. Indeed, I shall serve her with the last breath of my body; and it seems to me—bear this in mind!—it seems to me, death already takes me by the hand. *(to Agnes)* That is the word of a nobleman of Bavaria; not one of the lesser ones, either. And may I be called a dishonorable wretch if anything happens to you now, as long as I can prevent it. *(to Albrecht)* But you, my lord, be not angry because I drew aside the veil rather rudely! It was to your advantage, as well as hers, that I looked into her face. *(steps back)*

ALBRECHT: She is silent! You offended her, not me. Follow me outside. When she sees how I avenge her she will know how much I love her.

AGNES: For God's sake, no! Only from you was the thrust a deadly one. Now, father—

BERNAUER: She's sorry for her severe words, your lordship—she would like to recall them. You see, she is almost overcome.

ALBRECHT: And not for the world would I have missed them. Good master, two children must have been exchanged in their cradles. An emperor's daughter was brought to you, and an emperor has reared your son. Gaze upon her—do you still know her? Agnes, in your earliest childhood you heard a fairy tale about such an event, only then you did not know that the tears you shed were for yourself. Yet this hour has caused you to remember. But now you know at last who you are, Agnes! That is proved by the noble fire flashing in your eye and glowing on your cheek. You have forgotten now that you have not always worn the purple and drunk from a goblet of gold. Come to my arms before you have time to recollect!

BERNAUER: Agnes!

AGNES: Father, not a word about the danger! Do not remind me that it needs great courage, or else I might—

ALBRECHT *(opens his arms to her):* What? What?

AGNES *(sinks on his breast):* If I should have to pay for this with death, now it would not matter.

ALBRECHT *(embracing her):* My Agnes!

AGNES *(drawing away):* But no amount of courage can justify it. You are a prince!

ALBRECHT: And, as such, like any one of my ancestors, I may make a fresh start.

AGNES: But your father!

ALBRECHT: I am his son, not his slave.

AGNES: And suppose your people should object?

ALBRECHT: They may object, until they once more rejoice. And if they were to band together and openly revolt against me: I would confront them with your picture instead of soldiers and they would return to their ploughing shamefacedly.

AGNES: And should your father pronounce a curse?

ALBRECHT: Even so, God will give His blessing.

AGNES: And if your father draws his sword?

ALBRECHT: Then he gives me the right to lay hand on my own.

AGNES: And still we could—and yet, you could be happy?

ALBRECHT: Far happier than if I had to give you up. The one would be war, and it is a part of war that one does not know its outcome beforehand; the other would be death, death without wounds and honor, a cowardly death of strangling by my own hand, and I should choose that? To reach for my throat rather than my sword? Never! I would be the very last to do such a thing. But, Agnes, now I know your heart—come to me! *(enfolding her)* There is nothing more for you to do. The rest is my affair. Upon what did God found this world, if not on this depth of love which draws me to you and you to me? The Countess of Würtemberg whom they had put between you and me, would fall down dead this very minute if she had not run off. I am sure of it, so do not be afraid!

(enter Frauenhoven *and* Wernberg*)*

Is everything ready?

FRAUENHOVEN: Yes, we have found a priest who will risk the disfavor of the old Duke for the favor of the young one.

WERNBERG: But only on condition that the affair be kept secret as long as possible.

ALBRECHT: What do you say to that, my Agnes?

AGNES: As long as only God knows it, none of my dreadful forebodings will be fulfilled.

ALBRECHT: Well, then. Now, my friends, where and when?

FRAUENHOVEN: This evening, at the stroke of ten, in the Chapel of St. Mary's. We must all come in disguise, as if to a burial.

ALBRECHT: Agreed. And tomorrow to Vohburg. Agnes! Vohburg is a little red castle on the green banks of the Danube, which my mother—peace to her ashes!—gave me as a reward for my first battle. Just heed what I am saying. You will smile at yourself there, whenever you think of this morning. There are more larks there than sparrows elsewhere; and for nearly every tree, a nightingale. I shall settle it upon you. Pray accept the merry bird cage as it is; you will like it there. The sky is always blue. And if you can express gratitude for a gift you have never seen, call me now by my name!

AGNES *(weeping):* My Albrecht!

ALBRECHT: And with tears?

AGNES: Forgive me! How could I help suffering still for those bitter words, more for your sake than my own? It seemed to me as if the brightest star in all the firmament had suddenly left its course and I had encountered it at my feet in the horrible state in which one sometimes sees such stars extinguished here on earth. But now I feel as if life had already bestowed upon me more than is my due. My father!

BERNAUER *(coming forward):* They shall leave father and mother to cling to one another. My blessings on you, my child. You are following God's command, I suppose. May He be with you. *(places his hand upon her head)*

ALBRECHT: For me, your blessings, too.

BERNAUER: You fear that you will have otherwise to do without any? *(lays his hand on* Albrecht's *head)*

Act 3

Scene 1

Munich. The Royal Cabinet. On one wall hang two maps; on the other the portraits of the Bavarian princes.
(Duke Ernest *is discovered standing in front of the maps*)
ERNEST: I cannot leave it, and it always arouses my anger anew. That was Bavaria once, and this is Bavaria now. Like full moon and new moon, side by side! And if five centuries had even intervened between the two phases! But there must be many an old man still living who can plainly remember the time when all *that* belonged to us—Tyrol, Brandenburg, and sturdy Holland, and what not, besides—who, moreover, can enumerate the whole list of follies which lost us all of them. *(steps in front of the portraits)* What wretched havoc you have made! Even twenty-four hours before the judgment day it would have been too bad. And you had such a good example in your neighbor, Austria! Rudolph von Hapsburg, by clever turning and constant overturning on a sticky soil, could have rolled a grain of sand to a globe; and what have you done? Through your manipulations a globe has dwindled to a grain of sand! *(walks on, stops in front of one of the portraits)* Emperor Louis, bold warrior, who withstood every enemy save the last one, concealed and nameless, you are frowning down upon your grandson! I understand you, you are right: fault finding is for women; the man's work is to mend. Well, I have been patching and piecing for a whole lifetime, trying to get the old Elector's mantle together again, and I think you will give me your hand in approval when we meet. You would have probably saved me the work if the poisoner had not conspired against you with bread and wine and thus ended your life prematurely.[3] But your sons— Well! They are dead! *(enter Stachus)* What is it?
STACHUS: The man from Cologne has come—the clever one with the strange name. He says he was sent for.
ERNEST: He has brought something, then. Bring it to me! *(exit Stachus)* He is bringing the designs for the decoration of the Memorial Chapel, where lies the dust of her who bore my son. *(Enter Stachus, with a roll of papers. The Duke looks through*

papers carefully) The designs are all too elaborate. Come here, Stachus, can you tell me what this is?

STACHUS: Oh, your Grace, I am only a simple man!

ERNEST: That does not matter. You should be able to understand it, too. Tombs should be silent, or talk so plainly that even the simplest can understand. He was ordered to make it exactly as I told him: the Saviour, our all merciful Redeemer, with His arms extended over my dear wife, kneeling at his feet, just as they paint St. Martha, but with her face covered since we cannot know what she looks like now. And below—bowed before them—my son Albrecht and myself praying for her good soul. Tell him that! He can put this thing upon his own tomb. I do not want it. I had expected something different from Cologne. That is not worth the cost of a journey here. *(Stachus carries out paper)* That would have been something to the liking of your sweet, pious soul, my gentle Elizabeth—all those winged angels, with trumpets blowing, as if the Mother of Heaven were making a second ascension! And I had explained everything to him so carefully. But they are always bowing and scraping. It would not be surprising if we forgot in the end that we are made from dust and to dust we return. Yet, many seem to like this fawning attitude, otherwise those people would not try it with everyone. *(enter Chancellor Preising)* Are you there, Preising? It is well. Do you know what I have decided? We are going to begin an hour earlier after today. What man knows whether he may not have to stop his work before he is tired? How many plans my wife, the Duchess, had; and now she lies there! What have you brought?

PREISING: First of all, there are constantly increasing complaints about the usury of the Jews.

ERNEST: People must arrange their business affairs so that they can get along without the Jews. No one can be impoverished by them, who does not borrow of them; not even if they ask fifty percent.

PREISING: I mention it again simply for the sake of the Jews themselves. In Nürnberg they are being killed like dogs, and, as you know, bad examples are more contagious than good ones.

ERNEST: My Jews shall so act that they do not deserve death; and that will probably put an end to it. I shall not interfere with these affairs. You can ask my brother if he wishes to.

PREISING: If he should desire to, it would be the first time that Duke

William wished something you opposed.

ERNEST: Just on that account, one must never neglect him. Now, continue.

PREISING: As to the dispute over the electoral crown, the court in Bohemia has finally—

ERNEST: Nothing of that! Emperor Rudolph's controversial edict has made the matter so complicated that now it can only settled by the sword.[4] And we can only draw that if Munich, Ingolstadt and Landshut get back together. And so far there is little hope of that since my dear cousins Louis and Henry would prefer to embrace me if they could turn their backs to me at the same time. Let's go on. —But stop! this, first. Money has come to us from an unexpected source. The Count of Würtemberg has to hand over all that he has saved on birch rods in the education of his daughter, and pay heavy interest into the bargain. We can accomplish many things with his twenty-five thousand guldens.

PREISING: Let us have our hands on them first.

ERNEST: Don't you think the Count is an honest man?

PREISING: The most honest in the world.

ERNEST: Well, then, he's surely not a beggar? We could use it to redeem our mortgaged cities, and I know who would let us do it the cheapest way and where our money is most needed.

PREISING: That would certainly be a coup!

ERNEST: Yes, and there would be one place less in the country where we would not be allowed to pick up our ducal staff if we should happen to drop it. Or I could buy unlimited free passage for Lech so that our access to him cannot be blocked again by Augsburg at the Emperor's whim as in the year nineteen during the bishops' quarrels.

PREISING: The merchants would agree with that!

ERNEST: And you?

PREISING: Your Lordship, the Count of Würtemberg will not forfeit such a sum, I tell you.

ERNEST: He will not? Have I not his promise? Have not hostages been sent me? What objections can he have?

PREISING: He is displeased, because Duke Albrecht made no effort at all to regain his runaway bride—because he went to the Augsburg ball, instead of helping in the pursuit of the abductor.

ERNEST: What was there left to regain? She had become another's wife before we heard of the elopement. The Count would better be careful! I'll seize the Castle of Göpping before he is aware. One ride more does not matter.

PREISING: I beg and beseech you not to become incensed! As the victor at Alling, your son was never talked about so much as he was as the cavalier of the Augsburg ball.

ERNEST: I know, I know—and it vexes me sorely. Preising, it is the punishment for our own youthful sins that we have to indulge our children. You know how much I am spending for Andechs, but believe me, one doesn't build chapels without reason. But I have already put an end to that. Two years ago Erick of Brunswick said to me, "It is too bad, Ernest, that you have only one son, and that one promised." I remembered that, and the very day when I learned of the elopment of Albrecht's betrothed I sent a proposal for the hand of the Countess of Brunswick. Just yesterday the acceptance arrived.

PREISING: And Albrecht, will he consent?

ERNEST: Consent? What do you mean? You may be sure, I have made no inquiries in regard to that, but take it as a matter of course.

PREISING: You sent a messenger to him?

ERNEST: One? Three, four, I sent to him with warnings and admonitions; and with the last one I sent a letter.

PREISING: Well, the last one has just returned and is dismounting.

ERNEST: It took him long enough.

PREISING: And still, he made a speedy journey, for he is not returning from Augsburg, but from Vohburg. The Duke had left the imperial city before your messenger's arrival.

ERNEST: Then the affair with the barber's daughter is over, and I might have spared myself the stupid letter.

PREISING: Anything but ended; for he had taken the girl with him.

ERNEST: That is going too far! I should never have done such a thing during my father's lifetime. Is that the messenger's news?

PREISING: Yes, and—

ERNEST: What else? Why do you hesitate? That is not like you.

PREISING: You will have to know it. Rumor goes very much further.

ERNEST: Rumor has a thousand tongues, and truth but one. Who can detect the one among the many? But, how far? I am curious.

PREISING: There are rumors of a secret marriage. The girl would not consent to anything else.

ERNEST: And you tell me that with a serious face, Preising? Is that the messenger's news?

PREISING: I immediately enjoined the strictest silence upon him.

ERNEST: Not by any means. Let him talk; but let him add that all Bavaria has been settled upon a mistress. *(he laughs)* Isn't that the truth of the matter? Even the part which we have lost shall be reconquered especially for her! I shall do it, you understand?

PREISING: Are you sure there is nothing back of all this, nothing at all?

ERNEST: Quite sure. *(raises his hand)* And you should also be sure of that, and if you were on your death bed. My own flesh and blood deserves that much respect. The barber's daughter has simply started the report in order to gloss over her guilt. That is as plain as day. But that is no reason why we should look on calmly until it is known throughout the empire. I am doubly glad now that the Count of Brunswick has made reply, for it enables us to send down a cleansing shower to wash away the mud before it has time to harden. You must set out again immediately to bear this message.

PREISING: But if he should not receive it as you expect?

ERNEST: Let us not dwell on impossibilities. That's a quite different thing. He says yes. Whether gladly or not, or quickly or not, that's my concern, not yours. Although there is one person to whom that would seem of more importance than to the two of us, but I am not worried about her. She'll turn him around once she is here. Everything is just fine in Brunswick, except for those witches who meet on a mountain, on Halloween in the dark of night. Erick's Anna is said to outshine all other women. You probably know the little tale that was told about her at the last gathering of princes. When people talked about her simple manner and her modest attire, the Count of Nürnberg, the short hump-back, who always has such scurrilous ideas, called her a light which burns even brighter unadorned than adorned, and the younger men among us swore with much clamor that this was true while we older ones laughed. By the devil, surely she can compete with the barber's daughter.

PREISING: All right then.

ERNEST: You may, furthermore, summon him to a tournament at Regensburg. Yes, yes, to Regensburg. I owe it to them. Let him not stand there any longer like a boy whose bird flew away and who cannot catch another. My knights are to know immediately that Guelph and Wittelsbach are finally going to kiss and make up; and we shall formally announce his betrothal at the tournament. The whole plan must be carried out as expeditiously as possible. My brother must issue the summons at once. He will be glad to do so, for it is a task that he likes. Do you know how his little son is? It is a long time since I have seen him. They hide him from me, as if they were ashamed to let me see him; and I hardly like to ask about him.

PREISING: I hear he is much better since the old herb-woman has been attending him.

ERNEST: I am glad to hear it, though it doesn't signify much. For all the ills of the flesh play catch with this poor child. I would never have thought there were so many as he has already suffered from in his brief life. Such a pity! Preising, poor little Adolf will never do anything reckless, at most, nothing worse than enter a monastery. That would be the best thing for him, after all.

PREISING: But weak children often grow to be strong men.

ERNEST: God grant it! I wish it from my heart! But how different my Albrecht was! There wasn't anything that he was not up to when he was four years old. He let no man leave the castle with an unruffled beard, and wherever he was playing, there was not a window within reach unbroken. Of course, he has gone too far now. He has besmirched his record; I would never have thought it of him. Well, we will make it clean again; and afterwards I can demand so much the more from him. For all the ten commandments together cannot lash a man so madly onward, as his youthful follies peering over his shoulder every time he turns his head. That's the reason God allows them, I suppose.

PREISING: And if—Your Lordship, never was a consent in such a matter quickly given—if he does not send back his reply at once, am I still to summon him to the tournament?

ERNEST: Then most of all; for then, before the assembled knights, I shall—But, what folly! To horse and away, Preising! *(exeunt quickly)*

Scene 2

Tower room in Vohburg Castle.

(Albrecht *enters, with* Agnes; *the* Chamberlain *follows*)

ALBRECHT *(to* Agnes, *who shrinks from entering):* What is the matter? *(to the* Chamberlain*)* So this is the room?

CHAMBERLAIN: This is the room.

ALBRECHT: A perfect watch-tower!

CHAMBERLAIN: Yes, here enemies as well as friends can first be seen. That is what your dear mother said the first time she entered it, and, like you, stepped over to the balcony.

ALBRECHT: We should have come here immediately after our arrival, should we not? For, I see, you enjoyed my mother's confidence.

CHAMBERLAIN: Oh, I need not be told why you come five days later than she expected you! I know what I shall answer now, when the steward and the butler put their heads together; for now you are here, as well as my gracious lady, Elizabeth of Würtemberg, or, rather, of Bavaria now.

ALBRECHT: It is true, she is your lady; however, it is not Elizabeth of Würtemberg.

CHAMBERLAIN: Not Elizabeth of Würtemberg? Of course, I had imagined it all very different. Usually, when a princess marries in the Holy Roman Empire, one bell peals it out merrily to the other, banners wave, trumpets blare, and gay heralds dash hither and thither; but this time there was nothing of that sort. May God bless the duchess of this land and the lawful wife of my lord. *(exit)*

ALBRECHT: What a queer, old fellow! Just like a withered leaf which the wind has left hanging in the midst of green foliage.

AGNES: Albrecht, he reminds me of my father. Some day *he* will look just like that.

ALBRECHT *(turning quickly away):* Oh, we are really here! How that old fellow did go on! Kindly as my feelings are towards him, it almost vexed me to see him go ahead of us, jingling his keys.

AGNES: And I felt almost ashamed—but still I was touched. He cannot tolerate a blemish in his Duke; and in his eyes I am your blemish.

ALBRECHT: Now, you walls, if you have tongues, speak! So that I may find out why we were to come to this room first. I thought there was a surprise here, but there is nothing to be seen.

AGNES: How beautiful it is here! This brown woodwork is so

polished that we can see ourselves. That was surely made in Regengsburg. What wonderful windows, with all their beautiful colors, and the many pictures in them.

ALBRECHT: Yes, they do that work on the Rhine now, since they have begun to build the cathedral at Cologne. Each window is a pictured legend. It makes one pious merely to look through them. However, I cannot believe we were summoned hither merely to look at them.

AGNES: And oh, the view!

ALBRECHT: It is all your own now, my Agnes. But do not be too glad. You have to put up with a good deal into the bargain. For example, that old gnarled tree there, and that poor, dilapidated hut.

AGNES: My Albrecht, you are so happy; that is my greatest happiness.

ALBRECHT: But I am a mere sulker, compared with what I shall be tomorrow and the day after, and the day after that, and so on. Yes, Agnes, with me one delight is always the forerunner of the next greater one; and now, for the first time, I understand why man is immortal.

AGNES: I can stand no more, or my heart will burst with joy! *(catching sight of the prie-dieu)* There! There! *(falls on her knees and prays)*

ALBRECHT *(with a glance upward):* This is thy blessing! (Agnes *arises from the prie-dieu, where she has been kneeling, and a secret drawer springs open without her noticing it*)

ALBRECHT: Now my mother is no longer in heaven, but here on earth with us! But her bliss is undiminished.

AGNES: Ah, Albrecht, she was not expecting *me!*

ALBRECHT *(catching sight of the secret drawer):* But see, what is that?

AGNES: Pearls and jewels! Oh, what splendor!

ALBRECHT: Her jewels! At least, I suppose so; for she probably wore them only before my birth; and here's a letter, too. *(reads)* "To that one of my children who first prays here." *(hands letter to Agnes)* Then it's for you, and that is the secret. So there was an object in our coming here, after all? How splendid they would have been for your wedding day! But of course that was over before we even came here. Well? (Agnes *hands the letter back to Al-*

brecht, *who reads*) If I had been the one, I might have adorned you with them; but now you must do it for yourself.

AGNES: No, neither the one nor the other.

ALBRECHT: And underneath there is something for the one who did not pray. Surely that will not shine and sparkle so! Good mother, you knew even then who that would be. I can see you admonishing me! (*to* Agnes) But hurry. How long shall I dance around the last Christmas tree which she set up for me before I can get to my presents? Make haste to remove your things, so that I can get at mine.

AGNES: How could I touch them?

ALBRECHT: Well, if you will not, you surely will not prevent me from being a dutiful son. Now then— *(he picks up the pearls to put them on for her)*

AGNES: Oh, you must not! What would there be left for a princess?

ALBRECHT: Would you separate what belongs together? You would provide my father, whom you fear so, with a bad example. Quickly, undo the damage, so that he cannot refer to it. Come, let us match like with like. *(shakes the pearls, then fastens them around her throat)* But these are like hailstones against snow. Let us see which one is whiter.

AGNES: Flatterer!

ALBRECHT: Agnes, did anyone ever tell you that, when you drink red wine, it gleams through the alabaster of your throat, just as if it were being poured from one crystal into another? But what foolishness! *(takes up a golden diadem)* Here is another match to be made! *(tries to place it on her head)*

AGNES: Oh, it would weigh me down!

ALBRECHT: I can understand your making a stronger resistance than before, for here the similarity is even more doubtful. This gold and that— *(points to her hair)* The contrast is too great! This is a sun ray as it first went though the soil and gave its best to the earth's million plants, and then the coarse residue was condensed in heavy, dead grain. And that is a ray of sun—if it had ever touched the earth it would have created a flower of such beauty that even roses and lilies would have bowed to it, but it preferred to cover your head, lovingly, as a shimmering net. *(places the tiara on her head)* But you must not be too exacting when there is nothing better.

AGNES: Then you may put it on—only to see how she must have worn it.

ALBRECHT: The eye is itself a precious jewel that brooks no ornament, but this ring for the finger—it has gone unadorned long enough—this bracelet for your arm, and behold, the empress is perfect! For you did not dream that I wished to make an empress of you, did you? Now she stands before me. If you should step upon the first throne in the world, the next thousand years could produce no one who could have the right to say, "Arise!" But now, I must see what is my share. *(he removes from the drawer some faded flowers, and other objects)* Withered flowers and leaves ready to crumble at a touch! What is their message? But here— *(he catches sight of a skull and picks it up)*—is it you, Silent Admonisher? You are a better preacher than Solomon; but for me you have no message. A man who has grown up on battlefields does not need you to warn him that he must die. But first, I will *live!* I am sure there are many in heaven whose joy is still incomplete, because they gaze back upon the earth without knowing why. But I know why. They did not empty their cup of earthly bliss. They never loved! Ah, Agnes—*(enter* Chamberlain) Stop, not one word, if the fate of the world depends upon it! Yes, Agnes, if I am to end in God, I must begin with you. For me there is no other way to Him. Do not you feel that, too?

AGNES: Even if death should come this very instant, I could not say, "You have come too soon."

ALBRECHT *(embraces her)*: All our supremest joy is one with Him. What our hearts cannot contain overflows into His. He is only happy in our happiness. *(kisses her)* And sometimes the overflow rolls back and engulfs us, and we are suddenly transported and find ourselves wandering in Paradise without realizing a change. If that could only happen now!

AGNES: No more, I beg you. No more!

ALBRECHT: This has been an hour! Now let the second come. *(to* Chamberlain) What is it?

CHAMBERLAIN: A message from your father. Chancellor Preising—

ALBRECHT: Let him enter. (Agnes *is going to leave the room; exit* Chamberlain) No, Agnes, I do not intend to deny you. Remain! I can judge of my father's attitude in the matter by the way in which his Chancellor meets you. So we shall know immediately how things stand.

AGNES: Oh, let me go, Albrecht! Something bids me go. This— *(points to a diadem)* would be a challenge.

ALBRECHT: Then step into the adjoining room. You can be back at my side immediately. *(exit Agnes)* Now I am ready to be found!

(enter Chancellor Preising, accompanied by Törring, Frauenhoven, and Nothaft von Wernberg)

ALBRECHT: What is your message, Chancellor?

PREISING: Good news!

ALBRECHT: That would be adding joy to joy.

PREISING: This news would have been better brought to you by Sir Haydeck rather than by me.

ALBRECHT: Oh, I understand.

PREISING: He was to notify you of the flight of your first betrothed—

ALBRECHT: I forgot to reward him for that. I will make it up to him when I see him next.

PREISING: At the same time he was to bring you the consent of the second.

ALBRECHT: Preising, don't beat about the bush. I am bad at solving puzzles, but good at cracking heads. What is it?

PREISING: Your father has demanded the hand of the fairest princess in all Saxony for you, his son.

ALBRECHT: I regret it most sincerely.

PREISING: And Erick of Brunswick has given his consent.

ALBRECHT: My regret is so much the deeper then.

PREISING: And I—

ALBRECHT: And you are sent to make me nod my head in consent, like a Nürnberg jumping-jack? You will not succeed in doing so; and that is my deepest regret, for you will be the loser.

PREISING: I can assure you it would greatly amaze your father, if you should but for a moment be opposed to an alliance which never has been possible since the proscription of Henry the Lion, though often enough attempted—one that would amicably settle an ancient and ofttimes dangerous hostility, once and for all. Not to grasp this opportunity with both hands would be deliberately trampling rare fortune under foot. Not only that; it would also arouse again the slumbering feud between Guelph and Wittelsbach, and strengthen it; it would turn an unjust hatred into a justifiable scorn; it would be challenging revenge and offering the weapons to the enemy.

ALBRECHT: Oh, I know all that! It would surprise me if it were otherwise. No one dares to cross my father's plans without offending half the world. It never concerns him alone. However great his skill may be in spinning his threads so fine, it is not infallible; and this time they are going to break.

PREISING: And your reason for this?

ALBRECHT: You know it.

PREISING: I hope not.

ALBRECHT: You need not remain in ignorance long. I am a man, like any other man. I have the right to swear love and fidelity to a woman with whom I stepped before the sacred altar; therefore, I have to make my own choice, like any one else.

PREISING: You are a prince. You are to rule over millions, who must labor today for you in the sweat of their brow, who tomorrow must spill their blood for you, and the next day must give their lives for you. Do you expect all this for nothing? That is not the way God has made the world or else it wouldn't be round now. To them you also owe a sacrifice; and you will surely not be the first one of your far-famed line to refuse it?

ALBRECHT: One sacrifice? One with every breath, you mean. Do you know what you are demanding? Surely you do not; or you would have to lower your eyes, and not stand there as if the ten commandments flamed in golden letters on your brow. What do you do when the day has been a gloomy one, when everything has gone wrong, and you have found even yourself unbearable? You toss aside all that has bothered you and hasten to your wife's side. Perhaps she has just been doubly blessed by God and can share her happiness with you. And even if that is not so you cannot look at her without remembering all your happy hours together and that memory always brings new happiness. What would my life be? Could I hasten to my wife for consolation? Impossible! Rather would I have to place a sentinel before my door to keep her out, so that she would not come to me of her own accord and make me quite insane, for she would be my greatest curse. But still, I could not do that either. I should have to embrace and caress her, even though longing to push her from me. You shudder? Do you understand now what you are demanding? Not only am I to renounce my happiness; I am even to embrace and caress my misery, and to pray for it. But, no, no, never in all eternity!

PREISING: Your ancestor Louis had a consort who was always called involuntarily by another name than the one she had received in sacred baptism. She was Margaret of Kärnten, who to this day among the people is known as Margaret of the Large Mouth. He was young, like you, and it was never said that he was blind. However, by marrying her he brought back into possession of Bavaria the baronetcy of Tyrol; and, even though he could not take pleasure in her beauty, he must have consoled himself with the thought that his subjects during his reign could get their salt for half the former tax, and give him their blessing morning, noon, and night with joyous faces.

ALBRECHT: Do you happen to know whether he refused them a request every time he looked upon his wife?

PREISING: I only know that he left four heirs to the throne. Your lordship, I have delivered my message, and shall announce to your father that you have not given your consent. If you would add anything, you can do so when you see him. But there is one thing more. I am also to summon you to a tournament which your father has proclaimed at Regensburg, and you surely will not wish to increase his displeasure by staying away?

ALBRECHT: Of course not. I have not forgotten how to tilt, not even in Augsburg, and it will give me pleasure to prove it.

PREISING: Then you will have to leave this very day.

ALBRECHT: Today?

PREISING: The tournament occurs day after tomorrow.

ALBRECHT: That is quicker work than a peasant's brawl. What is it for? Has a daughter been born to the Emperor in his old age?

PREISING: Your father, the Duke, probably intended to announce your betrothal to his knights; for, never dreaming your refusal possible, he is feeling very proud of having accomplished what his ancestors failed in for three whole centuries. But now, there will probably be nothing but a crossing of lances.

ALBRECHT: Notwithstanding, I consider myself his obedient son in all reasonable things, and will enter the lists for a pea-pod, if he desires it.

PREISING: You have given me your word that you will be present.

(*exit* Preising, *with* Törring, Frauenhoven, *and* von Wernberg)

ALBRECHT (*alone*): That is over. I can hardly say that I am sorry. It is not intended that I shall enjoy my happiness like a boy munching the cherries he has stolen. Now, if the storm blows off the magic cap, the priest in Augsburg surely cannot complain of my having betrayed the secret.

(*enter* Agnes, *without the jewels*)

AGNES: Now, my Albrecht?

ALBRECHT: Yes, Agnes, I shall now see if you have learned anything from your father. Just to try you, I am going to bring back a few bruises from Regensburg. But what have you been doing? Undoing all my handiwork? Oh, no, you simply mean you have restored God's. And it is true. I had only destroyed it. Like a boy tossing carnation petals at a lily! You were right to shake off these gaudy superfluities.

AGNES: I heard everything, everything! I could not help it.

ALBRECHT: Everything, except my last answer. Do not be afraid of my temper. I will keep it at bay as long as I can. Even now. But just in case: Here is my answer (*embraces her*) We are united. Only death can part us, and *he* is his own master. And there is no one in the world who gives in more quickly than my father when he sees that things cannot be changed. Now to the armory. I'll take Nothaft and Törring with me and leave Frauenhoven here for your protection.

AGNES: It is not fear that excites me, but—You see, my Albrecht, it does hurt to have to think that all Augsburg does not know I am your wife; and the consolation of being pure before God does not always suffice, nor, I must confess, the feeling of paying for my happiness thus. But I will willingly bear it, however hard, my whole life long, if you and your father only remain on friendly terms. How I used to hate it when friends and brothers were fighting over me. I stayed away from many a dance in order not to see that happen. But that was nothing compared with this!

ALBRECHT: There is no cause for worry this time. Even a prince's son may say, "I do not want her, at any rate, I do not want her yet!" Oh, but I shall beat them down in the jousts. Whoever considered me a good lance before will be ashamed of ever having thought so. And I will make every one vow to himself that he will never cross my path again—even those who get no scratches. (*exeunt both*)

Scene 3

Regensburg: the tilting place.
(The spectators are already assembled. The Marshal *stands at the lists, with a book under his arm. A long procession; banners, torches, trumpets.* Duke Ernest *enters, accompanied by his knights. Among these are:* Hans von Laubelfing, Wolfram von Pienzenau, Otto von Bern, Ignace von Seyboltsdorf, *and* Hans von Preising. *The knights, with exception of* Preising, *take their places in line, at the right of the* Marshal)

PREISING *(walking at Ernest's side):* Your Lordship, do not misinterpret my making another appeal to you. But this hour is decisive. It may be impossible ever to undo what you are about to do now; and usually you do not treat my humble advice with scorn.

ERNEST: I can protect you from everyone but my successor; therefore, I can now only heed my own counsel.

MARSHAL *(calling):* Wolfram von Pienzenau, Otto von Bern!

WOLFRAM AND OTTO: Here! (Marshal *admits them to lists*)

PREISING: I am afraid to guess what you intend to do; surely the marshall does not carry that book around for no reason. I beg you to give the matter a little more consideration, and not to take his hasty reply for the defiance of a son—but rather, the obstinacy of a lover who cannot so easily transfer his affections from an Agnes to an Anna.

ERNEST: They will call your name any time now. (Preising *walks over to the knights*)

ERNEST *(to himself):* A gash is sometimes necessary. If it does not work immediately, it does later. Well, well! Who would have ever dreamed it possible? And all for the sake of a courtesan?

(enter Albrecht *with* Norhaft von Wernberg *and* Törring)

ERNEST *(as he passes* Albrecht): Once more I ask you, am I to announce to my assembled knights your betrothal to Anna of Brunswick?

ALBRECHT: Father, there is too much of you in me, that I should give two different answers to one and the same question on one and the same morning. God above! Was it all for nothing that I prostrated myself before you like the humblest suppliant?

ERNEST: Very well. *(walks on)* Marshal, I have nothing to say. *(ascends the platform)* Go on!

MARSHAL *(calling names):* Hans von Preising! Ignace von Seyboltsdorf!

(von Preising *and* von Seyboltsdorf *move forward to the lists)*

ALBRECHT: Preising! Seyboltsdorf! Back! Wittelsbach is here, and comes first. *(moves forward to the lists)*

MARSHAL: Halt!

ALBRECHT: Marshal von Pappenheim! Take heed! When I have to open a blind man's eyes I make use of my lance.

ERNEST: Article ten!

MARSHAL *(open the book and reads):* "Further, it was decreed at Heilbron for all time, he who is born and descended from nobility and seduces a woman—"

ALBRECHT *(knocking the book from his hand):* Is not allowed to enter the tournament. Are there vagabonds here who do not know that, without having it read to them?

MARSHAL: You are accused of living in dishonor with a Swabian maid at your Castle at Vohburg.

ALBRECHT: My accuser? (Duke Ernest *arises)*

ALBRECHT: Duke of Munich-Bavaria, have your spies beaten for reviling your own people. The honorable and virtuous daughter of Augsburg, Agnes Bernauer, is my wife. Here are my witnesses.

ERNEST *(aside):* Preising, that is enough to—make one grow young again.

ALBRECHT: Since one cannot live in dishonor with his own wife— Page, just show the Marshal how to let down the barriers! *(page quickly opens for him, and* Albrecht *enters)* Well, gentlemen, it is customary to extend good wishes to your adversary.

ERNEST *(grasps his sword and is about to descend):* I shall wish you good luck.

PREISING *(blocks his way):* Your Highness, you will have to stab me first, if you do!

ERNEST: Oh, I only intended to give him a beating as a reward for his impudence; but you are quite right. 'Tis better so. Why need I permit my wrath to be aroused, when my authority as reigning duke suffices? *(calls out in clear tones)* Noblemen of Bavaria, Counts, Barons, and Knights—as you know, William, my brother, also has a son!

ALBRECHT *(aside):* What does this mean?

ERNEST: My sincere respects to the virtuous maiden who can only be gained with the sanction of the church. She must indeed be a shrewd person! But the one who wins her thus has to take into the bargain the blessing and mercy of all the heavenly host. *However,* his crown and ducal robes must be left on the altar steps. My brother's son, by the name of Adolph, I hereby declare—my successor!

ALBRECHT: By the memory of my mother, it cannot be!

LAUBELFING: Albrecht von Wittelsbach, Ingolstadt stands by you! Do not fear for your rights, Louis of Ingolstadt will help you to protect them!

ERNEST: Louis of Ingolstadt, or whoever may be his spokesman, the whole empire will stand by me, with all its ban and banishment. Woe unto him who disturbs the peace of the empire!

MARSHAL *(together with many other knights, all clashing their swords):* Ay, woe be to him!

ERNEST: Citizen of Augsburg, barber's son-in-law, accept now your blessing and wedding gift at one and the same time! Long live my successor! *(descends from the tribune)* Let all good Bavarians hail him with me! Long live Adolph, the child!

MARSHAL *(with many knights, gathering around* Duke Ernest): Long live, Adolph, the child!

ALBRECHT *(draws his sword and advances toward the* Marshal, *but is surrounded by his followers):* Otto, my grandfather, be our protector!

ERNEST: The tournament is ended.

ALBRECHT: No, it is only beginning. If the noblemen are deserting me, then citizens and peasants will stand by me. *(waves his sword toward the audience) (great commotion prevails)*

Act 4

Scene 1

Munich. The Ducal Cabinet
(Chancellor Preising, seated at a table, holding a sealed document in his hand)

PREISING: This I am to open and examine? And of all days, on this day of sorrows? *(turns over the document)* Not even an address!

Nothing but a cross! But, seven times sealed by his own hand; besides, it was lying in a copper casket with a triple lock. Its content must be very serious indeed. This dust on my fingers proves that it cannot be of very recent date. *(breaking the seal)* It is plainly a secret which he has long kept from me. My courage almost fails me! *(enter Stachus)*

STACHUS: There is a farmer outside, with an extraordinarily large ear of grain, which he wants to show to the duke.

PREISING: Not today. When he returns from the death bed he won't have eyes for such things.

STACHUS: I told him that, but he won't change his mind, and you know that we are not to treat the common folk unkindly.

PREISING: So let him stand out there till he leaves on his own. Have you heard any news of Prince Adolph? Not even a little better? With God there is nothing impossible, you know.

STACHUS: Better? But half an hour ago the last sacrament was administered to him. Sir, the Witch of Augsburg is on the alert, and the devil will not desert her. How should the poor child be able to recover?

PREISING: What nonsense you are talking again, Stachus!

STACHUS: It is just what everyone else is saying; in castle and cloister, market and street, wherever you go, everybody, everybody! A reverend Franciscan father has pronounced a curse upon this Bernauer girl, saying she deserves to be burned at the stake; so it must be true. And why should it not be true, pray tell? First the father died, good, noble Duke William (he gave me this doublet), then, before the time for mourning his loss was over, his fair wife followed him, and now the Prince, their son, dear little Adolph, the Crown Prince, lies at death's door. *(the chapel bell tolls)* There, do you hear? It is tolling. The end has come. *(clenching his hands as if with a curse)* How can I help it? *(falls on his knees and prays. Preising kneels also)* With my own hands I would light the fire to destroy her. She would find as many executioners as there are good Bavarians. The next victim will be the Duke, our reigning lord, mark my words! *(exit Stachus)*

PREISING *(who has risen with Stachus)*: Yes, the end has come. The child has drawn his last breath, and Duke Ernest is now without an heir, since he has cast off his own son. A heavy hour for this land! May God be merciful unto us. *(picks up the document)* He will probably be here soon now. He was over there the entire night. *(draws the document from the cover and unfolds it)* What is this? *(reads)* "Legal proof from the imperial authorities, that on account of criminally misleading young Duke Albrecht into unlawful marriage, or indeed, if nothing else can be proved, simply on account of being a party to such a marriage, Agnes Bernauer may be put to death by whatever means chosen as a precaution against grievous calamity." *(stops reading)* Oh, now I understand everything! This Prince in dying will cause another death, this dead child will drag a victim after him! Horrible! *(looks at the document again)* "The young Duke!" He is five years older than she, and probably had won his first battle before she had laid aside her dolls. Poor girl, what a fate is about to befall you! *(turns over the pages)* Who are the signers of the document? Adlsreiter, Kraitmayr, Emeran zu Kalmperg! All famous jurists, worthy to sit at Justinian's feet and rule the world! Who would dare to defy them? She is lost! This must have been drawn up just after the tournament at Regensburg. I remember they all met here in Munich, I thought, by chance, but now I see they were summoned. That was two years and a half ago. How little she must be expecting this now! *(continues to turn the pages)* And below stands the formal death sentence, lacking nothing but the Duke's signature. That he will doubtless affix shortly. The thought of it makes me shudder! Many such documents have passed through my hands, but the stern sentence was always prefaced by a long list of atrocious crimes; murders, robberies, criminal violations of the law—which deserved severe punishment. But what is the offense in this case? The worst one could plead against her is, she did not enter a cloister. *(reads again)* "By the executioner's axe, by drowning or even from ambush!" And is there no other way? No possible way of saving her?

(enter Duke Ernest)

DUKE ERNEST: I have kept you waiting, Preising! But you see I have been kept waiting myself.

PREISING: My Lord!

ERNEST: Enough! Enough! One soul more has joined the countless throng. Have you read the document?

PREISING: I had but broken the seal, your lordship, when the bell began to toll.

ERNEST: Pray, finish it at once. *(turns away)* I am quite undone. To think the child would die so hard! A life so brief, and a death struggle lasting twelve hours! Father in heaven! But now, it is over. *(the great cathedral bell begins to toll)*

ERNEST *(paces back and forth):* The great bell at last! That is what I have been waiting for. Now the city will know the sad news, too! From place to place, from house to house, from mouth to mouth! Prayers! prayers! prayers! We need them all. *(turning to Preising)* Well?

PREISING *(lays the document on the table):* Is there anything for me to say?

ERNEST: Whatever you are able to! Test it point for point; I'll answer you now as always. Have you any objections to the men who pronounced the sentence?

PREISING: To such renowned judges? If the code of laws had not already been established, to these I would entrust the commission, if I were the Emperor!

ERNEST: Are they open to bribery? Is there one among them who can be suspected of venality?

PREISING: Most surely, no! But even so, Duke Ernest would never tempt any man by bribery.

ERNEST: You give me only my just dues there, Preising. I did not even pay the fees which they would have deserved. And that is the only debt I will never repay.

PREISING: I would vouch for you. But also for her.

ERNEST: Well, such men of the most scrupulous honesty, after a careful, conscientious investigation of the case, submitted this document to me two years and a half ago! From that time to this it has never seen the light of day. Could I be accused of unseemly haste?

PREISING: Not even by an enemy, my lord!

ERNEST: If I put this sentence into execution now, can it be asserted that it is not the Duke who is doing his duty, but the knight who wishes to remove a blemish from the family escutcheon, or a father who will be avenged?

PREISING: No, not that, my lord!

ERNEST *(picking up the pen):* Then—

PREISING: Your Lordship, one moment!

ERNEST *(drops the pen):* Well? I am not a tyrant, nor do I desire to become one! But it shall never be said of me, I wore my sword simply as an ornament. It is taken away from him who draws it unnecessarily, but if he does not use it when it is needed he will call down the ten plagues of Egypt on his people, and then the just and the injust are punished alike, for our Lord above does not pull out only the weeds when he has to mete out punishment: he simply mows everything down. Take that into consideration. And now: What have you to say?

PREISING: The sentence I cannot refute! You are right. There is but one inevitable result when the rights of succession are in dispute; sooner or later it means civil war, with all its horrors and no one can foretell what the outcome may be.

ERNEST: This inevitable result is now impending, whether there would be born an heir to Albrecht or not! In the one case, the right of succession would have to be established, in the other there would be no possibility of agreement between the rival factions of Ingolstadt and Landshut, for both would claim the lion's share. Indeed, I doubt if they would wait until the succeeding reign! Even now they are trying to arouse my wrath by courting my son's favor!

PREISING: But it is horrible that she must die just because she is beautiful and virtuous!

ERNEST: Alas, too true! Therefore I placed it in God's hands. Now he has spoken. I even went so far as to cast off my own son, and put my nephew in his place. This nephew's death was God's answer.

PREISING: And is there no other way? None at all?

ERNEST: Your appeal strikes me to the heart! You think I might do even more? And it is true: the blood of our ancestors flows just as pure in the veins of Louis of Ingolstadt and Henry of Landshut as it does in mine.

PREISING: I had not even thought of that.

ERNEST: But I did! True, the solution would be so bad that even a saint would ask, "Why are you punishing me, Lord?" But if it should be thus? The last of the Hohenstaufen line died by the executioner's hand; God's unfathomable ways are not always clear to us. But this could not be God's intent, for it would not do any good, and that is my consolation. If I were to say to Henry, "Come, you old fox, all my life you have set traps and dug pits for me. Now take my dukedom as the reward," Louis would interfere at once. And if I said to Louis, "I owe you thanks for all the times you have tried to stab me in the back: Here it is," Henry would want a share. But only one of them could take over. Is that not so?

PREISING: It is!

ERNEST: Thus it would be all the same. Everything would be topsy-turvy, and the thousands who came to my country trusting me, who turned my villages into towns, and who raised my towns to such importance that even the proud Hansa League cannot disregard them without retaliation, they would curse me and my memory.

PREISING: That was not what I had in mind. Have her abducted; let her disappear! That will be quite easily accomplished now, for he does not deem it necessary to keep her so closely guarded as heretofore.

ERNEST: What would be gained by such a step? He would never give up searching for her to his dying day! You were a poor prophet in Regensburg.

PREISING: Have the report circulated that she is dead; he found a priest to marry them, do you think it would be difficult to find one who would issue a death certificate for you?

ERNEST: And I should bestow upon him a second wife, with the first one still living? Preising, I hold the sacrament sacred and my son shall never be able to testify against me on the day of wrath: "Lord of this I am innocent, for it was done without my knowledge." The cloister is of no avail here. There is nothing but death!

PREISING: But there is the Pope, and, if he refuses, the Emperor! Frederick Barbarossa divorced himself; why not Louis of Bavaria divorce his son?

ERNEST: How divorce, when neither party desires it? Preising, I have had two years and a half to weigh this matter, and I have found no other solution *(picks up the pen)* No, it is God's will, thus, and no other way! Now is the time to put it into execution, for Albrecht will be setting out either today or tomorrow for the tournament at Ingolstadt. One might almost say, he is to be restored to his full honor there, for Louis of Ingolstadt has summoned thither all of my enemies, thinking that the wider the gulf between father and son, the better his own chances. Well, while they are waving their standards about them, I'll see to it that they need not be ashamed of so doing afterwards! Nothing vexed me so sorely as the splendid pageant at the time he took her from Vohburg to Straubing, attended by all the magnificence belonging to a duchess. But now it is my turn. Emeran zu Kalmperg is the judge of Straubing, and Pappenheim can be there with a hundred soldiers inside of twenty-four hours!

PREISING: And afterwards? Gracious sir, you were right. I made a poor prophecy at Regensburg. Do you think he will submit to such a thing? In his rage may not he threaten his own life, or rise in open rebellion against you?

ERNEST: The first, possibly; the second, certainly. I am simply doing what I must—the issue is with God. I'll offer him to God as Abraham did Isaac. If he succumbs to his despair—and it is quite possible that he will—I'll have him buried, like her; if he confronts me openly I will subdue him or hold him till the emperor arrives, to whom I am reporting this event before it has even happened. He will not hesitate to come, for he wants his realm in order just as I want order in my house. For her it is unfortunate, and for me it is surely no joy; but in the name of the widows and orphans whom civil war would create, in the name of the cities which it would lay in ashes, of the villages it would destroy— Agnes Bernauer, go to thy doom! *(he affixes his signature, then turns and leaves the room.* Preising *follows with the document)*

Scene 2

Straubing. The court of the castle and an adjoining garden.
(Törring, Frauenhoven, Nothaft von Wernberg, in full armor, sitting at a stone table drinking. The Chamberlain *passes)*

WERNBERG: Well, my good man—on your way to the chapel? *(lifts his goblet)* Come and have a drink, so that you will be convinced that the prayers of the pious are not in vain.

CHAMBERLAIN: The knight said to the wine cup—I am going to overturn you—and did so seven times in succession; but finally the wine cup overturns him, and right into the devil's arms, who was standing behind. Take heed—nor be unduly scornful. *(exit)*

FRAUENHOVEN: Where is the Duke? The horses are growing restless.

TÖRRING: He is inspecting the mausoleum, which she has had built for herself and which was to be finished either yesterday or today. I saw them walking over together.

WERNBERG: What a strange idea for a young woman! A mausoleum!

TÖRRING: To begin with, it was not so strange. She probably felt uneasy enough just after the marriage, and with reason. Of course matters stand differently now. And yet, who can tell what may happen? The sickly child successor in Munich has not been strengthened by the weight of the crown—which the old Duke bestowed upon him. Indeed, he may have put it upon the child's head merely because he expected it to roll off again.

FRAUENHOVEN: In that you are wrong. How often he tried—through his brother—to force a formal abdication from Albrecht.

TÖRRING: That was always just an insult, a veiled inquiry if he was not fed up with her yet. If Ernest had not had ulterior motives why did he stand between him and the Emperor who wanted to be informed about the Regensburg affairs. Old Sigismund was serious; gout has made a valiant "Reichsvogt" of him, and his emissaries, we might as well admit it, would not have needed glasses to notice open rebellion. Why did they so suddenly return to Munich?

FRAUENHOVEN: You always see the worst in things.

WERNBERG: There they come. Let us mount, so that we do not delay the start. But first— *(lifts his glass)*

TÖRRING: Here's to good luck! *(clink glasses and drain them. Exeunt.)*

> *(Albrecht, in armor, enters with* Agnes. *A bell rings.)*

AGNES: So you'll bring me the swinging lamp I want? A bronze one, with a long chain, that will hang from the ceiling in the chapel?

ALBRECHT: I would rather bring something else, I admit, but I have promised. So you shall have it.

AGNES: Are you angry?

ALBRECHT: How could I be angry? But I am worried because you are so absorbed in this erection of your mausoleum. Is it because you are disturbed by forebodings of misfortune? I cannot see why you should be—but there must be something!

AGNES: There is nothing at all, my Albrecht. If there were, I would speak of my coffin, of torches and bells ringing and all the other things I would want. And if I feared to hurt you I would say, "Just think, I dreamed I was being buried, and you must be glad about it, for it means a long life; yet the burial was so beautiful that when the time comes I want it like that and no other way." And then I would describe it to you.

ALBRECHT: Then I will give you the lamp after thirty years.

AGNES: If that's how you want it. I was not expecting to light it yet. You simply do not understand. We girls of the common people always make our shrouds as soon as we have finished our wedding gowns, and with reason, too, for we would never be sure of having one otherwise. You see, I belong to that class, and I have not yet been the wife of a duke long enough to be completely transformed. But I have lost some of my humility, for instead of pricking my fingers over my shroud, as my former playmates must do, I am making mason and carpenter do my work for me by building me a mausoleum. Now that it is finished, I am happy to know the place where I shall sleep my last long sleep, and to be able to say my prayers there now. That's why I would like to hang a lamp there now, so that the place would not feel quite so strange to me in my last hour.

ALBRECHT: If only that is all!

AGNES: But what else could it be? I am simply getting my bed ready, while it is still day! Nothing more! Perhaps you imagine I still feel a little of that fear and anxiety that oppressed me on coming here to Straubing with you after the tournament at Regensburg? Then, I did tremble for both of us! At that time I was not yet accustomed to my castle at Vohburg, and was still running from apartment to apartment in a vain effort to find one small enough for my comfort. And then the change from my little castle of Vohburg to this magnificent palace was just as great as the difference between my father's humble house and the castle of Vohburg! Oh, how well I remember all the music on the way—the cheers of the peasants, following us with their scythes and ploughshares—the flowers they scattered in front of us, everything struck terror to my heart. Even you seemed almost a stranger, because you permitted it, nay, even gloried in it! I was almost frightened to death when you wanted to have the bells rung at our arrival here! But now, my Albrecht, all that feeling has long since vanished. You just heard me call Vohburg small; I no longer am amazed when the supplicants crowd around me in the morning—and I can make inquiries like a born duchess—I can shake my head, and almost refuse. I should be ashamed.

ALBRECHT: That is the way I like you!

AGNES: But in my dreams everything is so different, else I might grow too proud. When I am asleep, visions of the old days return, when I had to sweep up all the crumbs from the floor—oh, so carefully! And when my birthday usually consisted of not being scolded for having done something that was not quite right. Just last night (your generous heart will smile at this) in a dream I blushed and stammered when I asked my father for a trifle, and he replied, as was his wont: "Very well—you may have it—but then I must do without my wine for half a year!" I was still very angry at him when I awoke. But then—I at least saw him again, if only in a dream!

ALBRECHT: You *are* going to see him—*(stops abruptly)* There! I have spoiled a surprise for you.

AGNES: No, my Albrecht—I know what you are planning, but it is useless. If he had ever intended to come, he would have come long ago. I can understand what keeps him from coming—and you must respect him for it.

ALBRECHT: I think he is going to yield, this time! If he does not, we'll go to the carnival in Augsburg!

(enter Törring)

TÖRRING: Pray pardon me for intruding, your Grace!

ALBRECHT: I am tarrying too long for you?

TÖRRING: If you intend to go at all—

ALBRECHT: If I intend to go at all? I most surely do not intend to disappoint all the knights that Duke Louis has assembled with such difficulty.

TÖRRING: Do you not hear the cathedral bell?

ALBRECHT: It has been ringing for some time, but what of that? It does not concern me.

TÖRRING: More than you dream! Your cousin Adolph is dead!

ALBRECHT: Adolph!

TÖRRING: The news of his death has just been brought from Munich!

ALBRECHT: Peace to him! His life was never anything but a burden to himself, and surely not a pleasure to anyone else.

AGNES: God in Heaven! The third of the family to die within six months!

TÖRRING: You, my lady, understand!

AGNES: Do they say that I am to blame this time, too? Oh, of course! Who else? Who else?

ALBRECHT: God knows, I am not glad to hear this news. Why should I be? As far as I am concerned, he never existed. But I can shed no tears for him. There is only one thing I am thinking of! Now my father will be able to retract with honor.

TÖRRING: Your Grace, shall I have the horses unsaddled?

ALBRECHT: What an idea! Of course—I am not eager to have the tournament continue—but I surely should be the last one to be absent. I must go at once—but I shall be back much sooner than I anticipated. Agnes, now—*(he whispers something in her ear, then holds his hand against her cheek)* Ouch, it's burning.

AGNES: May God forgive you for thinking of that.

ALBRECHT: Amen! I agree. But we will see. I always had the feeling that my last wish could not be fulfilled before that. Well, our son must have a grandfather. And now—*(embraces her)* You see, you are not really angry with me. You are holding me tight. I know that you will not believe in God's blessing until then. You are superstitious in this. But do not change, for I love that in you, too. *(he kisses her)* My love, my life—farewell! *(embraces* Agnes, *then moves away a few steps)* You see, Törring—one can part from his life, and still not need to die immediately! So you must not stay single! *(he goes back to kiss her again)* And now, I am to be in Ingolstadt and you in Straubing, here! Can you still see me? You can? I don't see you anymore. *(exit.* Törring *follows)*

AGNES *(hurries into the garden):* Here I can see him mount! *(she turns back)* If only he could pick me up and let me look over the wall, as he did when the dark Egyptians passed by with their cymbals and bells. But I must be able to hear him! *(hurries back again)* Silence! trumpeter—else I cannot hear him! Hark! That is his voice. "You are good and kind, Törring." Why should he be telling him that now? Now they are setting out. Farewell, my—But wait! They are stopping! Can anything have happened? Someone is talking, low and indistinct. There, that is his voice again! "Take him to her!" To me! Who can it be? "It will make her very happy."

Make me happy! Ah! my Albrecht, you do not know me, after all! I wish the night would fall this very minute, and the day would not return for three times twenty-four hours! Or could it be my father? My father! Oh, surely not! But now, they are riding on. Fly on your way, swift-footed steeds! Just so much more quickly will you bring him back to me! *(she stands in a listening attitude)* I can hear no sound now. *(listens again)* Yes—I can! *(thoughtlessly picks a flower, then drops it again)* I am sorry I picked the pretty blossom—it is no time to wear flowers. *(walks slowly along)* And now, things have turned out just as they prophesied! He is dead! Can that possibly signify a change for the better for Albrecht and me? What am I to do now? Put on mourning? If I do—they will again accuse me of being proud—and of considering myself one of the family; the criticism that dreadful, steel-eyed judge is said to have pronounced upon me. If I continue to wear colors, then it will be said that I am glorying in his death. I shall simply follow the dictates of my heart, which tells me to mourn with the mourners. Do not laugh, Sir Emeran. Sometimes one owes thanks to a person and doesn't know it. It is a good thing that this heart is so gentle, even if you are not aware of that. *(enter* Count Törring*)* What! Are you still here?

TÖRRING: I am to stay here, my lady. Someone has just arrived from Augsburg. Do you wish to see him?

AGNES: From Augsburg? *(exit* Törring. Theobald *enters immediately)* Theobald!

THEOBALD: Agnes? Your ladyship, I mean—That is the way I must address you, is it not?

AGNES: Never mind that now! Tell me—is my father coming, too? But why ask such a question? Of course, you could not both leave at once!

THEOBALD: Well—that might be possible now—but you know him. He thinks you ought to forget your old father and stop sending messages to him; it will do no good, anyway, for he knows his place and does not intend to remind people here of the old barber—your father! He is sincerely glad that you do not forget him—that your lord is not ashamed of him—but he understands the ways of the world better than you, and wishes to be left in peace.

AGNES: And that is the only message you have for me from him! You have taken this long journey only to tell me that!

THEOBALD: Oh, that was not the only reason!

AGNES: Perhaps there is a secret one—that I am not to know?

THEOBALD: No reason on earth why you should not know it. We have heard many conflicting reports about you, during these years since you left us, and I was overcome by the desire—I felt I had to see—

AGNES: Whether I was really happy or not? Oh, if you only had come an hour sooner! Then you might have seen it with your own eyes! But no, it is better as it is! And you, Theobald? And Augsburg? Tell me everything! Everything!

THEOBALD: As far as your father is concerned, you need not be worried. Just after you went away he built the new laboratory furnace, which he never could afford before, and it has made money for him.

AGNES: Thank Heaven!

THEOBALD: He has made more chemical discoveries than he dares to make known, for fear he might fall into ill repute as a magician. Marvels—I tell you—perfect wonders! Too bad you cannot see them! They will have to perish with him. Some of them, however, he does not have to conceal; and, besides, he is successful enough. He is quite able to buy a little garden now; do you remember how you always longed for one?

AGNES: And what about yourself, Theobald?

THEOBALD: Oh, my wages have been doubled!

AGNES: Really?

THEOBALD: Yes, indeed—and sometimes I have to laugh at myself! For instance, just now, when I met the Duke, your lord, riding away on horseback. What a man he is! One can judge how much he loves you by the way he kept his people waiting for him. That is not at all the usual way; I passed them fully an hour ago, and they were growing very impatient with the delay.

AGNES: That is quite impossible, for they all set out together with him.

THEOBALD: Yes, I know, ten or twelve of them. But I mean the others.

AGNES: What others? He was only going to the tournament at Ingolstadt, and no one else was to accompany him.

THEOBALD: Nevertheless, an hour ago, as I passed the pine-covered hill, I saw a hundred and fifty or two hundred men waiting there, one foot in the stirrup, lance in hand, and eagerly gazing towards Straubing as if waiting for their leader or expecting some signal.

AGNES: I am terrified! Where did you say it was?

THEOBALD: Back there, on the Munich road.

AGNES: On the Munich road? But Albrecht is going in the opposite direction—to Ingolstadt.

THEOBALD: Somewhat farther on, a knight in full armor dashed past me—coming from the castle. I thought he was to announce his lord's approach! It just occurs to me that he wore a mask.

AGNES: That looks most suspicious! Törring must know of this at once. God above! Do you hear that? A terrific blast from the gates! Trumpet calls on all sides—close at hand—coming nearer—nearer! That portends nothing good—that comes from Duke Ernest!

THEOBALD: Nothing good? Shouts! Clashing weapons! Is that for you? There is no doubt of it—they are storming the castle—they are already inside!

AGNES: It cannot be! The castle is surrounded by walls and moats!
(Chamberlain *rushes in*)

CHAMBERLAIN: My lady! Follow me to the mausoleum! I am sent by Count Törring.

AGNES: I depend upon his protection!

CHAMBERLAIN: Some traitor let down the drawbridge, or else did not pull it up again! The enemy is entering—no one can hold them back!

AGNES: At least they are not murderers—and as for me, what am I?
(*the tumult approaches*)

CHAMBERLAIN: I implore you to follow me! Perhaps they will not think of looking for you there!

AGNES: Theobald, you go with him.

THEOBALD: You mean, to find me a weapon? This tree will provide me the nearest one. (*tears off a branch*)
(*enter* Törring *and* Pappenheim, *fighting; in the background soldiers are fighting.* Preising, *too, comes into view, but without sword drawn*)

PAPPENHEIM: Surrender, Törring!

TÖRRING: Wretch!

PAPPENHEIM: Then, take that! I have spared you long enough!

TÖRRING: Bah!

PAPPENHEIM: Wasn't that a good thrust?

TÖRRING: Ah! *(strikes, but falls on his knees)* There! My lady! You see—how can I help you now?

PAPPENHEIM *(bending over him):* You made me do it!

TÖRRING *(falls):* The sign of the cross over me, I beseech you— friend—or— *(dies)*

THEOBALD *(casts aside his stick, and bends over the lifeless* Törring, *taking his sword from him):* Here I fall heir to something!

AGNES: Theobald!

THEOBALD: I know it is presumption on my part—but I cannot help it.

PAPPENHEIM *(turning):* Where is the witch who caused me to spill this noble blood?

AGNES *(steps toward* Pappenheim*):* Whom do you seek?

PAPPENHEIM *(involuntarily lowers his sword, and puts his hand to his helmet, but then beats his brow):* The devil! What am I doing?

THEOBALD: Serfs, gather around your mistress to defend her! Surely every one of you owes her some gratitude!

(the servants surround Agnes*)*

PAPPENHEIM *(to his followers):* Seize her! She is the one.

THEOBALD *(steps in front of* Agnes*):* Not as long as I live!

PAPPENHEIM: What do you want?

THEOBALD: She is the daughter of my master.

PAPPENHEIM: Barber's apprentice. Can you count? Down with him if he will not step back. And off with her.

(the soldiers start toward Agnes, *but hesitate, as if dazzled by her beauty)*

SOLDIERS: Oh! Her?

PAPPENHEIM: Well, why do you stare so? Has she cast her spell over you, too, as she did over the poor Duke? Are you going to wait until you are completely under her charm? Just give her time, and gaze into her dangerous eyes, and she will turn your hairs into bristles and your nails into claws! I thought you were familiar enough with her maddening witchery! Are you going to force me to do the bailiff's duty myself? *(approaches* Agnes. Theobald *swings his sword in a circle about his head, making approach impossible)* I shall have to— *(strikes at* Theobald*)*

AGNES *(throws herself between them):* Spare him! He is only thinking of my poor old father! I will follow you! But I beg you to remember it is Duke Albrecht's wife whom you are attacking in his own castle!

PAPPENHEIM (*attacking* Theobald *again*): That, fellow!

PREISING (*quickly approaching*): In the name of my lord, Duke Ernest, every sword in its scabbard!

PAPPENHEIM (*sheathing his sword*): I am willing. My orders were only to capture her!

AGNES: Theobald, do not return to Augsburg yet, for this is not the end. (*passes on*)

(Pappenheim *follows with his soldiers*)

THEOBALD (*is about to follow, but stops suddenly*): No! I shall go to Ingolstadt to Duke Albrecht! The first horse I find is mine! (*rushes out*)

PREISING: God grant she will listen to me, for then I may save her from death even yet!

Act 5

Scene 1

Straubing. A prison.

AGNES (*alone*): "Ingolstadt is far away!" he said. Those dreadful words could drive me wild! It is not twenty-four hours to Ingolstadt—and yet, when Theobald rushed past and the marshal was going to stop him, they looked at me and said, "Let him go, wherever he will—Ingolstadt is far away." Does it mean that I have not even twenty-four hours left to live? God in heaven, desert me not in this hour of need!

(*enter* Preising)

AGNES (*goes to meet* Preising): What do you bring?

PREISING: What you yourself desired.

AGNES: What I desired? Pray, do not mock me! You are not going to throw open the gloomy gates, so closely barred to hold me!

PREISING: Most willingly will I do so, if you will submit to the condition.

AGNES: What is the condition?

PREISING: I stand before you in the place of the Duke of Bavaria. (Agnes *shrinks back*) But I will be honest with you, and tell you that my noble lord is not your enemy.

AGNES: Not my enemy? Why am I here, then?

PREISING: You know the state of affairs. Duke Ernest is an old man now—and, if God should summon him, his throne would be left vacant, unless his only son and heir were ready to fill his place. To that exalted position Albrecht will never be able to lift you—and since he refuses to leave you, it is your duty to leave him.

AGNES: I—him! Rather perish!

PREISING: There is no escape for you! Believe me—believe a man who knows your fate as well as God himself, and one who would like to save you! You must trust me. Why would I have have come if it were not out of concern for you. My arm cannot protect you. You saw yourself how superfluous I was and of what use my sword was. I drew it because I felt sorry for you. Therefore, I come to you here in your prison, when you stand at the very threshold of death, because I am your one and only helper. But, again I repeat—you must give him up!

AGNES: A short while ago you saved the poor man who risked his life for me; I must believe that you are honest. But you are a man and cannot know what you are asking of me. *Never*, not in all eternity!

PREISING: Not too hasty, I implore you! I know it would be a terrible sacrifice, but if you refuse, you will—Can you have any doubt of your impending fate, after all that has happened today? You yourself will be the victim! I am even now perhaps saying more than I should by offering you this condition; I am doing so at my own risk.

AGNES: You want to frighten me—but you will not succeed! *(leans against the table for support)* I am not easily frightened. It is from the attack that my knees are still shaking. My God, first the trumpet blows, than the bloody swords and dead men! But I do not fear for my own safety. I am not in a robber's den—and Duke Ernest must be as just as he is severe! *(sits down)* Do not look at me like that! I only felt faint for a moment—I fancied I saw poor Törring again, lying dead before me. Now I am myself again. *(rises)* What could befall me? Until the judge has pronounced the final sentence, even a criminal is as safe in his prison cell as though God's angels guarded him; and as yet I have not even had a glimpse of my judge. No—I could not believe it of my husband's father—after all the son has told me of him! Oh, it is impossible, quite impossible, I know—but, even if death awaits me on the threshold this very minute, I could not decide differently!

PREISING: Death stands even now at your door—and, as soon as I leave, he will enter—Indeed, if I tarry too long, he will knock. Look out through the bars at the bridge—across the Danube! What do you see?

AGNES: A great crowd of people—some lift their arms to the sky as if in supplication, others peer over into the water. Can someone have fallen into the stream?

PREISING *(looking at her significantly):* Not yet!

AGNES: Merciful God! Do you mean—? (Preising *nods*) And for what crime?

PREISING *(holding up the death sentence):* You have disturbed the law and order of the state, have come between father and son, have separated the Prince from his people, and have brought about a condition of affairs which is not concerned with guilt or innocence—but simply with cause and effect. Thus have your judges decreed! For the judgment which you are facing now was made against you years ago by men above and beyond reproach, and God Himself has confirmed the harsh sentence by taking to Him the young prince who alone stood between you and the execution of your sentence. You are shivering. Do not deceive yourself any longer. That is how it is. If there were a gem more precious than all those that gleam in royal coronets, or still sleep in mountain depths, and on account of its wondrous beauty it aroused the wildest passions, and incited both the good and the wicked to murder and to theft—should not this jewel be seized by the only one still undazzled, and be hurled by a strong hand into the depths of the sea, in order to avert universal destruction? Yours is a parallel case! Once more, consider—I implore you, for the last time!

AGNES: But do you not see that you are asking something worse than death of me? I will not give up my husband—I cannot—I dare not! Am I the same Agnes Bernauer as of old? Have I done nothing but receive? Have I given nothing? Are he and I not one, indissolubly one—through mutual giving and receiving, like body and soul? I can answer for him, that he will most willingly renounce all claims to the throne! Do not fear I am giving a promise he will not keep! From his own lips I have it,—like a talisman in time of greatest danger! I never thought I should be forced to make use of it, but this hour makes it imperative. Use it as you will.

PREISING: Even that has no power to save you now! Duke Albrecht can as little cast off his inherited rank as he can bestow it upon you! To him it is as inseparably linked, as to you the beauty which enchains him. If he cannot call it a blessing, he must call it a curse—But he belongs to his people and must ascend his throne—and you must go to your doom! Your one means of escape is to declare your marriage to him illegal and take the veil at once!

AGNES: How gentle Duke Ernest is! *He* only wants my life. But you ask for even more than that. Do you think I would have to do no more than take that terrible step to wipe out all memory of me from my husband's soul forever—and that he would afterwards blush at remembering having loved me at all? My Albrecht—your Agnes deny you? Never! O God! At this moment how rich am I in my poverty, how strong in my powerlessness! At least I can spare him *one* sorrow. No reigning duke can drive me to it by his commands! Now, Chancellor, I am ready; you may be sure you will not see me tremble with weak fears again!

PREISING: If only your father stood here with me and supported me. He would say to you, "Child, why not give up a position voluntarily which you were forced to accept in the first place?" For I know that this was so.

AGNES: Was forced? Is that how my fear, my fretting and hesitating are interpreted? If you felt pity for me because you believed that then take your pity back and do not torture me any longer. I make no claim to it. No, no, I was never forced. Just as certainly as I saw him before he saw me, just as certainly did I love him before he loved me, and from the beginning it was as if it had always been thus and would be for all eternity. Therefore do not accuse him. I am more guilty than he. Although I would never have admitted it. Perhaps I would not even have given him a second glance. I might have sooner crushed my heart and, crying and laughing at the same time, made a silent pledge. I was ashamed before God and before myself. My blood seemed to rush to my head, and I returned poor Theobald's smile, just to hurt myself. And when Albrecht approached me in the evening I turned away at first, but only as a person would do who is to enter Heaven and knows that she has not yet paid her debt to Death. When an angel pushes you gently across the threshold, can that be considered force?

PREISING: And this is your final word?

(the door opens, revealing the executioner and troops beyond. Judge Emeran *stands on the threshold)*

AGNES *(moving forward):* Sir Emeran, if my husband had ever heard what I know of you, you would never have lived to betray me! Wholly without cause he hates you worse than anyone else in the whole world; I might have given him a reason for doing so if I had wished. Remembering this, your breast should be stirred by some feeling of compassion, if you are human. (Emeran *is silent*) Sir Emeran, did I fall into your hands by fair means or foul? Think what an end you are sending me to, without so much as a moment's warning! Grant me but a brief respite, and God himself shall forgive you for adding one Judas more to the record of the ages; I myself will pray for you! (Emeran *still silent*) Sir Emeran, as I stand now before you, imploring a moment's delay—even so will you stand before your God, and as you now give answer, so shall you then be answered. Give me but one minute of every year you are robbing me of—only one minute! I simply wish time to be at peace with myself before going to my doom!

PREISING: You are asking of him what he has no power to grant! He found out from your maid that you went to confession last night, and the hour is pressing. Believe me, for you one is quite as black as the other—Do consent to my proposition!

AGNES: Get thee behind me, Satan! (Emeran *motions to the bailiff, who enters and approaches* Agnes) Back, fellow! You would lay hands upon me, whom no one but your Duke has ever dared to touch! Only the person who digs my grave may do that. *(she walks toward the door)* O my poor Albrecht! How you will have to suffer!

PREISING: Yes, you would rather thrust this thorn into his soul, than—It is not too late yet!

AGNES: You may ask him, after I am gone—if he would have preferred to curse an unworthy wife than mourn for a murdered one! I know his answer. No, you will never bring your victim to the point of dishonoring herself! My first breath of life was pure—my last one shall be no less pure. Do what you may and must—I

will bear it. I shall soon know whether it was right or not!
(*walks out between the lines of guards,* Preising *and* Emeran
following)

Scene 2

*An open field not far from Straubing. Scattered peasants' huts—one
close by.*

(Duke Ernest, *with his knights and troopers.* Wolfram von
Pienzenau, Ignace von Seyboltsdorf, Otto von Bern)

ERNEST (*stepping forward with the three*): You, Pienzenau, ride on
to Haydeck's assistance; he is to advance as far as he can. I have to
remain here to wait for the Chancellor. (*exit* Pienzenau) You,
Seyboltsdorf—turn towards Straubing and take possession of the
hills! (*exit* Seyboltsdorf) You, Bern, attend to your troops; keep
them sober, and keep sober yourself. (Bern *is about to speak*) I
know what you are going to say—that your mind is in such a
befogged condition when you get up in the morning that you have
to clear it slowly by drinking; but I am not much impressed by
such proceedings, and you *must* be as ready to my hand today as
my sword! (*exit* Bern)

ERNEST: A peasant hut. I wouldn't mind seeing how these people
live. (*he walks to the hut, but finds it locked*) It's locked. They're
all in the fields working. Who is cooking their meal? Or did I
chase them all away? (*he walks back*) If everything went as
planned they will bring the news any minute. This is the first time
that time seems long to me.—Ernest, do not tempt fate. Who
knows what shadow lurks this very minute between heaven and
earth. (*enter* Preising, *with* Pappenheim)

ERNEST (*goes eagerly toward them*): You, Preising! Well?

PREISING: Dead!

ERNEST: God have mercy upon her! Pappenheim, set out immediately to join Pienzenau in Haydeck's support. He will get the
first blow that comes. (*exit* Pappenheim) Tell me of her death!

PREISING: Did she not appear before you at the eleventh hour?

ERNEST: What do you mean?

PREISING: Of course not! At the last moment the executioner refused
to do the deed—so Sir Emeran had to offer one of his serfs his
freedom before he could find anyone to hurl her from the bridge!

First, she seemed to shrink from the contamination of his hands—and was about to take the leap by herself—but fear overcame her—she faltered—and he had to push her over! The infuriated people were eager to stone him for it, though everyone knew the poor fellow did it only to earn his freedom. Not for the whole world would I witness such a sight again!

ERNEST: That will do, Preising. Some things have to be done blindly, as if in sleep. This is one of them. The great wheel rolled over her, and now she is with Him who turns it. And now Albrecht must be thought of.

PREISING: Oh, he doubtless has heard of it before this! A fellow from Augsburg was at the castle when Pappenheim stormed it; and tried to make a staunch resistance. But when she was led off to prison, he hurried away and surely went to Ingolstadt. He had come from her father!

ERNEST: Poor old man! Well, am I not putting my own flesh and blood at stake, quite as well as yours? Our fates may even now be identical!

PREISING: And then?

ERNEST: Come what may, I have done my part, and will look after the graves. But there is still a possibility of a different result! The prince in him was not dead, but slumbering. Why else would he not abdicate? Why did he insist so on the tournament? Perhaps he will awaken and then—It is silly to talk to the common people of bewitching, when a face which our Lord has painted twice can explain everything. But much is changed when heaven and earth have parted again in this mirage of a girl and only the corpse is left, which can no longer draw attention to the vanity of the world with its red lips and rouged cheeks, but whose broken eyes can only remind of the end to come.

     (A village is seen burning in the distance)

PREISING: Is that a fire?

ERNEST: That is my son! His sorrow is consuming itself in rage. Now, I foresee that all will end well! *(calls out)* Keep on, my son, keep on! The worse, the better!

PREISING: But is not that just what you wanted to prevent?

ERNEST: Oh, this is only one day! What he destroys I can build up again! Moreover, you may be sure, the Emperor's eagle has spread his wings ere now! And before Albrecht is aware, he will feel its talons. Then—*(lifts his ducal staff)* Preising, I have a surprise for you today! (Preising *is about to answer*) Come, come—to horse! *(calls)* Otto von Bern! *(exit with* Preising *and soldiers)* *(peasants, men, women, and children, screaming and running in confused crowds, and shouting)*

SOME: The Bohemian!

OTHERS: The Emperor!

OTHERS: Ingolstadt and Landshut!

ALL: Woe unto us! Whither, oh, whither?

(*enter* Duke Albrecht, *with many soldiers, fighting; among them* Theobald)

ALBRECHT *(with every shriek a blow)*: Agnes Bernauer! Agnes Bernauer! Before you perish, hear! Death's name today is Agnes Bernauer—and there is no such thing as pity! There is not a family in all Bavaria, high or low, who shall not weep tomorrow. There lies a Haydeck, here Pienzenau—there a Seyboltsdorf. But Pappenheim still lives. Robber, traitor, villain! Where are you hiding? All of you, all of you, shout with me until the whole world re-echoes: Pappenheim—robber, traitor, villain! Come forth!

PAPPENHEIM *(enters)*: Who seeks me?

ALBRECHT: Both the devil and I; but I have the first turn! Draw and see if an honest blade will still serve you. *(thrusts him back)*

THEOBALD *(comes forward)*: And I! Ha, ha, ha! It is all black before my eyes! I'll close them, and hew right and left! If I do not kill anyone, I'll surely make someone kill me.

(*re-enter* Albrecht)

ALBRECHT: Pappenheim is dead! What now? If I could only bring him back to life, and cut him down again with my every breath until the judgment day!

THEOBALD *(stepping in front of* Albrecht): Slay me!

ALBRECHT: You? And why? What are you thinking of?

THEOBALD: Do you think I can be the bearer of such news to Augsburg?

ALBRECHT: Do not go back! Stay with me, thou good, faithful soul!

THEOBALD: With you! With you! If it had not been for you—There! *(makes a thrust at* Albrecht) That comes from Agnes Bernauer! And that! And that!

ALBRECHT *(wards off the blows)*: Are you mad? Rather, give me your hand! You cannot force me to do you an injury!

THEOBALD: But you must! *(makes another thrust at* Albrecht)

ALBRECHT: Then I would have to do what I have never done before!

(turns his back to Theobald.*)* What red face is that I see? That is a Degenberg. They must not escape! *(rushes out)*

THEOBALD: Everyone shall die, friend or foe! *(rushes towards his fellow soldiers, who are following* Albrecht*)* Where to? Halt! *(is pierced by a sword)* Now I am content! *(falls and dies)*

(enter Wernberg*)*

WERNBERG: Victory! Victory! Victory! Where is Duke Albrecht? They are retreating before us, as though we were monsters!

(enter Albrecht*)*

ALBRECHT: But they shall all fall! The Danube, that choked her, I shall in turn choke with their corpses!

WERNBERG: Straubing has been stormed and is as good as taken.

ALBRECHT: They must be sure to capture the judge—but on no condition to injure him. From his blood I will drink my last draught.

(enter Frauenhoven*)*

FRAUENHOVEN: Hurrah! Hurrah! Now it is done! We have taken him captive! *(to* Albrecht, *as soon as he sees him)* We have taken your father. You can bid him good day shortly. He has just been captured.

ALBRECHT: Who commanded you to do so?

FRAUENHOVEN: What objection can there be? His own soldiers left him in the lurch, when he tried to put a stop to their flight. There they come with him and the chancellor, too.

ALBRECHT *(turns away):* Release him at once!

FRAUENHOVEN: Will not tomorrow be soon enough?

ALBRECHT: At once, I say! Man, have you no feelings?

WERNBERG: Now? Before he has sworn peace and insured our heads?

ALBRECHT *(stamps impatiently):* Immediately!

WERNBERG: Then tell him yourself.

(enter Duke Ernest *with* Preising *and* Hans von Laubelfing *and followers)*

ERNEST: That is my son! If he demands his father's surrender, here is my sword!

ALBRECHT: No—I remember you saved my life at Alling! Away! I beg you!

ERNEST: At Alling, I did nothing but my duty, and desire no thanks for it.

ALBRECHT *(turns away):* This hour brings a like rescue to you! *(catches sight of* Preising) But there is someone else who will not escape so easily! Chancellor Preising, you have but one choice now—to follow your companion Marshal von Pappenheim down to hell! *(draws his sword)*

ERNEST: For shame! For shame! My chancellor has done nothing but execute my orders—and I had to give them twice before they were carried out.

ALBRECHT: Then there is no one responsible but you—no one I can blame but you? And still you dare to cross my path? Do not seek to avoid me?

ERNEST: Why should I? At Straubing, as at Alling and at Regensburg, I have simply done my duty.

ALBRECHT: Your duty? And God lets you fall into my hands? Is that His sentence upon one who has done his duty?

ERNEST: It is His way of testing you! Take heed lest you fall! Never before have two people stood before him as you and I now stand. *(draws near to* Albrecht) My son, you allied yourself with my worst enemy—your false uncle: he was glad enough to scatter firebrand that should bring destruction to my innocent country, but he would never have snatched your sword from you, if you had pointed it at your own heart. Come back to your father's side! That is the only way! Believe me—I *had* to do what I have done! Some day you will understand, even if not before the last hour of your life. But I can weep with you, for I sympathize with your sorrow!

ALBRECHT: I beg you, cease! Let me think you know no more about it than the cold waters that took her life! Unless I call down curses upon you, I must feel you are the dread Death-angel in a new disguise. No human being could ever have attacked her—for by daylight he would have seen her, and at night he would have heard her—and in either case he would have been completely disarmed. Assure me that you are not human, that your servants were not human—then I will make the sign of the cross and flee!

ERNEST: But I am a human being, like yourself—and ought to have been spared this dreadful task. But when you rise in open revolt against the existing order of things—both divine and human— then I am the one appointed to preserve it, at whatever cost.

ALBRECHT: The divine and human order of things! Ha, ha! You

speak as if they were two rainbows, joined and bound about the world like a glowing ring of magic. It was the divine order that called her into life, that she might uplift what is degraded and debase what is falsely uplifted. The human—*(approaches* Ernest) The human—*(turns quickly away towards his followers)* Forward, friends! Onward! Who wishes to cease his work in the middle of the day? Duke Ernest is free—let none touch a hair of his head. There is not another Agnes he might kill—But we shall not rest until we have put the torch to his capital city!

ERNEST: Very well, my boy! You will only make Bavaria heap curses upon her, instead of bewailing her sad fate. You will be murdering her brothers, not mine—and, even if you massacre the whole race of man, you will never be able to stir again a single drop of blood in her veins. Are you going to force things to a point where even her own father will curse the hour of her birth, and she herself will steal out of Paradise with horror and shame, the first and the last one to leave without being damned? (Albrecht *stops and lets his sword fall. Trumpets are heard in the distance)* That must be Louis of Ingolstadt. The destroyer grows impatient. On God's whole earth there is no man who can so utterly demolish what another has built up as he! One admonition I give you—on earth, as well as in heaven, there is One who judges over you—and before ooth your sentence will be severe! *(tumpets draw nearer)*

VOICES: Make way for the Imperial standard!

OTHER VOCIES: The Emperor's herald!

(*enter* Imperial Herald *with followers; the colors in the lead*)

HERALD *(flourishing his sword):* In the name of His majesty, the Emperor, let no sword be shown, save this! *(all the knights except* Albrecht *sheathe their swords)* Albrecht von Wittelsbach, Duke of Bavaria, you are summoned by your Emperor!

(Albrecht *approaches, with hesitating step, and slowly sheathes his sword)*

ALBRECHT: Is this the place?

HERALD: Any spot will do—for pronouncing the proscription!

WERNBERG AND FRAUENHOVEN: The bann! Has it come to this?

(blare of trumpets from without)

PREISING (*to* Ernest): Still something more?

ERNEST: More than I desired, I fear.

VOICES: A legate! A legate from the Holy See!

HERALD: And with him comes excommunication from the Church.

MANY VOICES *(of the knights and the troopers):* Proscribed and excommunicated at one and the same time? Then it is high time— *(throw down their arms)*

(enter the Legate *with followers, a burning taper borne before him and takes his positon at the right of the* Herald)

HERALD *(unfolding document):* "We, Sigismund, Emperor of Rome by the Grace of God, and King of Hungary, Bohemia and Dalmatia, Protector of the Church and highest judiciary of the world, hereby announce and declare: Inasmuch as you, Albrecht von Wittelsbach, two years and a half ago disturbed the order of the empire by open revolt at Regensburg, and therefore were liable to the penalty of proscription, which was withheld only on account of your father's intervention; inasmuch as you, undeserving of such intervention and of our mercy, have persisted in your defiance of both divine and human law and order, and have a second time, with drawn sword, entered the field in open rebellion; we hereby command you by this, our order, that you surrender your sword at once unto your lord and father, Duke Ernest of Bavaria, and as his prisoner humbly await our further sentence—" *(breaks off and looks at* Albrecht. Albrecht *thrusts his sword into the earth and leans upon it)* "In default thereof, with our imperial authority, we banish you from the empire."

ERNEST: My son, will you bear still more? Say the word, and I will raise my ducal staff!

FRAUENHOVEN: Now he'll talk about the creatures of the woods, and the birds in the sky, and the fish in the water.

WERNBERG: Look around you. They're all turning away. No one will stay with you except for us.

ALBRECHT: And how could they. The mountains are beginning to move in order to bury me.

ERNEST: Is the church, too, to interfere? Do you want the candle extinguished, your soul cursed in eternity, and your name erased from the book of life?

ALBRECHT *(to* Wernberg *and* Frauenhoven): Go away from me so that I can answer.

FRAUENHOVEN: Do we deserve that from you? The devil, that hurts.

ALBRECHT: Shall I bow to that violence because you are with me? Let it crush me today!

ERNEST: Violence? If that is violence being done to you, then it comes from all your forefathers, who have taken it upon themselves and carried it uncomplainingly for half a millenium, and that is the strength and power which comes with justice. Woe to him who slings a stone at it in order to destroy it. The stone will rebound and destroy him. Is it just I talking to you and not the whole German Empire?

ALBRECHT: So be it! I did not know it was a capital crime to pick up a pearl instead of treading upon it. That is what I have done, and I will pay the penalty. Come on, Bear and Wolf—swoop down, Eagle and Vulture, and tear me to pieces! Not one move will I make to defend myself, if you obey the imperial command!

ERNEST: Are you in such haste to appear before your judge? He has not yet counted the dead and the wounded. Are you so certain how He will receive you?

ALBRECHT: I am not afraid of Him. He will surely forgive that I took His dearest child by her hand. He knows how beautiful and noble He had made her.

ERNEST: My son, take heed! You can make your guilt greater, you can force death upon yourself, or, who would prevent you, leave this world in a cowardly way. But it is also in your power to have something good come of all this. Do that, and make a decision which will allow you to be proud before your ancestors. Do what is necessary. The battlefield will bear terrible witness against you some day; all these ghastly dead will accuse you, saying: "We perished through Duke Albrecht's wrath." Woe unto you, if on that day a much mightier host does not rise up and declare for you, silencing your accusers—if millions do not shout in reply: "But, behold us! We all lived and died in peace and harmony because he conquered himself." That can come only through your clinging to life instead of cowardly renouncing it.

ALBRECHT: And she, the innocent victim, must crumble to dust, while I—what a wretch I would have to be to listen to you!

ERNEST: You are not one of those who can reconcile justice by repentantly baring your breast to her sword. From you she demands just the opposite! Behold this banner, and learn a lesson! It is woven of the same thread as the doublet worn by every knight who follows it, and will likewise some day turn to dust and be scattered to the winds. But under it the Germans have been victorious in a thousand battles, and beneath its folds another thousand battles will vanquish the enemy; no one but a boy would wish to tear it to pieces; no one but a fool, to patch it, instead of shedding his blood for it, holding every shred of it sacred! It is just the same for the prince who carries it. In our great need we poor mortals cannot tear a star from the skies to fasten to our standard—and the Angel with the flaming sword, who drove us from paradise into the desert, did not remain to pronounce judgment upon us. We have to put the mark upon a thing, worthless in itself, that gives it value; we have to raise dust above dust, until we are in the presence of Him who knows neither prince nor pauper, but only good and evil and holds His representatives here to strict account. Woe to him who does not understand this wise regulation of the race; woe to him who does not respect it! Look into the depths of your own heart, and say: "Father, before heaven and you, have I sinned, but I will make atonement; I will live!"

ALBRECHT: Does it depend upon me alone?

ERNEST: This question suffices. God will give you strength, and even your poor dead wife will pray for you.

ALBRECHT: My wife?

ERNEST: What I was forced to refuse her in life, I can grant her in death, for I know she is worthy. I could not acknowledge her in life; but I myself will attend to her funeral rites and at her tomb perpetuate a memorial service for future generations, so that she will ever be cherished in sacred memory as the purest victim ever sacrificed to necessity in the course of the centuries.

ALBRECHT: I will—I will do what I can! *(to the* Herald*)* To his Imperial Majesty, my respect! *(to* Ernest*)* To you, my lord and father— *(is about to surrender his sword.* Ernest *goes toward him with open arms.* Albrecht *draws back and takes a stand)* No, no! I cannot. May hell take me—but let it be blood for blood!

ERNEST: Stop! Take this first! *(extends his ducal staff, which* Albrecht *involuntarily grasps)* This makes you your father's judge; why be his murderer?

PREISING: Duke Ernest!

ERNEST: That was the decision—not merely to spend the evening of my life in peace. I need his consent. If he can conscientiously refuse, I am undone!

ALBRECHT: I am reeling; take it back—it burns my fingers!

ERNEST: In the fear of our Lord, wield it for one year as I have done. Then, if you cannot acquit me, summon me; and I shall pronounce upon myself whatever sentence you may see fit. I shall be in the monastery at Andecks.

ALBRECHT *(kneeling):* Not to the Emperor nor the empire do I kneel, but to you! To you! My father!

ERNEST: Only wait, my son! My day's task was a hard one, but perhaps I may still survive the year. *(is about to go,* Preising *following him)* Remain! One monk is enough!

Translated by Loueen Pattee
Adapted by Hannelore M. Spence

Notes to
King Ottocar's Rise and Fall

1. A town on the river March. The battle took place July 12, 1260. *König Ottokars Glück und Ende. Grillparzers Werke*, Band 3, Hrsg. v. Rudolf Franz (Leipzig und Wien, n.d.), p. 269, footnote 2. All subsequent endnotes are taken from this edition and will be identified as *GW*, with the page and footnote number.

2. In the original, Grillparzer called Cunigunda Bela's niece. The translator correctly identified her as Bela's grandchild. *GW*, p. 271, 1.

3. They were related in the fourth degree: their great-grandfathers were brothers. *GW*, p. 276, 5.

4. Ottocar was twenty-three years old then, Margaret forty-seven. *GW*, p. 278, 2.

5. Refers to Mongols then living in Southern Russia. *GW*, p. 281, 1.

6. Ottocar founded the town of Marchegg, on the right of the March, in 1268, in order to commemorate his victory. *GW*, p. 283, 1.

7. A fortress in Prague, on the right bank of the Moldau river. Fortified in 1252 against the Bavarians and Hungarians. *GW*, p. 284, 1.

8. In the eastern part of Bohemia, south of the Elbe river. *GW*, p. 285, 1.

9. Grillparzer has Rudolph take part in Ottocar's crusade (in 1254) against the Prussian heathens. *GW*, p. 296, 1.

10. A Turkish tribe which Bela had established in the region between the Danube and Theiss rivers. Bela's successor, Stephan V (1270–72), had a Kuman wife. *GW*, p. 311, 1.

11. The name of a town which occurs several times (near Landskron and the Moravian town of Neustadt). *GW*, p. 315, 1.

12. Today, the location of this island is no longer known. *GW*, p. 338, 1.

13. In memory of Grillparzer's bride. *GW,* 343, 1. See Egon Schwarz's introduction to this edition, p. ix.
14. A town on the Thaya river, in Moravia. *GW,* p. 359, 1.
15. After the victory at Croissenbrunn, Ottocar had a monastery built here for the Cistercian Order. *GW,* p. 365, 1.
16. In Moravia, near the Bohemian border. *GW,* 381, 1.
17. Margaret had been ordered to withdraw to Krems, on the Danube. *GW,* p. 389, 1.
18. Rudolph is addressing his son, Albrecht, who is later to receive the duchies. *GW,* p. 394, 1.
19. Directed at his younger son, Rudolph. *GW,* p. 407, 1.

Notes to *The Talisman*

1. The "Titus-head" was a fashionable Nineteenth Century French hair style, modeled on the bust of the Roman emperor.
2. A coppery red, the traditional color for this instrument.
3. The guardian of church buildings (he died trying to put out a church fire), St. Florian became in time the patron of buildings in general. In Austrian farmyards, an image of the saint often appeared as a talisman to ward off fires.
4. An obvious play on Goethe's *Wahlverwandtschaften (Elective Affinities)*.
5. November 11, feast day of St. Martin, whose iconography almost always includes a goose. A goose is the traditional main course of a Martinmas dinner.
6. A candle protected by a glass lens, usually reddish in color, against the wind. Wind lanterns were a part of the paraphernalia of funeral cortèges.
7. Old fashioned, unstylish, and stiff.
8. An inexpensive vacation community just outside Vienna in the Vienna Woods.
9. A tributary of the Danube in Vienna, noted for its fruit market.
10. One of the more infamous coffeehouses in the Prater, Vienna's amusement park.
11. Here Nestroy is playing on Franz Grillparzer's popular tragedy, *König Ottokars Glück und Ende,* which treats of the medieval Bohemian monarch's meteoric rise and equally spectacular downfall.
12. A wordplay on the Eastern Question, one of the most compelling issues in Europe in the 1820s and 1830s. The Eastern Question had ostensibly to do with recognition of the Greeks in their struggle to win

independence from the Ottoman empire. Its moral effect was far more wide-ranging, however; liberals all over Europe saw in the Greek rebels the champions of their own causes, and Philhellenism became a thinly-veiled metaphor for resistance to established authority all over the continent. By throwing his support to the sultan, Metternich reaffirmed Austria's reputation as the bastion of reactionary politics and thereby succeeded in isolating Austria from the other major European powers, all of whom were in open sympathy with the Greeks.

13. A German proverb often used in the context of "misunderstood genius" and "unappreciated good deeds."

14. The Vienna Burgtheater, the most illustrious (hence most coveted by actors) of Austrian stages, usually performed "serious" dramas by established authors.

15. The Linigraben, a moat enclosing Vienna's twenty-three suburbs, was dug in 1703 and later converted into an avenue. In Nestroy's time it was a dumping ground and haven for indigents.

16. Belisarius, a general of the Byzantine emperor Justinian I, was well known to Nestroy's audience through Donizetti's opera which bears his name.

17. Nestroy is here punning on the two meanings of *englisch:* English and angelic.

Notes to *Agnes Bernauer*

1. According to the chronicler Engelbertus Werlechius, whose chronicle of Augsburg was one of Hebbel's sources, Augsburg was indeed founded during Drusus' times. "Anmerkungen" zu *Friedrich Hebbels Werke,* Siebenter Teil. Hrsg. v. Hermann Krumm (Leipzig, 1913), pp. 208, 210.
2. Unofficial secret tribunals held in the fourteenth and fifteenth centuries.
3. In a history of Bavaria by Konrad Mannert, which may have served as another of Hebbel's sources, it is stated (although this piece of information is not authenticated) that Emperor Louis was poisoned on October 11, 1347: "It can hardly be doubted that his life was shortened by poisoning; no one knows where the poison came from." "Anmerkungen," p. 208 and 213.
4. According to Mannert, Emperor Rudolph had decided that Bavaria deserved an electoral vote, and he thus turned the representatives of King Ottocar away. However, Bavaria's vote was given to both Louis of Ingolstadt and Henry of Landshut. Later Rudolph publicly changed his opinion in favor of his son-in-law, King Wenceslav of Bohemia. Thus Bavaria lost its electoral vote while Louis retained his vote for the Palatinate. "Anmerkungen," p. 213.

ACKNOWLEDGMENTS

Every reasonable effort has been made to locate the owners of rights to previously published translations printed here. We gratefully acknowledge permission to reprint the following material:

The Talisman from *Three Viennese Comedies* by Johann Nepomuk Nestroy, translated by Robert Harrison and Katharina Wilson. Copyright © Camden House, Inc.

THE GERMAN LIBRARY
in 100 Volumes

Gottfried von Strassburg
Tristan and Isolde
Edited and Revised by Francis G. Gentry
Foreword by C. Stephen Jaeger

German Medieval Tales
Edited by Francis G. Gentry
Foreword by Thomas Berger

German Humanism and Reformation
Edited by Reinhard P. Becker
Foreword by Roland Bainton

Immanuel Kant
Philosophical Writings
Edited by Ernst Behler
Foreword by René Wellek

Friederich Schiller
Plays: Intrigue and Love and *Don Carlos*
Edited by Walter Hinderer
Foreword by Gordon Craig

Johann Wolfgang von Goethe
The Sufferings of Young Werther
and *Elective Affinities*
Edited by Victor Lange
Forewords by Thomas Mann

German Romantic Criticism
Edited by A. Leslie Willson
Foreword by Ernst Behler

Philosophy of German Idealism
Edited by Ernst Behler

Heinrich von Kleist
Plays
Edited by Walter Hinderer
Foreword by E. L. Doctorow

E. T. A. Hoffman
Tales
Edited by Victor Lange

Georg Büchner
Complete Works and Letters
Edited by Walter Hinderer and Henry J. Schmidt

German Fairy Tales
Edited by Helmut Brachert and Volkmar Sander
Foreword by Bruno Bettelheim

German Literary Fairy Tales
Edited by Frank G. Ryder and Robert M. Browning
Introduction by Gordon Birrell
Foreword by John Gardner

Heinrich Heine
Poetry and Prose
Edited by Jost Hermand and Robert C. Holub
Foreword by Alfred Kazin

Heinrich von Kleist and Jean Paul
German Romantic Novellas
Edited by Frank G. Ryder and Robert M. Browning
Foreword by John Simon

German Romantic Stories
Edited by Frank Ryder
Introduction by Gordon Birrell

German Poetry from 1750 to 1900
Edited by Robert M. Browning
Foreword by Michael Hamburger

Gottfried Keller
Stories
Edited by Frank G. Ryder
Foreword by Max Frisch

Wilhelm Raabe
Novels
Edited by Volkmar Sander
Foreword by Joel Agee

Theodor Fontane
Short Novels and Other Writings
Edited by Peter Demetz
Foreword by Peter Gay

Theodor Fontane
Delusions, Confusions and The Poggenpuhl Family
Edited by Peter Demetz
Foreword by J. P. Stern
Introduction by William L. Zwiebel

Wilhelm Busch and Others
German Satirical Writings
Edited by Deiter P. Lotze and Volkmar Sander
Foreword by John Simon

Writings of German Composers
Edited by Jost Hermand and James Steakley

German Lieder
Edited by Philip Lieson Miller
Foreword by Hermann Hesse

Arthur Schnitzler
Plays and Stories
Edited by Egon Schwarz
Foreword by Stanley Elkin

Rainer Maria Rilke
Prose and Poetry
Edited by Egon Schwarz
Foreword by Howard Nemerov

Robert Musil
Selected Writings
Edited by Burton Pike
Foreword by Joel Agee

Essays on German Theater
Edited by Margaret Herzfeld-Sander
Foreword by Martin Esslin

German Novellas of Realism I and II
Edited by Jeffrey L. Sammons

Friedrich Dürrenmatt
Plays and Essays
Edited by Volkmar Sander
Foreword by Martin Esslin

Hans Magnus Enzensberger
Critical Essays
Edited by Reinhold Grimm and Bruce Armstrong
Foreword by John Simon

Gottfried Benn
Prose, Essays, Poems
Edited by Volkmar Sander
Foreword by E. B. Ashton
Introduction by Reinhard Paul Becker

German Essays on Art History
Edited by Gert Schiff

Max Frisch
Novels, Plays, Essays
Edited by Rolf Kieser
Foreword by Peter Demetz

All volumes available in hardcover and paperback editions at your bookstore or from the publisher. For more information on The German Library write to: The Continuum Publishing Company, 370 Lexington Avenue, New York, NY 10017.